BUSHMAN
Life in a New Country

KANGAROO HUNTING.

Lieut. A H Irby 51ˢᵗ Regᵗ del.

E. Radcly sc.

The
BUSHMAN
Life in a New Country

EDWARD WILSON LANDOR

SENATE

The Bushman

First published in 1847 by Richard Bentley, London

This edition published in 1998 by Senate,
an imprint of Tiger Books International plc,
26A York Street, Twickenham,
Middlesex TW1 3LJ, United Kingdom

Cover design © 1998 Tiger Books International

1 3 5 7 9 10 8 6 4 2

ISBN 1 85958 538 8

Printed and bound in the UK by
Cox & Wyman, Reading, England

PREFACE.

———◆———

THE British Colonies now form so prominent a portion of the Empire, that the Public will be compelled to acknowledge some interest in their welfare, and the Government to yield some attention to their wants. It is a necessity which both the Government and the Public will obey with reluctance.

Too remote for sympathy, too powerless for respect, the Colonies, during ages of existence, have but rarely occupied a passing thought in the mind of the Nation; as though their insignificance entitled them only to neglect. But the weakness of childhood is passing away: the Infant is fast growing into the possession and the consciousness of strength, whilst the Parent is obliged to acknowledge the increasing usefulness of her offspring.

The long-existing and fundamental errors of Government, under which the Colonies have hitherto groaned in helpless subjection, will soon become generally known and understood—and then they will be remedied.

In the remarks which will be found scattered through this work on the subject of Colonial Government, it must be observed, that the system only is assailed, and not individuals. That it is the system and not THE MEN who are in fault, is sufficiently proved by the fact that the most illustrious statesmen and the brightest talents of the Age, have ever failed to distinguish themselves by good works, whilst directing the fortunes of the Colonies. Lord John Russell, Lord Stanley, Mr. Gladstone— all of them high-minded, scrupulous, and patriotic statesmen—all of them men of brilliant genius, extensive knowledge, and profound thought—have all of them been but slightly appreciated as Colonial rulers.

Their principal success has been in perpetuating a noxious system. They have all of them conscientiously believed their first duty to be, in the words of Lord Stanley, to keep the Colonies dependent upon the Mother Country; and occupied with this belief, they have legislated for the Mother Country and not for the Colonies. Vain, selfish, fear-inspired policy! that keeps the Colonies down in the dust at the feet of the Parent State, and yet is of no value or advantage to her. To make her Colonies useful to England, they must be cherished in their infancy, and carefully encouraged to put forth all the strength of their secret energies.

It is not whilst held in leading-strings that they can be useful, or aught but burthensome: rear them kindly to maturity, and allow them the free exercise of their vast natural strength, and they would be to the parent country her truest and most valuable friends.

THE COLONIES OF THE EMPIRE ARE THE ONLY LASTING AND INALIENABLE MARKETS FOR ITS PRODUCE; and the first aim of the political economist should be to develope to their utmost extent the vast resources possessed by Great Britain in these her own peculiar fields of national wealth. But the policy displayed throughout the history of her Colonial possessions, has ever been the reverse of this. It was that grasping and ungenerous policy that called forth a Washington, and cost her an empire. It is that same miserable and low-born policy that still recoils upon herself, depriving her of vast increase of wealth and power in order to keep the chain upon her hapless children, those ambitious Titans whom she trembles to unbind.

And yet poor Old England considers herself an excellent parent, and moans and murmurs over the ingratitude of her troublesome offspring! Like many other parents, she means to do well and act kindly, but unhappily the principles on which she proceeds are radically wrong. Hence, on the one side, heart-burning, irritation, and resentment; on the other, disappointment, revulsion, and alarm.

Is she too deeply prejudiced, or too old in error, to attempt a new system of policy?

In what single respect has she ever proved her-

self a good parent to any of her Colonies? Whilst
supplying them with Government Officers, she has
fettered them with unwholesome laws; whilst
giving them a trifling preference over foreign states
in their commerce, she has laid her grasp upon
their soil; whilst allowing them to legislate in a
small degree for themselves, she has reserved the
prerogative of annulling all enactments that interfere with her own selfish or mistaken views; whilst
permitting their inhabitants to live under a light-
ened pressure of taxation, she has debarred them
from wealth, rank, honours, rewards, hopes—all
those incentives to action that lead men forward to
glory, and stamp nations with greatness.

What has she done for her Colonies—this careful
and beneficent parent? She has permitted them
to exist, but bound them down in serf-like dependence; and so she keeps them—feeble, helpless,
and hopeless. She grants them the sanction of her
flag, and the privilege of boasting of her baneful
protection.

Years—ages have gone by, and her policy has
been the same—darkening the heart and crushing

the energies of Man in climes where Nature sparkles with hope and teems with plenty.

Time, however, too powerful for statesmen, continues his silent but steady advance in the great work of amelioration. The condition of the Colonies must be elevated to that of the counties of England. Absolute rule must cease to prevail in them. Men must be allowed to win there, as at home, honours and rank. Time, the grand minister of correction—Time the Avenger, already has his foot on the threshold of the COLONIAL OFFICE.

CONTENTS.

CHAP.   PAGE

I.—Colonists 1

II.—St. Jago 8

III.—The Mutiny 18

IV.—The Prison-Island 29

V.—First Adventures 44

VI.—Perth.—Colonial Juries 62

VII.—Boating up the River 80

VIII.—Farms on the River 97

IX.—The Moral Thermometer of Colonies . . 107

X.—Country Life 118

XI.—Persecutions 129

XII.—Michael Blake, the Irish Settler . . . 140

XIII.—Wild Cattle Hunting 152

XIV.—Woodman's Point 177

XV.—How the Laws of England affect the Natives 186

XVI.—Remarks on the Physical Organization of the Natives 196

XVII.—Sketches of Life among the Natives . . 208

XVIII.—The Model Kingdom 217

XIX.—Trials of a Governor 223

XX.—Mr. Sails, my Groom.—Over the Hills.—A Sheep Station 233

XXI.—Extracts from the Log of a Hut-keeper . 257

XXII.—Pelican Shooting. — Gales. — Wrestling with Death 265

CONTENTS.

CHAP.   PAGE

XXIII.—The Desert of Australia.— Cause of the Hot Winds.—Geology 283

XXIV.—Colonial Government 298

XXV.—One of the Errors of Government.— Adventures of the " Bramble " . . . 307

XXVI.—Scientific Discoveries.—Kangaroo Hunting.—Emus.—Lost in the Bush . . . 323

XXVII.—The Comet. — Vital Statistics.—Meteorology 349

XXVIII.—The Botany of the Colony 356

XXIX.—Misfortunes of the Colony 370

XXX.—Resources of the Colony :—Horses for India—Wine—Dried Fruits—Cotton —Coal—Wool—Corn—Whale-Oil.— A Whale Hunt.—Cured Fish.—Ship Timber 381

XXXI.—Rise and Fall of a Settlement.—The Sequel to Captain Grey's Discoveries. —A Word at Parting 403

PLATES.

              Refers to page

Kangaroo Hunting *(Frontispiece)* 335

              To face page

The Bivouac 160

Spearing Kangaroo 215

Death of the Kangaroo 336

Emu Hunt *(woodcut)* 338

THE BUSHMAN;

OR,

LIFE IN A NEW COUNTRY.

———◆———

CHAPTER I.

COLONISTS.

THE Spirit of Adventure is the most animating impulse in the human breast. Man naturally detests inaction; he thirsts after change and novelty, and the prospect of excitement makes him prefer even danger to continued repose.

The love of adventure! how strongly it urges forward the Young! The Young, who are ever discontented with the Present, and sigh for opportunities of action which they know not where to seek. Old men mourn over the folly and recklessness of the Young, who, in the fresh and balmy spring-time of life, recoil from the confinement of the desk or the study, and long for active occupation, in which all their beating energies may find employment. Subjection is the consequence of civilized life; and self-sacrifice is necessary in those who are born to toil, before they may partake of its enjoyments. But though the Young are conscious that this is so, they repine not the less; they feel that the freshness and verdure of life must first die away; that the promised recompense will probably come too late to the exhausted frame; that the blessings which would now be received with prostrate gratitude will cease to be felt as boons; and that although the wishes and wants of the heart will take new directions in the progress of years, the consciousness that the spring-time of life—that peculiar season of happiness which can never be known again—has been consumed in futile desires and aspirations, in vain hopes and bitter experiences, must ever remain deepening the gloom of Memory.

Anxious to possess immediate independence, young men, full of adventurous spirit, proceed in search of new fields of labour, where they may reap at once the enjoyments of domestic life, whilst they industriously work out the curse that hangs over the Sons of Adam.

They who thus become emigrants from the ardent spirit of adventure, and from a desire to experience a simpler and less artificial manner of living than that which has become the essential characteristic of European civilization, form a large and useful body of colonists. These men, notwithstanding the pity which will be bestowed upon them by those whose limited experience of life leads to the belief that happiness or contentment can only be found in the atmosphere of England, are entitled to some consideration and respect.

To have dared to deviate from the beaten track which was before them in the outset of life; to have perceived at so vast a distance advantages which others, if they had seen, would have shrunk from aiming at; to have persevered in their resolution, notwithstanding the expostulations of Age, the regrets of Friendship, and the sighs of Affection —all this betokens originality and strength of character.

Does it also betoken indifference to the wishes of others? Perhaps it does; and it marks one of the broadest and least amiable features in the character of a colonist.

The next class of emigrants are those who depart from their native shores with reluctance and tears. Children of misfortune and sorrow, they would yet remain to weep on the bosom from which they have drawn no sustenance. But the strong blasts of necessity drive them from the homes which even

Grief has not rendered less dear. Their future has never yet responded to the voice of Hope, and now, worn and broken in spirit, imagination paints nothing cheering in another land. They go solely because they may not remain—because they know not where else to look for a resting place; and Necessity, with her iron whip, drives them forth to some distant colony.

But there is still a third class, the most numerous perhaps of all, that helps to compose the population of a colony. This is made up of young men who are the wasterels of the World; who have never done, and never will do themselves any good, and are a curse instead of a benefit to others. These are they who think themselves fine, jovial, spirited fellows, who disdain to work, and bear themselves as if life were merely a game which ought to be played out amid coarse laughter and wild riot.

These go to a colony because their relatives will not support them in idleness at home. They feel no despair at the circumstance, for their pockets have been refilled, though (they are assured) for the last time; and they rejoice at the prospect of spending their capital far from the observation of intrusive guardians.

Disgusted at authority which has never proved sufficient to restrain or improve them, they become enamoured with the idea of absolute license, and are far too high-spirited to entertain any apprehensions of future poverty. These gallant-minded and truly enviable fellows betake themselves, on their arrival, to the zealous cultivation of field-sports instead of field produce. They leave with disdain the exercise of the useful arts to low-bred and beggarly-minded people, who have not spirit enough for anything better; whilst they themselves enthusiastically strive to realize again those glorious times,—

" When wild in woods the noble savage ran."

In the intervals of relaxation from these fatigues, when they return to a town life, they endeavour to prove the activity of their energies and the benevolence of their characters, by getting up balls and pic-nics, solely to promote the happiness of the ladies. But notwithstanding this appearance of devotion to the fair sex, their best affections are never withdrawn from the companion of their hearts—the brandy flask. They evince their generous hospitality by hailing every one who passes their door, with " How are you, old fellow? Come in, and take a nip." Somehow or other they are always liked, even by those who pity and despise them.

The women only laugh at their irregularities—

they are such "good-hearted creatures!" And so
they go easily and rapidly down that sloping path
which leads to ruin and despair. What is their
end? Many of them literally kill themselves by
drinking; and those who get through the seasoning,
which is the fatal period, are either compelled to
become labourers in the fields for any one who will
provide them with food; or else succeed in exciting
the compassion of their friends at home, by their
dismal accounts of the impossibility of earning a
livelihood in a ruined and worthless colony; and
having thus obtained money enough to enable
them to return to England, they hasten to throw
themselves and their sorrows into the arms of their
sympathizing relatives.

Nothing can be more absurd than to imagine
that a fortune may be made in a colony by those
who have neither in them nor about them any of
the elements or qualities by which fortunes are
gained at home.

There are, unfortunately, few sources of wealth
peculiar to a colony. The only advantage which
the emigrant may reasonably calculate upon enjoying, is the diminution of competition. In England
the crowd is so dense that men smother one
another.

It is only by opening up the same channels of
wealth under more favourable circumstances, that

the emigrant has any right to calculate upon success. Without a profession, without any legitimate calling in which his early years have been properly instructed; without any knowledge or any habits of business, a man has no better prospect of making a fortune in a colony than at home. None, however, so circumstanced, entertains this belief; on the contrary, he enters upon his new career without any misgivings, and with the courage and enthusiasm of a newly enlisted recruit.

Alas! the disappointment which so soon and so inevitably succeeds, brings a crowd of vices and miseries in its train.

CHAPTER II.

ST. JAGO.

THE reader may naturally expect to be informed of the reasons that have induced me thus to seek his acquaintance.   In one word—I am a colonist. In England, a great deal is said every day about colonies and colonists, but very little is known about them.   A great deal is projected; but whatever is done, is unfortunately to their prejudice. Secretaries of State know much more about the distant settlements of Great Britain than the inhabitants themselves; and, consequently, the latter are seldom able to appreciate the ordinances which (for their own good) they are compelled to submit to.

My own experience is chiefly confined to one of the most insignificant of our colonies,—insignificant in point of population, but extremely important as to its geographical position, and its prospects of future greatness,—but the same principle of government applies to all the British settlements.

A few years ago, I was the victim of medical skill; and being sentenced to death in my own country by three eminent physicians, was comparatively happy in having that sentence commuted to banishment. A wealthy man would have gone to Naples, to Malta, or to Madeira; but a poor one has no resource save in a colony, unless he will condescend to live upon others, rather than support himself by his own exertions.

The climate of Western Australia was recommended; and I may be grateful for the alternative allowed me.

As I shall have occasion hereafter to allude to them incidentally, I may mention that my two brothers accompanied me on this distant voyage.

The elder, a disciple of Æsculapius, was not only anxious to gratify his fraternal solicitude and his professional tastes by watching my case, but was desirous of realizing the pleasures of rural life in Australia.

My younger brother (whose pursuits entitle him to be called Melibœus) was a youth not eighteen, originally designed for the Church, and intended to cut a figure at Oxford; but modestly conceiving that the figure he was likely to cut would not tend to the advancement of his worldly interests, and moreover, having no admiration for Virgil beyond the Bucolics, he fitted himself out

with a Lowland plaid and a set of Pandæan pipes,
and solemnly dedicated himself to the duties of a
shepherd.

Thus it was that we were all embarked in the
same boat; or rather, we found ourselves in the
month of April, 1841, on board of a certain ill-
appointed barque bound for Western Australia.

We had with us a couple of servants, four
rams with curling horns — a purchase from the
late Lord Western; a noble blood-hound, the gift
of a noble Lord famous for the breed; a real old
English mastiff-bitch, from the stock at Lyme
Park; and a handsome spaniel cocker. Besides
this collection of quadrupeds, we had a vast assortment of useless lumber, which had cost us many
hundred pounds. Being most darkly ignorant of
every thing relating to the country to which we
were going, but having a notion that it was very
much of the same character with that so long
inhabited by Robinson Crusoe, we had prudently
provided ourselves with all the necessaries and
even non-necessaries of life in such a region.
Our tool chests would have suited an army of
pioneers; several distinguished ironmongers of the
city of London had cleared their warehouses in
our favour of all the rubbish which had lain on
hand during the last quarter of a century; we
had hinges, bolts, screws, door-latches, staples, nails

of all dimensions—from the tenpenny, downwards
—and every other requisite to have completely
built a modern village of reasonable extent. We
had tents, Macintosh bags, swimming-belts, several sets of sauce-pans in graduated scale, (we
had here a distant eye to kangaroo and cockatoo
stews,) cleavers, meat-saws, iron skewers, and a
general apparatus of kitchen utensils that would
have satisfied the desires of Monsieur Soyer himself. Then we had double and single-barrelled
guns, rifles, pistols, six barrels of Pigou and
Wilkes' gunpowder; an immense assortment of
shot, and two hundredweight of lead for bullets.

Besides the several articles already enumerated,
we had provided ourselves with eighteen months'
provisions, in pork and flour, calculating that by
the time this quantity was consumed, we should
have raised enough to support our establishment
out of the soil by the sweat of our brows. And
thus from sheer ignorance of colonial life, we had
laid out a considerable portion of our capital in
the purchase of useless articles, and of things
which might have been procured more cheaply in
the colony itself. Nor were we the only green-
horns that have gone out as colonists: on the
contrary, nine-tenths of those who emigrate, do so
in perfect ignorance of the country they are about
to visit and the life they are destined to lead.

The fact is, Englishmen, as a body, know nothing and care nothing about colonies. My own was merely the national ignorance. An Englishman's idea of a colony (he classes them altogether) is, that it is some miserable place—the Black-hole of the British empire—where no one would live if he were allowed a choice; and where the exiled spirits of the nation are incessantly sighing for a glimpse of the white cliffs of Albion, and a taste of the old familiar green-and-yellow fog of the capital of the world. Experience alone can convince him that there are in other regions of the world climes as delightful, suns as beneficent, and creditors as confiding, as those of Old England.

The voyage, of course, was tedious enough; but some portion of it was spent very pleasantly in calculating the annual profits which our flocks were likely to produce.

The four noble rams, with their curly horns, grew daily more valuable in our estimation. By the sailors, no doubt, they were rated no higher than the miserable tenants of the long-boat, that formed part of the cuddy provisions. But with us it was very different. As we looked, every bright and balmy morning, into the pen which they occupied, we were enabled to picture more vividly those Arcadian prospects which seemed now brought almost within reach. In these grave and respectable animals we recognised the patriarchs of a vast and invaluable progeny; and it was impossible to help feeling a kind of veneration for the sires of that fleecy multitude which was to prove the means of justifying our modest expectations of happiness and wealth.

Our dogs also afforded us the most pleasing subjects for speculation. With the blood-hound we were to track the footsteps of the midnight marauder, who should invade the sanctity of our fold. The spaniel was to aid in procuring a supply of game for the table; and I bestowed so much pains upon his education during the voyage, that before we landed, he was perfectly *au fait* in the article of " down-charge !" and used to flush the cat in the steward's pantry with the greatest certainty and satisfaction.

Jezebel, the mastiff-bitch, was expected to assist in guarding our castle,—an honourable duty which her courage and fidelity amply warranted us in confiding to her. Of the former quality, I shall mention an instance that occurred during the voyage. We had one day caught a shark, twelve feet long; and no sooner was he hauled on deck than Jezebel, wild with fury, rushed through the circle of eager sailors and spectators, and flew directly at the nose of the struggling monster. It was with difficulty that she was dragged away by the admiring seamen, who were compelled to admit that there was a creature on board more reckless and daring than themselves.

We were now approaching the Cape Verd Islands. I daresay it has been frequently mentioned, that there is in these latitudes a vast bed of loose sea-weed, floating about, which has existed there from time immemorial, and which is only found in this one spot of the ocean ; as though it were here com-pelled to remain under the influence of some magic spell.   Some navigators are of opinion that it grows on the rocks at the bottom of the sea, beneath the surface on which it floats.   Others maintain that it has been drifted across the Atlantic, having issued from the Gulf of Mexico.   Here, however, it is doomed to drift about hopelessly, for ever lost in the wilderness of waters; on the surface of which it now vegetates, affording shelter to small crabs, and many curious kinds of fishes.

One of the latter which we caught, about an inch in length, had a spike on his back, and four legs, with which he crawled about the sea-weed.

We approached the Island of St. Jago, sailing unconsciously close to a sunken rock, on which (as we afterwards learnt) the "Charlotte" had struck about six weeks before whilst under full sail, and had gone down in a few minutes, barely allowing time for the crew to escape in their boat.

Notwithstanding we had been five weeks at sea when we dropped anchor in Porto Praya roads, the appearance of the land was by no means inviting to the eyes. A high and extremely barren hill, or large heap of dry earth, with a good many stones about it, seemed to compose the Island. Close to us was the town, a collection of white houses that looked very dazzling in the summer sun. Beside, and running behind it, was a greenish valley, containing a clump of cocoa-nut trees. This was the spot we longed to visit; so, getting into the captain's boat, we approached the shore, where a number of nearly naked negroes rushing into the sea (there being no pier or jetty) presented their slimy backs at the gun-wale, and carried us in triumph to the beach. The town boasted of one hotel, in the only sitting-room of which we found some Portuguese officers smoking pipes as dirty as themselves, and drinking a beverage which had much the appearance of rum and water. There was no one who could speak a word of English; but at length a French waiter appeared, who seemed ravished with delight at the jargon with which we feebly reminded him of his own lively language " when at home." Having ordered dinner, we wandered off in search of the cocoa-nut valley, and purchased bananas for the first time in our lives, and oranges, the finest in the world.

Those who have been long at sea know how pleasant it is to walk once more upon the land. It is one of the brightest of the Everlasting flowers in the garland of Memory.

We walked along the sea-beach, as people so circumstanced must ever do, full of gladsome fancies. There was delight for us in the varied shells at our feet; in the curious skeletons of small fishes, untimely deceased; in the fantastic forms of the drifted sea-weed; in the gentle ripple of the companionable waves by our side. And little Fig, the spaniel, was no less pleased than ourselves. He ran before us rejoicing in his fleetness; and he ran back again in a moment to tell us how glad he was. Then as a wave more incursive than its predecessor unexpectedly wetted his feet, he would droop his tail and run faster with alarm, until the sight of some bush or bough, left high and dry by the last tide, awakened his nervous suspicions, and dreading an ambuscade, he would stop suddenly and bark at the dreadful object, until we arrived at his side, when, wagging his tail and looking slyly up with his joyous eyes, he would scamper away again as though he would have us believe he had been all the time only in fun.

What profound satisfaction is there in the freedom of land after so long a confinement! The sunshine that makes joyous every object around us finds its way into the deeps of the heart.

And now we determined to bathe. So we crossed over a jutting rock, on the other side of which was a beautiful and secluded little bay, so sheltered that the waves scarcely rippled as they came to kiss the shell-covered beach. Here we soon unrobed; and I was the first to rush at full speed into the inviting waters. Before I got up to my middle, however, I saw something before me that looked like a dark rock just below the surface. I made towards it, intending to get upon it, and dive off on the other side; but lo! as I approached, it stirred; then it darted like a flash of lightning towards one side of the bay, whilst I, after standing motionless for a moment, retreated with the utmost expedition.

It was a ground-shark, of which there are numbers on that coast.

We lost no time in putting on our clothes again, and returned in rather a fluttered state to the inn.

CHAPTER III.

THE MUTINY.

WE remained a week at St. Jago, the captain
being busily engaged in taking in water, and quar-
relling with his crew.   One day, at the instigation
of our friend, the French waiter, we made a trip of
seven miles into the interior of the island, to visit a
beautiful valley called Trinidad.   Mounted on donkeys, and attended by two ragged, copper-coloured
youths, we proceeded in gallant style up the main
street, and, leaving the town, crossed the valley
beyond it, and emerged into the open country.   It
was a rough, stony, and hilly road, through a barren
waste, where there scarcely appeared a stray blade
of grass for the goats which rambled over it in
anxious search of herbage.

At length, after a wearisome ride of several hours,
we descended suddenly into the most fertile and
luxuriant valley I ever beheld, and which seemed
to extend a distance of some miles.   A mountain
brook flowed down the midst, on the banks of

which numerous scattered and picturesque cottages appeared. On either side the ground was covered with the green carpet of Nature in the spring of the year. Everywhere, except in this smiling valley, we saw nothing but the aridity of summer, and the desolation caused by a scorching tropical sun. But here—how very different! How sudden, how magical was the change! Every species of vegetable grew here in finest luxuriance. Melons of every variety, pine-apples, sweet potatoes, plantains, and bananas, with their broad and drooping leaves of freshest green and rich purple flower, and ripe yellow fruit. Orange-trees, cocoa-nut trees, limes— the fig, the vine, the citron, the pomegranate, and numerous others, grateful to the weary sight, and bearing precious stores amid their branches, combined to give the appearance of wealth and plenty to this happy valley. It was not, however, destined to be entered by us without a fierce combat for precedence between two of our steeds. The animal whom it was the evil lot of Melibœus to bestride, suddenly threw back its ears, and darted madly upon the doctor's quadruped, which, on its side, manifested no reluctance to the fight.

Dreadful was the scene; the furious donkeys rearing and striking with their fore-feet, and biting each other about the head and neck without the smallest feeling of compunction or remorse; the two guides shrieking and swearing in Portuguese at the donkeys and each other, and striking right and left with their long staves, perfectly indifferent as to whom they hit; the unhappy riders, furious with fright and chagrin, shouting in English to the belligerents of both classes to "keep off!" The screams of two women, who were carrying water in the neighbourhood, enhanced by the barking of a terrified cur, that ran blindly hither and thither with its tail between its legs, in a state of frantic excitement—altogether produced a *tableau* of the most spirited description. Peace was at length restored, and we all dismounted from our saddles with fully as much satisfaction as we had experienced when vaulting into them.

There is little more to say about the valley of Trinidad. The cottagers who supply the town of Porto Praya with fruits and vegetables are extremely poor, and very uncleanly and untidy in their houses and habits. We had intended to spend the night with them, but the appearance of the accommodations determined us to return to our inn, in spite of the friendly and disinterested advice of our guides.

St. Jago abounds with soldiers and priests; the former of whom are chiefly convicts from Lisbon, condemned to serve here in the ranks.

The day for sailing arrived, and we were all on

board and ready. Our barque was a temperance ship; that is, she belonged to owners who refused to allow their sailors the old measure of a wine-glass of rum in the morning, and another in the afternoon, but liberally substituted an extra pint of water instead.

There is always one thing remarkable about these temperance ships, that when they arrive in harbour, their crews, excited to madness by long abstinence from their favourite liquor, and suffering in consequence all the excruciating torments of thirst, run into violent excesses the moment they get on shore. St. Jago is famous for a kind of liquid fire, called *aguadente*, which is smuggled on board ship in the shape of pumpkins and water-melons. These are sold to the sailors for shirts and clothing; there being nothing so eagerly sought for by the inhabitants of St. Jago as linen and calico.

Our crew, being thoroughly disgusted with their captain, as indeed they had some reason to be, and their valour being wondrously excited by their passionate fondness for water-melons, came to a stern resolution of spending the remainder of their lives on this agreeable island; at any rate, they determined to sail no farther in our company. The captain was ashore, settling his accounts and receiving his papers; the chief-mate had given orders to loose the fore-topsail and weigh anchor; and we

were all in the cuddy, quietly sipping our wine,
when we heard three cheers and a violent scuffling
on deck.   In a few moments down rushed the mate
in a state of delirious excitement, vociferating that
the men were in open mutiny, and calling upon us,
in the name of the Queen, to assist the officers of
the ship in bringing them to order.   Starting up
at the call of our Sovereign, we rushed to our cabins
in a state of nervous bewilderment, and loading our
pistols in a manner that insured their not going off,
we valiantly hurried on deck in the rear of the exasperated officer.   On reaching the raised quarter-
deck of the vessel, we found the crew clustered
together near the mainmast, armed with hand-
spikes, boat-oars, crow-bars, and a miscellaneous
assortment of other weapons, and listening to an
harangue which the carpenter was in the act of delivering to them.   They were all intoxicated ; but
the carpenter, a ferocious, determined villain, was
the least so.

At one of the quarter-deck gangways stood the
captain's lady, a lean and wizened Hecate, as
famous for her love of rum as any of the crew, but
more openly rejoicing in the no less objectionable
spirit of ultra-methodism.   Screaming at the top
of her voice, whilst her unshawled and dusky shoulders, as well as the soiled ribands of her dirty cap,
were gently fanned by the sea-breeze, she com-

manded the men to return to their duty, in a volume of vociferation that seemed perfectly inexhaustible. Fearing that the quarter-deck would be carried by storm, we divided our party, consisting of the two mates, three passengers with their servants, and Mungo the black servant, into two divisions, each occupying one of the gangways.

In a few moments the carpenter ceased his oration ; the men cheered and danced about the deck, brandishing their weapons, and urging one another to " come on." Then with a rush, or rather a stagger, they assailed our position, hoping to carry it in an instant by storm. The mate shouted to us to fire, and pick out three or four of the most desperate ; but perceiving the intoxicated state of the men we refused to shed blood, except in the last extremity of self-defence ; and determined to maintain our post, if possible, by means of our pistol-butts, or our fists alone. In the general *mêlée* which ensued, the captain's lady, who fought in the van, and looked like a lean Helen Mac-Gregor, or the mythological Ate, was captured by the assailants, and dragged to the deck below. Then it was that combining our forces, and inspired with all the ardour which is naturally excited by the appearance of beauty in distress, we made a desperate sally, and after a fearful skirmish, succeeded in rescuing the lady, and replacing her on the quarter-deck, with the loss only of her cap and gown, and a few handfuls of hair.

After this exploit, both parties seemed inclined to pause and take breath, and in the interval we made an harangue to the sailors, expressive of our regret that they should act in so disgraceful a manner.

The gallant (or rather ungallant) fellows replied that they were determined to be no longer commanded by a she-captain, as they called the lady, and therefore would sail no farther in such company.

I really believe that most of them had no serious intention whatever in their proceedings, but the officers of the ship were firmly convinced that the carpenter and one or two others had resolved to get possession of the vessel, dispose of the passengers and mates somehow or other, and then slip the cable, and wreck and sell the ship and cargo on the coast of South America.

Whilst the truce lasted, the second mate had been busily engaged making signals of distress, by repeatedly hoisting and lowering the ensign reversed, from the mizen-peak. This was soon observed from the deck of a small Portuguese schooner of war, which lay at anchor about half a mile from us, having arrived a few hours previously, bringing the Bishop of some-where-or-other on a visitation to the island. The attention of the officer of the watch had been previously attracted towards us by the noise we had made, and the violent scuffle which he had been observing through his glass. No sooner, therefore, was the flag reversed, than a boat was lowered from the quarter-davits, filled with marines, and pulled towards our vessel with the utmost rapidity. The mutineers, whose attention was directed entirely to the quarter-deck, did not perceive this manœuvre, which, however, was evident enough to us, who exerted ourselves to the utmost to prolong the parley until our allies should arrive.

The carpenter now decided upon renewing the assault, having laid aside his handspike and armed himself with an axe; but just at this moment the man-of-war's boat ran alongside, and several files of marines, with fixed bayonets, clambering on to the deck, effected a speedy change in the aspect of affairs. Perceiving at once how matters stood, the officer in command, without asking a single question, ordered a charge against the astonished sailors, who, after a short resistance, and a few violent blows given and received, were captured and disarmed.

There was a boy among the party called Shiny Bill, some fifteen years of age, who managed to escape to the fore-shrouds, and giving the marine

who pursued him a violent kick in the face, succeeded in reaching the fore-top, where he coiled
himself up like a ball.   Two or three marines, exasperated by the scuffle, and by several smart raps
on the head which they had received, hastened
up the shrouds after the fugitive, who, however,
ascended to the fore-top-mast cross-trees, whither
his enemies, after some hesitation, pursued.   Finding this post also untenable, he proceeded to swarm
up the fore-top-gallant-mast shrouds, and at last
seated himself on the royal yard, where he calmly
awaited the approach of the enemy.   These, however, feeling that the position was too strong to be
successfully assailed by marines, deliberately commenced their retreat, and arrived on deck, whilst
their officer was hailing the immovable Bill in
Portuguese, and swearing he would shoot him unless
he instantly descended.

Disdaining, however, to pay the least attention
to these threats, Shiny William continued to occupy
his post with the greatest tranquillity ; and the
officer, giving up the attempt in despair, proceeded
to inquire from us in Portuguese-French the history
of this outbreak.   The scene concluded with the
removal of the mutineers in one of the ship's boats
to the man-of-war, where, in a few moments,
several dozen lashes were administered to every
man in detail, and the whole party were then sent

on shore, and committed to a dungeon darker and
dirtier than the worst among them had ever before
been acquainted with. But before all this was
done, and when the boats had pulled about a hundred yards from the vessel, Shiny Bill began to
descend from his post. He slipped down unob-
served by any one, and the first notice we had of
his intentions was from perceiving him run across
the deck to the starboard bow, whence he threw
himself, without hesitation, into the sea, and began
to swim lustily after his captive friends. Our
shouts—for, remembering the abundance of sharks,
we were very much alarmed for the poor fellow—
attracted the attention of the officer in the boat, to
whom we pointed out the figure of Bill, who
seemed as eager now to make a voluntary surrren-
der, and share the fate of his comrades, as he had
previously been opposed to a violent seizure. The
swimmer was soon picked up, and, to our regret,
received in due season the same number of stripes
as fell to the lot of his friends captured in battle.

The prisoners remained several days in their
dungeon, where they were hospitably regaled with
bread and water by the Portuguese Government;
and at the end of this period (so unworthy did
they prove of the handsome treatment they received) the British spirit was humbled within them,
and they entreated with tears to be allowed to

return to their duty. The mates, however, refused to sail in the same vessel with the carpenter, and it was accordingly settled that he should remain in custody until the arrival of a British man-of-war, and then be returned to his country, passage free.

CHAPTER IV.

THE PRISON-ISLAND.

It was nearly the end of August when we approached the conclusion of our voyage. The wind was fair, the sun shone brightly, and every heart was gay with the hope of once more being upon land. We drew nigh to the Island of Rottnest, about sixteen miles from the mouth of the river Swan, and anchored to the north of it, waiting for a pilot from Fremantle.

And there we had the first view of our future home. Beyond that low line of sand-hills, which stretched away north and south, far as the eye could reach, we were to begin life again, and earn for ourselves a fortune and an honourable name. No friendly voice would welcome us on landing, but numberless sharpers, eager to prey upon the inexperienced Griffin, and take advantage of his unavoidable ignorance and confiding innocence. There was nothing very cheering in the prospect; but supported by the confidence and ambition of youth, we experienced no feelings of dismay.

In order to wile away the time, we landed on the island, and, passing through a thick wood of cypresses, came to a goodly-sized and comfortable-looking dwelling-house, with numerous out-buildings about it, all built of marine lime-stone.

As the particulars which I then learned respecting this island were afterwards confirmed by experience and more extended information, I may as well enter upon its history at once.

The gentleman who was then Governor of Western Australia, was Mr. JOHN HUTT, a man of enlightened mind, firm, sagacious, and benevolent. From the first, he adopted an admirable policy with regard to the native inhabitants.

Exhibiting on all occasions a friendly interest in their welfare, he yet maintained a strict authority over them, which they soon learned to respect and fear. The Aborigines were easily brought to feel that their surest protection lay in the Government; that every act of violence committed upon them by individual settlers was sure to be avenged by the whites themselves; and that, as certainly, any aggression on the part of the natives would call down the utmost severity of punishment upon the offenders. By this firm administration of equal justice the Aboriginal population, instead of being, as formerly, a hostile, treacherous, and troublesome race, had become harmless, docile, and in some degree useful to the settlers.

But it was not the policy of Mr. Hutt merely to punish the natives for offences committed against the whites; he was anxious to substitute the milder spirit of the British law in lieu of their own barbarous code; and to make them feel, in process of time, that it was for their own interest to appeal for protection on all occasions to the dominant power of Government, rather than trust to their own courage and spears. This was no easy task, and could only be accomplished by firmness, discrimination, and patience; but in the course of a few years, considerable progress had been made in subduing the prejudices and the barbarous customs of the Aborigines. Although it had been declared by Royal Proclamation that the native inhabitants were in every respect subjects of the British throne, and as such entitled to equal privileges with ourselves, and to be judged on all occasions by the common and statute laws, it proved to be no easy matter to carry into practice these views of the Home Government. People in England, who derive their knowledge of savages from the orations delivered at Exeter Hall, are apt to conceive that nothing more is requisite than to ensure them protection from imaginary oppression, and a regular supply of spiritual comforts. They do not consider

that whilst they insist upon these unfortunate creatures being treated exactly as British subjects, they
are placing a yoke on their own necks too heavy
for them to bear in their present condition. Primitive and simple laws are necessary to a primitive
state of society; and the cumbrous machinery of
civilized life is entirely unsuited to those who in
their daily habits and their intellectual endowments
are little superior to the beasts that perish. By
declaring the savages to be in every respect British
subjects, it becomes illegal to treat them otherwise
than such. If a settler surprise a native in the
act of stealing a pound of flour, he of course
delivers him over to a constable, by whom he is
conveyed before the nearest magistrate. Now this
magistrate, who is an old settler, and well acquainted with the habits of the natives, is also
a man of humanity; and if he were allowed to
exercise a judicious discretion, would order the
culprit to be well flogged and dismissed to his ex-
pectant family. But thanks to Her Majesty's
well-meaning Secretaries of State for the Colonies,
who have all successively judged alike on this
point, it is declared most unadvisable to allow a
local magistrate the smallest modicum of discretion.
He has only one course to pursue, and that is,
to commit the offender for trial at the next Quarter Sessions, to be held in the capital of the

colony. Accordingly, the poor native, who would rather have been flayed alive than sent into confinement for two months previous to trial, whilst his wives are left to their own resources, is heavily ironed, lest he should escape, and marched down some sixty or seventy miles to Fremantle gaol, where the denizen of the forest has to endure those horrors of confinement which only the untamed and hitherto unfettered savage can possibly know.

Among savages, the *Lex talionis*—the law of retaliation—is the law of nature and of right; to abstain from avenging the death of a relative would be considered, by the tribe of the deceased, an act of unpardonable neglect. Their own customs, which are to them as laws, point out the mode of vengeance. The nearest relative of the deceased must spear his slayer. Nothing is more common among these people than to steal one another's wives; and this propensity affords a prolific source of bloodshed.

They have also a general law, which is never deviated from, and which requires that whenever a member of a tribe dies, whether from violence or otherwise, a life must be taken from some other tribe. This practice may have originated in a desire to preserve the balance of power; or from a belief, which is very general among them, that a man never dies a natural death. If he die of some disorder, and not of a spear-wound, they say he is "quibble gidgied," or speared by some person a long distance off. The native doctor, or wise man of the tribe, frequently pretends to know who has caused the death of the deceased; and the supposed murderer is of course pursued and murdered in turn. This custom necessarily induces a constant state of warfare. Now it is very right that all these barbarous and unchristian practices should be put an end to; but, whilst endeavouring to suppress them, we ought to remember that they are part and parcel of the long-established laws of this rude people, and that it is not possible all at once to make them forego their ancient institutions and customs. The settlers would gladly see punished all acts of violence committed among the natives in their neighbourhood. Were they permitted to inflict such punishments as are best suited to the limited ideas and moral thraldom of the Aborigines, these, without cruelty or injustice, might gradually be brought within the pale of civilization; but when the law declares it to be inevitable that every British subject who is tried and found guilty of having speared his enemy shall be hanged without benefit of clergy, the colonists, out of sheer humanity and pity for the ignorance of the culprit, refrain from bringing him to trial and punishment—a proceeding which, by the way, would cost the colony some fifteen or twenty pounds—and thus he goes on in his errors, unreproved by the wisdom or the piety of the whites. Sometimes, however, it happens that the officers who exercise the calling of Protectors of the Aborigines, anxious to prove that their post is no sinecure, make a point of hunting up an occasional law-breaker, who, being brought to trial, is usually found guilty upon his own evidence—the unfortunate culprit, conscious of no guilt in having followed the customs of his ancestors, generally making a candid statement of his offence. The sentence decreed by the English law is then passed upon him, and he would, of course, be duly subjected to the penalty which justice is supposed to demand, did not the compassionate Governor, in the exercise of the highest privilege of the Crown, think proper to step in and commute the sentence to perpetual imprisonment. As it would have entailed a serious expense upon the colony to have had to maintain these prisoners in a gaol in the capital, his Excellency determined to establish a penal settlement at Rottnest; and this he accordingly accomplished, with very good effect.

At the time we visited the island, there were about twenty native prisoners in charge of a superintendent and a few soldiers.

The prisoners were employed in cultivating a sufficient quantity of ground to produce their own food. It was they also who had built the superintendent's residence; and whenever there was nothing else to do, they were exercised in carrying stone to the top of a high hill, on which a lighthouse was proposed to be built.

The Governor has certainly shown very good judgment in the formation of this penal establishment. It is the dread of the natives throughout the colony; and those prisoners who are released inspire among their fellows the greatest horror and dismay by their tales of the hardships they have suffered. No punishment can be more dreadful to these savages—the most indolent race in the world—than being compelled to work ; and as their idleness brings them occasionally in contact with the superintendent's lash, their recollections and accounts of Rottnest are of the most fearful description. Certain, however, it is, that nothing has tended so much to keep the Aborigines in good order as the establishment of this place of punishment. It is maintained at very little expense to the colony, as the prisoners grow their own vegetables, and might easily be made to produce flour enough for their own consumption.

It was a clear, beautiful, sparkling day, and there was a sense of enjoyment attached to the green foliage, the waving crops, and the gently heaving sea, that threw over this new world of ours a charm which filled our hearts with gladness.

Having returned to our ship, we saw the pilot-boat rapidly approaching. As it came alongside, and we were hailed by the steersman, we felt a sensation of wonder at hearing ourselves addressed in English and by Englishmen, so far, so very far from the shores of England. With this feeling, too, was mingled something like pity; we could not help looking upon these poor boatmen, in their neat costume of blue woollen shirts, canvass trousers, and straw hats, as fellow-countrymen who had been long exiled from their native land, and who must now regard us with eyes of interest and affection, as having only recently left its shores.

No sooner was the pilot on board than the anchor was weighed, the sails were set, and we began to beat up into the anchorage off Fremantle. Night closed upon us ere we reached the spot proposed, and we passed the interval in walking the deck and noting the stars come forth upon their watch. The only signs of life and of human habitation were in the few twinkling lights of the town of Fremantle: all beside, on the whole length of the coast, seemed to be a desert of sand, the back-ground of which was occupied with the dark outline of an illimitable forest.

It was into this vast solitude that we were destined to penetrate. It was a picture full of sombre beauty, and it filled us with solemn thoughts.

The next morning we were up at daybreak. Certainly it was a beautiful sight, to watch the sun rise without a cloud from out the depths of that dark forest, rapidly dispersing the cold gray gloom, and giving life, as it seemed, to the sparkling waves, which just before had been unconsciously heaved by some internal power, and suffered to fall back helplessly into their graves.

How differently now they looked, dancing joyously forward towards the shore! And the sun, that seems to bring happiness to inanimate things, brought hope and confidence back to the hearts of those who watched him rise.

Flights of sea-birds of the cormorant tribe, but generally known as Shags, were directing their course landward from the rocky islands on which they had roosted during the night. What long files they form!—the solitary leader winging his rapid and undeviating way just above the level of the waves, whilst his followers, keeping their regular distances, blindly pursue the course he takes. See! he enters the mouth of the river; some distant object to his practised eye betokens danger, and though still maintaining his onward course, he inclines upwards into the air, and the whole line, as though actuated by the same impulse, follow his flight. And now they descend again within a few feet of the river's surface, and now are lost behind projecting rocks. All day long they fish in the retired bays and sheltered nooks of the river, happy in the midst of plenty.

The river Swan issues forth into the sea over a bar of rocks, affording only a dangerous passage for boats, or vessels drawing from four to five feet water. Upon the left bank of the river is the town of Fremantle. The most prominent object from the sea is a circular building of white limestone, placed on the summit of a black rock at the mouth of the Swan. This building is the gaol.

On the other side of the roadstead, about ten or twelve miles distant from the main, is a chain of islands, of which Rottnest is the most northern. Then come some large rocks, called the Stragglers, leaving a passage out from the roadstead by the south of Rottnest; after these is Carnac, an island abounding with rabbits and mutton-birds; and still farther south is Garden island.

Fremantle, the principal port of the colony, is unfortunately situated, as vessels of any burthen are obliged to anchor at a considerable distance from the shore. Lower down the coast is a fine harbour, called Mangles Bay, containing a splendid anchorage, and it is much to be lamented that this was not originally fixed upon as the site for the capital of the colony.

The first impression which the visitor to this

settlement receives is not favourable. The whole country between Fremantle and Perth, a distance of ten miles, is composed of granitic sand, with which is mixed a small proportion of vegetable mould. This unfavourable description of soil is covered with a coarse scrub, and an immense forest of banksia trees, red gums, and several varieties of the eucalyptus. The banksia is a paltry tree, about the size of an apple-tree in an English or French orchard, perfectly useless as timber, but affording an inexhaustible supply of firewood. Besides the trees I have mentioned, there is the xanthorea, or grass-tree, a plant which cannot be intelligibly described to those who have never seen it. The stem consists of a tough pithy substance, round which the leaves are formed. These, long and tapering like the rush, are four-sided, and extremely brittle; the base from which they shoot is broad and flat, about the size of a thumb-nail, and very resinous in substance. As the leaves decay annually, others are put forth above the bases of the old ones, which are thus pressed down by the new shoots, and a fresh circle is added every year to the growing plant. Thousands of acres are covered with this singular vegetable production; and the traveller at his night bivouac is always sure of a glorious fire from the resinous stem of the grass-tree, and a comfortable bed from its leaves.

We landed in a little bay on the southern bank of the river. The houses appeared to be generally two-storied, and were built of hard marine limestone. Notwithstanding the sandy character of the soil, the gardens produced vegetables of every variety, and no part of the world could boast of finer potatoes or cabbages. Anxious to begin the primitive life of a settler as speedily as possible, we consulted a merchant to whom we had brought letters of introduction as to the best mode of proceeding. He advised us to fix our head-quarters for a time near to Fremantle, and thence traverse the colony until we should decide upon a permanent place of abode. In the meantime we dined and slept at Francisco's Hotel, where we were served with French dishes in first-rate style, and drank good luck to ourselves in excellent claret.

In the early days of the colony, Sir James Stirling, the first Governor, had fixed upon Fremantle as the seat of government; and the settlers had begun to build themselves country-houses and elegant villa residences upon the banks of the river. These, however, were not completed before it was determined to fix the capital at Perth, some dozen miles up the river, where the soil was rather better, and where a communication with the proposed farms in the interior would be more readily kept up.

The government officers had now to abandon

their half-built stone villas, and construct new
habitations of wood, as there was no stone to be
found in the neighbourhood of Perth, and brick
clay had not then been discovered.

It was in one of these abandoned houses (called
the Cantonment), situate on the banks of the Swan,
about half a mile from Fremantle, that, by the
advice of our friend, we resolved to take up our
quarters. The building was enclosed on three sides
by a rough stone wall, and by a wooden fence,
forming a paddock of about three quarters of an
acre in extent. It comprised one large room, of
some forty feet by eighteen, which had a roof of
thatch in tolerable repair. The north side, protected by a verandah, had a door and two windows,
in which a few panes of glass remained, and looked
upon the broad river, from which it was separated
by a bank of some twenty feet in descent, covered
with a variety of shrubs, just then bursting into
flower. A few scattered red-gum trees, of the size
of a well-grown ash, gave a park-like appearance to
our paddock, of which we immediately felt extremely proud, and had no doubt of being very
comfortable in our new domain. Besides the large
room I have mentioned, there were two others at
the back of it, which, unfortunately, were in rather
a dilapidated condition; and below these apartments
(which were built on the slope of a hill) were two

more, which we immediately allotted to the dogs
and sheep. This side of the building was enclosed
by a wall, which formed a small court-yard. Here
was an oven, which only wanted a little repair to be
made ready for immediate use.

For several days we were occupied in superintending the landing of our stores, and housing them
in a building which we rented in the town at no
trifling sum per week. A light dog-cart, which I
had brought out, being unpacked, proved extremely
useful in conveying to our intended residence such
articles as we were likely to be in immediate
want of.

The two men had already taken up their abode
there, together with the rams and dogs; and at
last, leaving our comfortable quarters at the hotel
with something like regret and a feeling of doubt
and bewilderment, we all three marched in state,
with our double-barrels on our shoulders, to take
possession of our rural habitation.

CHAPTER V.

FIRST ADVENTURES.

WE had providently dined before we took possession; and now, at sunset, we stood on the bank
before our house, looking down upon the placid
river. The blood-hound was chained to one of the
posts of the verandah; Jezebel, the noble mastiff-
bitch, lay basking before the door, perfectly contented with her situation and prospects; and little
Fig was busily hunting among the shrubs, and
barking at the small birds which he disturbed as
they were preparing to roost.

One of the men was sitting on an upturned box
beside the fire, waiting for the gently-humming
kettle to boil; whilst the other was chipping wood
outside the house, and from time to time carrying
the logs into the room, and piling them upon the
hearth. As we looked around we felt that we had
now indeed commenced a new life. For some
months, at any rate, we were to do without those
comforts and luxuries which Englishmen at home,

of every rank above the entirely destitute, deem so essential to bodily ease and happiness.

We were to sleep on the floor, to cook our own victuals, and make our own beds. This was to be our mode of acquiring a settlement in this land of promise. Still there was an air of independence about it, and we felt a confidence in our own energies and resources that made the novelty of our position rather agreeable than otherwise.

There was something exhilarating in the fresh sea-breeze; there was something very pleasing in the gay appearance of the shrubs that surrounded us—in the broad expanse of the river, with its occasional sail, and its numerous birds passing rapidly over it on their way to the islands where they roosted, or soaring leisurely to and fro, with constant eyes piercing its depths, and then suddenly darting downwards like streams of light into the flood, and emerging instantly afterwards with their finny prey. The opposite bank of the river displayed a sandy country covered with dark scrub; and beyond this was the sea, with a view of Rottnest and the Straggler rocks. A few white cottages relieved the sombre and death-like appearance of that opposite shore. Unpromising as was the aspect of the country, it yet afforded sufficient verdure to support in good condition a large herd of cattle, which supplied Fremantle with milk and food.

Here, then, the reader may behold us for the
first time in our character of settlers. He may
behold three individuals in light shooting coats and
cloth caps, standing upon the bank before their
picturesque and half-ruinous house, their dogs at
their side, and their gaze fixed upon the river that
rolled beneath them.   The same thoughts probably
occupied them all : they were now left in a land
which looked much like a desert, with Heaven for
their aid, and no other resources than a small
capital, and their own energies and truth. The
great game of life was now to begin in earnest,
and the question was, how it should be played
with success ?   Individual activity and exertion
were absolutely necessary to ensure good fortune ;
and warmly impressed with the consciousness of
this, we turned with one impulse in search of
employment.

Æsculapius began to prepare their supper for
the dogs, and Melibœus looked after his sheep,
which were grazing in the paddock in front of the
dwelling.   As for myself, with the ardent mind of
a young settler, I seized upon the axe, and began
to chop firewood—an exercise, by the way, which
I almost immediately renounced.

And now for supper !

Our most necessary articles were buried somewhere beneath the heaps of rubbish with which we

had filled the store-room at Fremantle. Our
plates, cups and saucers, &c., were in a crate which
was not to be unpacked until we had removed our
property and abode to the inland station which we
designed for our permanent residence. There were,
however, at hand for present use eight or nine
pewter plates, and a goodly sized pannikin a-piece.
In one corner of the room was a bag of flour, in
another a bag of sugar, in a third a barrel of pork,
and on the table, composed of a plank upon two
empty casks, were a couple of loaves which Simon
had purchased in the town, and a large tea-pot
which he had fortunately discovered in the same
cask with the pannikins.

The kettle fizzed upon the fire, impatient to
be poured out; the company began to draw round
the hospitable board, seating themselves upon their
bedding, or upon empty packing-cases; and, in a
word, tea time had arrived. Hannibal, as we
called the younger of our attendants, from his
valiant disposition, had filled one of the pewter
plates with brown sugar from the bag; the doctor
made the tea, and we wanted nothing but spoons
to make our equipage complete. However, every
man had his pocket-knife, and so we fell to work.

Butter being at that time half-a-crown a pound,
Simon (our head man) had prudently refrained
from buying any; and as he had forgotten to boil

a piece of the salt pork, we had to sup upon dry bread, which we did without repining, determined, however, to manage better on the morrow.

In the meantime we were nearly driven desperate by most violent attacks upon our legs, committed by myriads of fleas. They were so plentiful that we could see them crawling upon the floor; the dogs almost howled with anguish, and the most sedate among us could not refrain from bitter and deep execrations. We had none of us ever before experienced such torment; and really feared that in the course of the night we should be eaten up entirely. These creatures are hatched in the sand, and during the rains of winter they take refuge in empty houses; but they infest every place throughout the country, during all seasons, more or less, and are only kept down by constant sweeping from becoming a most tremendous and overwhelming plague, before which every created being, not indigenous to the soil, would soon disappear, or be reduced to a bundle of polished bones. The natives themselves never sleep twice under the same wigwam.

After tea, the sheep and dogs being carefully disposed of for the night, we turned out before the house, and comforted ourselves with cigars; and having whiled away as much time as possible, we spread out our mattresses on the floor, and in a

state of desperation attempted to find rest. We
escaped with our lives, and were thankful in the
morning for so much mercy vouchsafed to us, but
we could not conscientiously return thanks for a
night's refreshing rest.

At the first dawn of day we rolled up our beds,
lighted the fire, swept out the room, let the dogs
loose, and drove the rams to pasture on the margin
of the river. After breakfast, which was but a
sorry meal, we determined to make our first
attempt at baking. Simon, a man of dauntless
resolution, undertook the task, using a piece of
stale bread as leaven. It was a serious business,
and we all helped or looked on; but the result,
notwithstanding the multitude of councillors, was a
lamentable failure. Better success, fortunately,
attended the labours of Hannibal, who boiled a
piece of salt pork with the greatest skill.

Mutton at this period, 1841, was selling at sixteen-
pence per pound (it is now two-pence), and we
therefore resolved to depend upon our guns for
fresh meat. We had brought with us a fishing-net,
which we determined to put in requisition the
following day.

The most prominent idea in the imagination of
a settler on his first arrival at an Australian colony,
is on the subject of the natives. Whilst in
England he was, like the rest of his generous-

minded countrymen, sensibly alive to the wrongs of these unhappy beings—wrongs which, originating in a great measure in the eloquence of Exeter Hall, have awakened the sympathies of a humane and unselfish people throughout the length and breadth of the kingdom.   Full of these noble and ennobling sentiments, the emigrant approaches the scene of British-colonial cruelty; but no sooner does he land, than a considerable change takes place in his feelings.   He begins to think that he is about to place his valuable person and property in the very midst of a nation of savages, who are entirely un-restrained by any moral or human laws, or any religious scruples, from taking the most disagreeable liberties with these precious things.

The refined and amiable philanthropist gradually sinks into the coarse-minded and selfish settler, who is determined to protect himself, his family, and effects, by every means in his power—even at the risk of outraging the amiable feelings of his brother philanthropists at home.   In Western Australia, the natives generally are in very good order; they behave peaceably towards the settlers, eat their flour, and in return occasionally herd or hunt up their cattle, and keep their larders supplied with kangaroo.

It is very rarely—I have never indeed heard of a single well-authenticated instance—that any amount of benefits, or the most unvarying kindness, can awaken the smallest spark of gratitude in the breasts of these degraded savages. Those who derive their chief support from the flour and broken meat daily bestowed upon them by the farm settlers, would send a spear through their benefactors with as little remorse as through the breast of a stranger. The fear of punishment alone has any influence over them; and although in this colony they are never treated with anything like cruelty or oppression, it is absolutely necessary to personal safety to maintain a firm and prompt authority over them.

When we first arrived, we were philanthropists, in the usual sense of that term, and thought a good deal about the moral and general destitution of this unfortunate people; but when we first encountered on the road a party of coffee-coloured savages, with spears in their hands, and loose kangaroo-skin cloaks (their only garments) on their shoulders, accompanied by their women similarly clad, and each carrying in a bag at her back her black-haired offspring, with a face as filthy as its mother's—we by no means felt inclined to step forward and embrace them as brethren.

I question, indeed, whether the most ardent philanthropist in the world would not have hesitated before he even held forth his hand to creatures whose heads and countenances were darkened over with a compound of grease and red clay, whose persons had never been submitted to ablution from the hour of their birth, and whose approach was always heralded by a perfume that would stagger the most enthusiastic lover of his species.

But it was not merely disgust that kept us at arm's length. We must confess we were somewhat appalled at this first view of savage life, as we looked upon the sharp-pointed spears, wild eyes, and well-polished teeth of our new acquaintance. Although, in truth, they were perfectly harmless in their intentions, we could not help feeling a little nervous as they drew nigh, and saluted us with shrill cries and exclamations, and childish bursts of wild laughter. Their principal question was, whether we were " cabra-man ?" or seamen, as we afterwards discovered their meaning to be. After a good deal of screaming and laughing, they passed on their way, leaving us much relieved by their absence. They seemed to be, and experience has proved to us that they are, the most light-hearted, careless, and happy people in the world. Subsisting upon the wild roots of the earth, opossums, lizards, snakes, kangaroos, or anything else that is eatable which happens to fall in their way, they obtain an easy livelihood, and never trouble themselves with thoughts of the morrow. They build a new house for themselves every evening; that is, each family erects a slight shelter of sticks covered over with bark, or the tops of the xanthorea, that just keeps off the wind; and with a small fire at their feet, the master of the family, his wife, or wives, and children, lie huddled together like a cluster of snakes—happier than the tenants of downy beds. Far happier, certainly, than we had lately been in ours. We had, however, devised a new plan for the next night. Having each of us a hammock, we suspended them from the rafters; and thus, after the first difficulty and danger of getting into bed was overcome, we lay beyond the reach of our formidable enemies, and contrived to sleep soundly and comfortably.

The next morning we breakfasted early. My brothers resolved to try the effect of the fishing-net, and I myself arranged a shooting excursion with a lad, whose parents rented a house situated about a quarter of a mile from our own. We were to go to some lakes a few miles distant, which abounded with wild ducks and other water-fowl. Preceded by Fig, and more soberly accompanied by Jezebel, we set out upon our expedition.

It was the close of the Australian winter, and the temperature was that of a bright, clear day in England at the end of September. The air was mild, but elastic and dry; the peppermint and wattle-trees were gay with white and yellow blos-

soms; an infinite variety of flowering shrubs gave
to the country the appearance of English grounds
about a goodly mansion; whilst the earth was
carpeted with the liveliest flowers. It was impossible to help being in good spirits.

We passed up a valley of white gum-trees, which
somewhat resemble the ash, but are of a much
lighter hue. They belong to the eucalyptus
species.

I shot several beautiful parroquets, the plumage of
which was chiefly green; the heads were black, and
some of the pinion feathers yellow. The country
presented very little appearance of grass, though
abounding with green scrub; and frequently we
passed over denuded hills of limestone-rock, from
which we beheld the sea on one side, and on the
other the vast forest of banksias and eucalypti,
that overspreads the entire country. The river
winding among this mass of foliage, relieved the
eye.

After a walk of two hours we approached the
lakes of which we were in search. Situated in a
flat country, and their margins covered with tall
sedges, it was difficult to obtain a view of the
water. Now, then, we prepared for action. Behind
those tall sedges was probably a brood of water-
fowl, either sleeping in the heat of the day, or
carefully feeding in the full security of desert soli-

tude. "Fig! you villain! what are you about?
are you going to rush into the water, and ruin me
by your senseless conduct? I have got you now,
and here you must please to remain quiet. No,
you rascal! you need not look up to me with such
a beseeching countenance, whilst you tremble with
impatience, eager to have a share in the sport.
You must wait till you hear my gun. I am now
shooting for my dinner, and perhaps for yours also,
if you will condescend to eat duck, and I dare not
allow you the pleasure of putting up the game.
You understand all this well enough, and therefore
please to be silent;—or, observe! I'll murder you."

Leaving the boy with the dogs, I began to steal
towards the lake, when I heard his muttered excla-
mation, and, turning round, saw him crouching
to the earth and pointing to the sky. Imitating
his caution, I looked in the direction he pointed
out, and beheld three large birds leisurely making
towards the spot we occupied. They were larger
than geese, black, with white wings, and sailed
heavily along, whilst I lay breathlessly awaiting
their approach. The dogs were held down by the
boy, and we all seemed equally to feel the awful-
ness of the moment. The birds came slowly
towards us, and then slanted away to the right;
and then wheeling round and round, they alighted
upon the lake.

Creeping to the sedges, I pushed cautiously through, up to the ankles in mud and water. How those provoking reeds, three feet higher than my head, rustled as I gently put them aside! And now I could see plainly across a lake of several acres in extent. There, on the opposite side, were three black swans sailing about, and occasionally burying their long necks in the still waters. With gaze riveted upon that exciting spectacle, I overlooked a myriad of ducks that were reposing within a few yards of me, and which, having discovered the lurking danger, began to rise *en masse* from the lake.

Never before had I seen such a multitude. Struck with amazement, I stood idly gaping as they rose before me; and after sweeping round the lake, with a few quacks of alarm, whirled over the trees and disappeared.

The swans seemed for a moment to catch the general apprehension, and one of them actually rose out of the water, but after skimming along the surface for a few yards, he sank down again, and his companions swam to rejoin him. Gently retreating, I got back upon the dry land, and motioning the boy to remain quiet, hastened round the lake to its opposite bank. More cautiously than before I entered the grove of sedges, and soon beheld two of the swans busily fishing at some distance from

the shore. What had become of the third? There
he is, close to the border of the lake, and only
about fifty yards from my position! My first shot
at a swan!—Now then—present! fire!—bang!
What a splutter! The shots pepper the water
around him. He tries to rise. He cannot! his
wing is broken! Hurrah! hurrah! "Here, Jonathan! Toby! what's your name? here! bring the
dogs—I've hit him—I've done for him!

"Fig, Fig!—O! here you are; good little dog
—good little fellow! now then, in with you! there
he is!"

With a cry of delight, little Fig dashed through
the reeds. The water rushed down his open throat
and half-choked him; but he did not care.
Shaking the water out of his nose as he swam, he
whimpered with pleasure, and hurried after the
swan, which was now slowly making towards the
middle of the lake. Its companions had left it to
its fate. We stood in the water watching the
chase. Jezebel, excited out of all propriety, though
she could see nothing of what was going on, gallopped up and down the bank, with her tail stiff
out, tumbling over the broken boughs which lay
there, and uttering every now and then deep barks
that awoke the astonished echoes of the woods.
Sometimes she would make a plunge into the

water, splashing us all over, and then she quickly
scrambled out again, her ardour considerably
cooled.

"Well done, Fig! good little dog! at him again!
never mind that rap on the head from his
wing."

Away swam the swan, and Fig after him, incessantly barking.

Had not the noble bird been grievously wounded
he would have defied the utmost exertions of the
little spaniel, but as it was, he could only get for a
moment out of the reach of his pursuer by a violent effort, which only left him more exhausted.
And now they approached the shore; and the
swan, hard pressed, turns round and aims a blow
with its bill at the dog.

This Fig managed to elude, and in return made
a snap at his enemy's wing, and obtained a mouthful of feathers; but in revenge he received on his
nose a rap from the strong pinion of the bird that
made him turn tail and fairly yelp with anguish.
"Never mind, brave Fig! good dog! at him again!
Bravo—bravo! good little fellow!" There he is,
once more upon him. And now, master Fig,
taught a lesson by the smart blows he had received,
endeavours to assail only the wounded wing of the
swan. It was a very fierce combat, but the swan

would probably have had the best of it had not loss
of blood rendered him faint and weak.

He still fought bravely, but now whenever he
missed his adversary, his bill would remain a moment in the water, as though he had scarcely
strength to raise his head; and as he grew mo-
mentarily weaker and weaker, so Fig waxed more
daring and energetic in his assaults; until at length
he fairly seized his exhausted foe by the neck, and
notwithstanding his struggles, and the violent flapping of his long unwounded wing, began to draw
him towards the shore. We hurried to meet and
help him. Jezebel was the first that dashed breast-
high into the water; and seizing a pinion in her
strong jaws, she soon drew both the swan and Fig,
who would have died rather than let go, through
the yielding sedges to the land.

The swan was soon dead; and Fig lay panting
on the sand, with his mouth open, and looking up
to his master as he wagged his tail, clearly imply-
ing, "Did not I do it well, master?" "Yes, my
little dog, you did it nobly. And now you shall
have some of this bread, of Simon's own baking,
which I cannot eat myself; and Jonathan and I
will finish this flask of brandy and water."

And now we set out on our return home, anxious
to display our trophy to envious eyes.

As we approached the Cantonment, I discharged
my unloaded barrel at a bird like a thrush in
appearance, called a Wattle-bird, from having two
little wattles which project from either side of its
head.

The salute was answered by a similar discharge
from the Cantonment, and soon afterwards Melibœus came running to meet us, preceded by the
blood-hound at full gallop. The dogs greeted one
another with much apparent satisfaction. Little Fig
was evidently anxious to inform his big friend of all
that he had done, but Nero was much too dignified
and important to attend to him, and bestowed all
his notice upon Jezebel.

The fishermen had succeeded in catching a dozen
mullet, which were all ready for cooking; and the
frying-pan being soon put in requisition, we were
speedily placed at table.

Being still without legitimate knives and forks,
the absence of the latter article was supplied by
small forked-sticks, cut from a neighbouring pepper-
mint tree. Those who did not like cold water alone
were allowed grog; and the entertainment, consisting of fish and boiled pork (which a few months
before we should have considered an utter abomina-
tion), being seasoned with hunger, went off with
tolerable satisfaction.

The following day we had the swan skinned and

roasted, but it certainly was not nearly so good as a Michaelmas goose. Nevertheless, it was a change from boiled pork, and we endeavoured to think it a luxury. Simon had been more successful in his latter efforts at baking, and, on the whole, things assumed a more comfortable aspect.

CHAPTER VI.

PERTH—COLONIAL JURIES.

So soon as we were well settled in our new abode, we began to think of pushing our researches a little farther into the country. We thought it high time that we visited the capital, and paid our respects to the Governor. About a mile and a half from our location, the Fremantle and Perth road crosses the river (which is there about four hundred yards wide) by a ferry. John-of-the-Ferry, the lessee of the tolls, the Charon of the passage, is a Pole by birth, who escaped with difficulty out of the hands of the Russians; and having the fortune to find an English master, after a series of adventures entered into the employment of an emigrant, and settled in Western Australia. He had now become not only the lessee of the ferry, but a dealer in various small articles, and at the time to which I refer, was the owner of several Timor ponies. Singular enough for a horse-dealer and a colonist,

John had the reputation of being an honest man, and his customers always treated him with the utmost confidence.

Having learnt his good character, we repaired to his neat, white-washed cottage on the banks of the river to inspect his stud; and soon effected a purchase of two of his ponies. These animals, about thirteen hands high, proved to belong to the swiftest and hardiest race of ponies in the world. They required no care or grooming; blessed with excellent appetites, they picked up their food wherever they could find any, and came night and morning to the door to receive their rations of barley, oat-meal, bread-crusts, or any thing that could be spared them. The colony had been supplied with several cargoes of these ponies from Timor, and they proved extremely useful so long as there was a scarcity of horses; but afterwards they became a nuisance, and tended greatly to keep back improvements in the breed of horses. Pony-stallions suffered to roam at large became at length such an evil, that special acts of Council were passed against them; and as these did not prove of sufficient efficacy, the animals were sometimes hunted like wild cattle, and shot with rifles.

It was some amusement to us to break in our small quadrupeds to draw my light cart; we had brought out tandem-harness; and in a short time we got up a very fair team. But, alas! there was no pleasure in driving in that neighbourhood—the road being only a track of deep sand. One bright and tempting morning, the doctor and myself mounted our steeds, and leaving our affairs at the castle in the faithful charge of Meliboeus, wended our way towards the capital of the colony. The river at the ferry has a picturesque appearance, precipitous rocks forming its sides, and two bays, a mile apart, terminating the view on either hand, where the river winds round projecting head-lands.

The old road to Perth was truly a miserable one, being at least six inches deep in sand the whole way. It was scarcely possible to see more than fifty yards ahead of you, so thickly grew the banksia trees. After crossing the ferry, we lost sight of the river for several miles, and then diverged from the dismal road by a path which we had been directed by the ferryman to look out for, and which brought us to a sandy beach at the bottom of a beautiful bay, called Freshwater Bay. From this point to the opposite side was a stretch of several miles, and the broad and winding river, or rather estuary, with its forest banks, presented a beautiful appearance.

We now ascended from the shore to the high land above. The forest through which we passed resembled a wild English park; below was the broad expanse of Melville water, enlivened by the white sails of several boats on their way from Perth to Fremantle. Farther on, the mouth of the Canning River opened upon us; and now we could see, deep below the high and dark hill-side on which we travelled, the narrow entrance from Melville water into Perth water. At length we obtained a full view of the picturesquely situated town of Perth.

It stands on the right bank of a broad and crescent-shaped reach of the river Swan, in an extremely well-chosen locality. The streets are broad; and those houses which are placed nearest to the river, possess, perhaps, the most luxuriant gardens in the world. Every kind of fruit known in the finest climates is here produced in perfection. Grapes and figs are in profuse abundance; melons and peaches are no less plentiful, and bananas and plantains seem to rejoice in the climate as their own.

The town has a never-failing supply of fresh water from a chain of swamps at the back, and the wells fed by them are never dry. Many of the houses are well built—brick having long since superseded the original structure of wood— and possess all the usual comforts of English residences.

In the principal street, most of the houses stand
alone, each proprietor having a garden, or paddock,
of three quarters of an acre in extent, about his
dwelling. The great misfortune of the town is,
that the upper portion of it is built upon sand,
which is many feet deep. The streets, not being
yet paved, are all but impassable; but happily,
each possesses a good foot-path of clay, and it is
to be hoped that the cart-ways will ere long be
similarly improved. Sydney was originally in the
state that Perth presents now; but *there* the
natural unfavourableness of the soil has been entirely overcome. Increasing wealth and population
will ere long do as much for us.

It is not until we reach Guildford, eight miles
farther inland than Perth, that the stratum of sand
ceases, and a cold and marly clay succeeds, which
reaches to the foot of the Darling range of hills,
and extends many miles down the coast.

The banks of the Swan River, as well as of the
Canning and most other rivers of the colony, contain many miles of rich alluvial soil, capable of
growing wheat sufficient for the support of a large
population. Many of these flats have produced
crops of wheat for sixteen years successively,
without the aid of any kind of manure. It must,
however, be owned, that a very slovenly system of
farming has been generally pursued throughout the

colony; and, in fact, is commonly observable in all colonies. The settlers are not only apt to rely too much upon the natural productiveness of the soil, but they are in general men whose attention has only lately been turned to agriculture, and who are almost entirely ignorant of practical farming in its most important details. The Agricultural Society of Western Australia has for some years exerted itself to improve this state of things, and has in some measure succeeded.

It must be observed that with the exception of the rich flats of the Swan and Canning rivers, the vast extent of country between the coast and the Darling Hills is a miserable region, scarcely more valuable for the purposes of cultivation than the deserts of Africa, except where occasional swamps appear like oases, and tempt the hardy settler to found a location. As all the worst land of the colony lies unfortunately near the coast, those who visit only the port and capital usually leave the country with a very unfavourable and a very erroneous impression of its real character.

It is not until the granite range of the Darling Hills is passed over, that the principal pastoral and agricultural districts are found. There are the farm settlements, the flocks, and herds of the colony. From the Victoria plains north of Toodyay, for hundreds of miles to the southward, comprising the fertile districts of Northam, York, Beverley, the Dale and the Hotham, is found a surface of stiff soil, covered over with straggling herbage, and many varieties of trees and shrubs. But I am travelling too fast : I must pause for the present at Perth.

Circumstances determined me to take up my residence there, instead of accompanying the rest of my party into the interior, as I had originally intended. I liked the appearance and situation of the town; and I liked the people generally. And here I may state, with many kindly feelings, that never was a more united or cordial society than that of the town of Perth, with its civil and military officers, and its handful of merchants. No political or religious differences have hitherto disturbed its harmony ; nor have there yet been introduced many of those distinctions which may be necessary and unavoidable in large communities, but which, though generally to be met with in all societies, are not only lamentable but highly ridiculous in small out-of-the-way colonies. Such divisions, however, must be apprehended even here in progress of time, and the period will come when we shall look back with regret to those days when we were all friends and associates together, and when each sympathized with the fortunes of his neighbour. The kindly feeling which thus held society together, was ever mani-

fested at the death of one of its members. Then
not only the immediate connexions of the deceased
attended his funeral, but every member of his circle,
and many also of the lower classes. It has more
than once happened that a young man has fallen a
victim to his rashness and nautical inexperience,
and met with an untimely fate whilst sailing on
Melville water. I myself twice narrowly escaped
such a calamity, as perhaps I may hereafter narrate.
Every boat belonging to the place is immediately
engaged in search of the body, and many of the
boatmen freely sacrifice their time and day's wages
in the pursuit. And when at length the object of
that melancholy search is discovered, and the day
of the funeral has arrived, the friends, companions,
neighbours, and fellow-townsmen of the deceased
assemble at the door of his late residence, to pay
the last testimonies of sympathy and regret for him
who has, in that distant colony, no nearer relative
to weep at his grave. It is a long procession that
follows the corpse to its home, passing with solemn
pace through the else deserted streets, and emerging
into the wild forest which seems almost to engulph
the town; and then pursuing the silent and solitary
path for a mile until, on the summit of a hill, surrounded by dark ever-green foliage, appears the
lonesome burial-ground. Ah! how little thought
the tenant of that insensible body, late so full of life

and vigour, that here he should so soon be laid, far
from the tombs of his family, far from the home of
his parents, to which his thoughts had so constantly recurred !   I do not think any one ever
witnessed the interment in that solitary place of
one whom perhaps he knew but slightly when
living, without feeling in himself a sensation of
loneliness, as though a cold gust from the open
grave had blown over him.   It is then we think
most of England and home—and of those who
though living are dead to *us*.

But these are only transient emotions ; they are
idle and unavailing, so away with them !

I shall now proceed to give an account of my
first appearance before a colonial public.   Some of
the crew of our vessel, exasperated by the conduct
of the captain, who refused to allow them any liberty
on shore after their long voyage, and encouraged
and even led on by the chief mate, had broken into
the store-room, and consumed a quantity of spirits
and other stores.   Now as we had been most
shabbily treated by the miserly and ruffian captain,
and as the stores thus stolen had been paid for by
the passengers, and withheld from them upon the
voyage (stolen, in fact, by the captain himself), we
were delighted with the robbery, and extremely
sorry to hear that the chief mate had been committed
to prison for trial as the principal offender.   In fact,

the captain thought proper to wink at the conduct of the others, as he could not afford to part with any more of his crew. The General Quarter Sessions drew nigh, and the day before they commenced I received a kind of petition from the prisoner, entreating me to aid him at this pinch, as he had not a friend in that part of the world, and would inevitably be ruined for what he considered rather a meritorious action—taking vengeance on the stinginess of the captain. Though I did not see exactly of what benefit I could be to him, I repaired to the court-house on the day of trial. It was crowded with people, as such places always are when prisoners are to be tried; and as I had met at dinner most of the magistrates on the Bench, I did not much like the idea of making my first public appearance before them as a friend of the gentleman in the dock, who had improperly appropriated the goods of his employer.

The amiable desire, however, of paying off old scores due to the captain, annihilated every other feeling; and when the prisoner, on being asked whether he was guilty or not guilty of the felony laid to his charge, instead of answering, cast his imploring eyes upon me, as though I knew more of the business than himself, I could not refrain from advancing towards the table occupied by the counsel and solicitors, and asking permission of the bench to give my valuable assistance to the prisoner. This being graciously accorded, the mate, with a most doleful countenance, and a very unassured voice, made answer to the plain interrogative of the Clerk of Arraigns—"Not guilty, my Lord."

Whilst the prosecutor was being examined by the Advocate General, I conned over the indictment with a meditative countenance, but without being able to see my way in the least. The captain, scowling atrociously at me and my persecuted friend, gave his evidence with the bitterest animosity. He proved his losses, and the facts of the store-room door having been broken open, and the prisoner and most of the sailors being found drunk by him on his repairing one evening to the vessel. It now became my turn to ask questions, as

Prisoner's Counsel. Your ship, Captain W., is commonly called a *Temperance ship*, is it not?

Captain (after a ferocious stare). I should think you knew that.

P. Counsel. And being a temperance ship, you do not allow the men, at any time, any other liquor than water?

Captain. No.

P. Counsel. In temperance ships, I suppose it sometimes happens that the men contrive to buy liquor for themselves?

Captain (*looking like a bull about to charge a matadore*). Boo!

P. Counsel. Do you remember the day we were off Madeira?

Captain stares and snorts.

P. Counsel. Do you remember on that day several of the sailors being remarkably light-headed —reeling about the deck?

Captain (*roaring, and striking the table with his hand*). Yes!

P. Counsel. Was this the effect of a *coup de soleil*, do you think?

Captain. No!

P. Counsel. Very well. Do you remember, whilst we were on the Line, the second-mate being in your cabin helping Mrs. W. to stow away some things in the lazarette, and both being found afterwards extremely unwell, and obliged to be taken to bed?

Chairman (*interfering*). I think the witness need not answer that question.

Advocate General. I should have made the same objection, Sir, but—(*aside*) I was laughing too much.

P. Counsel. Very well, Sir. I will not press it if it be disagreeable. Do you remember at St. Jago the whole of the crew being every day notoriously drunk—from eating water-melons?

Captain (*recovering from an apopletic fit*). Ah-h!

P. Counsel. Do you remember, when off the Cape, the sail-maker and several others being unable to do their duty, and being pronounced by the doctor to be in a state of liquor?

Captain. Yes.

P. Counsel. Then, as it appears that on board of a temperance ship, men ' do occasionally (and in your vessel very often) get drunk, might not the prisoner at the time of his alleged offence have been drinking other liquor than that which formed part of your stores?

Chairman (*the Captain being too full of rage to articulate*). The jury will be able to draw their own inference as to that.

Captain. It was he, gentlemen; it was this— *gentleman* (forsooth — ha! ha!) who gave the men money on landing in order to make them drunk.

P. Counsel. Thank you for that evidence. The intelligent gentlemen in the box will perceive that it was at my expense that the unfortunate prisoner got drunk, and not at the captain's.

The prosecutor was now permitted to retire, which he did growling like a bear, amid the jeers of the populace, who always sympathize with misfortune when it appears impersonated in the dock.

The jury were also evidently in high glee, and cast most friendly looks at the prisoner, and the *fidus Achates* who stood up for him so stoutly.

The next witness was the sail-maker, who reluctantly owned himself to have aided the prisoner in drinking some brandy which had come from the ship's stores.

P. Counsel. But, Sails, you do not mean to say that the prisoner told you he had himself taken it from the ship's stores?

Witness. Oh no, Sir, certainly not.

P. Counsel. In fact, of your own knowledge, you do not know where the liquor came from?

Witness. No, Sir; oh, no, Sir!

Here the Advocate-General administered such a lecture to the witness, who was considerably more than half-drunk at the time, that he entirely lost his wits and memory, and answered so completely at random, that the jury begged he might not be asked any more questions.

Advocate General. It is of no importance. I shall call no more witnesses, as I hold in my hand the prisoner's own confession, made before the committing magistrate, who was yourself, Mr. Chairman.

This was a knock-down blow to me, and made the jury look extremely blank. They gazed on

one another in despair. The document was duly
proved, and the case for the prosecution closed.
The chairman asked if I wished to address the
jury, but I declined, and observed that the prisoner
must explain for himself what he meant by this
extraordinary confession. Every thing seemed
dead against the prisoner, who hung his head and
looked remarkably simple. I read over the paper,
which stated that he, the prisoner, with several
others, on a certain day took a quantity of the
captain's brandy, and got drunk thereupon.

A ray of hope beamed upon me. I started up,
and the jury instinctively began to brighten; they
had given up the prisoner as lost, and now they
were ready to catch at a straw. I addressed the
unfortunate: " You state here, that you took the
captain's brandy with certain of the sailors. Do
you mean by that, you *partook* of the brandy which
other sailors were drinking ?"

Prisoner (balbutiant). I—I—ye—ye—

P. Counsel. What do you really mean, Sir, by
this written document ? Do you mean to say that
you yourself took this brandy, or that you partook
of it with others ?

Prisoner. Yes, Sir,—that I partook of it.

P. Counsel. Then, gentlemen of the jury, this
document does not convict the unfortunate man at
the bar; and what appears like an admission of

guilt is only to be attributed to his imperfect mode
of expressing himself.   He admits that he partook
of certain brandy stated to be the captain's, which
the captain, himself, however, would lead you to
suppose had been provided by me.   The witness
who has been examined throws no further light
upon the matter ; and though the prisoner himself
has admitted that he partook of liquor which he
believed belonged to the captain, that admission
does not convict him under the present indictment,
which charges him with having " feloniously taken
and carried away," &c.

The jury were evidently delighted with this con-
struction ; and the people in the gallery and body
of the court could scarcely be restrained from giving
three cheers.

The chairman recapitulated the evidence, and
left the matter in the hands of the jury, who jostled
one another out of the box, and retired to " consider their verdict."   As they passed through the
ante-room to the apartment in which they usually
held their solemn deliberations, they caught up a
bucket of water which the bailiff of the court
generally kept at hand for thirsty counsel or
magistrates ; and as soon as they had decently
secluded themselves, and indulged in a genial fit of
merriment, the foreman produced a bottle of brandy
from his pocket, and seizing the pannikin which

floated in the bucket, poured forth a good libation, and drank "towards all present." Each juryman in turn then drank the health of the foreman. After that, they all drank the prisoner's health; and, as one of the number afterwards assured me, they would have conscientiously toasted the prisoner's counsel, but the liquor unfortunately failed.

The foreman then said, "Come, my lads, there's no more left, so we may as well go back again." So they jostled one another out of the room, and with composed countenances returned to the court, where they were ostentatiously conducted to their box by the sheriff's officer amid loud cries of "Silence in the court! silence there!"

Their names having been called over, the Clerk of Arraigns asked the usual question, "Have you considered your verdict, gentlemen?"

"Not guilty!" interrupted the foreman, as if he feared lest the prisoner should be convicted in spite of the jury.

"How say you," continued the clerk, "is the prisoner at the bar guilty or not guilty?"

"Not guilty!" cried the whole jury to a man; and amid thunders of acclamations the prisoner was released from the dock, and turned out of court, where he was seized upon by a multitude of sympathizers, and carried in triumph to the next public-house. There he spent the ensuing four-and-twenty hours, the hero of the day.

In this slight sketch I am conscious that I have only been able to convey to the reader a very faint idea of

A COLONIAL JURY.

CHAPTER VII.

BOATING UP THE RIVER.

WHILST I was making acquaintances at Perth, my brothers, mounted on our Timor steeds, were making a tour of inspection beyond the Darling Hills. They fixed at length upon a farm at York, with about three thousand acres belonging to it, and having a good farm-house, with excellent barn and out-buildings attached. This evinced a more comfortable and luxurious state of things than they had anticipated, and they returned in high spirits to head-quarters.

It now became necessary to consider how the various goods and utensils were to be conveyed to the new settlement, which was seventy miles distant from Fremantle. We sold most of our flour and pork at a fair profit, and left by far the greater part of the other articles which we had brought out with us to be sold by a commission agent, as opportunity offered.

From various causes, but chiefly from our own

ignorance in selecting our goods in London, we lost a considerable sum upon the things we had brought out. Emigrants, unless they are men of great experience, should bring all their capital to a colony in bills or specie, and not attempt to increase their property by speculating in goods. On their arrival, they will most probably find the markets already glutted, and they will be compelled either to sell at a sacrifice, or leave their effects in the hands of an agent, who will charge enormously for warehouse-rent and other expenses, and will take especial care that the unfortunate emigrant is not the party who profits most by the sale of his goods.

We had brought out with us an old artillery waggon; and all hands now set to work to put it together, which was accomplished after a good deal of difficulty. We also purchased three pair of bullocks, which were at that date very dear. One pair—magnificent animals certainly—cost fifty guineas, and the other animals twenty pounds a-piece. Now, however, the best working bullocks may be obtained for about fifteen pounds a pair. As the road so far as Guildford was excessively heavy, we resolved to convey most of our goods by water to a spot a few miles beyond that town, where a friendly settler had placed at our disposal a wooden building, consisting of a single room,

situated on the banks of the river, and used occasionally by himself as a store-house for his own
goods on their transit to his dwelling. The
same friend lent us his own whale-boat; and by
determining to convey our effects ourselves we
avoided a very heavy expense. The cost of conveying necessaries from the coast to the farm settlements in the interior, has been one of the chief
drawbacks to the colony. The boatmen made
fortunes, whilst the farmers were nearly ruined by
their charges, and those of the storekeepers in the
towns.

For fifteen years, at least, the latter have
grumbled with violent indignation unless their
goods have realised from two to five hundred per
cent. profit. Resolved, therefore, to be our own
boatmen, we moored our vessel at a little wooden
jetty below our house, and began to pack up
such articles as were designed to compose the first
cargo.

I remember well the pleasure with which we
stood upon that wooden jetty one summer's evening, looking upon the boat in which we were to
perform our first voyage up the river, as she lightly
floated before us, scarcely giving a strain upon the
rope which held her to one of the posts at the end
of the pier. Fig and Jezebel, always intimate
friends, were hunting for bandicoots—animals less

than a kangaroo-rat—which abounded in the bank
below our dwelling.

Upon this bank, Hannibal was to be seen clean-
ing the tandem harness; suspended from the bough
of a tree, and occasionally casting an eye in the
direction of the sheep, for whose safety he was
responsible. By the river side, our bullocks were
busily engaged picking the scanty herbage. The
sea-breeze blowing steadily up the river cooled the
air, and seemed to bear health and spirits on its
wings.

The only sound that met the ear was a rushing
noise, which every now and then rose from the
water along the shore. It was caused by myriads
of little fish rushing into shoal water to escape
from some pressing foe.

There are some minds that draw pleasure from
things which in no degree affect others; to such,
this was one of those seasons of tranquil happiness
that leave no regrets behind. The consciousness
of independence—the pleasant nature of our
duties—the cheerful aspect of all around—the
flattering whispers of Hope, though false as usual—
all helped to form for the mental eye a picture
which it loved to look upon.

And now we were busied in loading our boat.
What pride we felt! no shame at being seen per-
forming manual labour; but pride, and pleasure,

and exultation. We had always been fond of boating, and now that it was about to be an useful employment, it seemed additionally agreeable. And what a noble scene for this our first adventurous voyage, upon that broad river or rather arm of the sea! We had found out the secret of human happiness, long hidden from us—business had become our pleasure. I was to be the captain, and my youngest brother and Simon composed the crew.

The boat was not loaded until late in the afternoon, and our departure was therefore postponed until the sea-breeze should set in on the following day. Still, we could not resist the delight of making an experimental trip, and so the sprit-sail and jib were set, and we shoved off into the tideway. A whale-boat goes very fast before the wind, but will not beat, nor will she go about well without using an oar; she is not, therefore, the craft best adapted for nautical evolutions, but we were too happy to find much fault with her on that occasion; and so we sailed several times across the river and back again in the very height of enjoyment. Then suddenly luffing-up in the middle of the stream, the anchor was let go, and the sail brailed up, in order that we might have the pleasure of sitting still in the very midst of the waters, and rest, as it were, in the plenitude of our satisfaction; and when the anchor dragged a few yards over the

sand before it held, and then suddenly brought up
the boat with a jerk, it seemed the climax of our
pleasure. This, the sagacious reader, in the depth
of his gravity, will consider extremely boyish. But
should we not rejoice and be thankful whenever we
find among the many simple pleasures of our
boyhood, a single one which retains the power of
gladdening our maturer years? Alas! one after
another they die down, and are no more to be
revived. We are apt to fancy that when the
pleasures of youth have lost their sweetness, and
are no longer desired, it is an evidence of our
increasing wisdom. But it proves only that our
tastes, grown more vitiated, have taken new directions. We have only changed our follies—and for
the worse.*

The breeze! the breeze! the glorious sea-breeze
comes stealing swiftly over the bar; it crosses the
first bay. Like a dark shadow it moves along the
face of the river, and now it has reached our

---

* " 'Tis sweet to think we grow more wise
    When Radcliffe's page we cease to prize,
    And turn to Malthus, and to Hervey,
    For tombs, or cradles topsy-turvy;
    'Tis sweet to flatter one's dear self,
    And altered feelings vaunt, when pelf
    Is passion, poetry, romance;—
    And all our faith's in three per cents."

R. R. MADDEN.

landing-place and gone swiftly forwards, bringing pleasure and thankfulness on its path. Now, my men, jump in! hand me the grog and provision basket—and now loose the sails, and shove off. There, we are fairly under weigh, and little Fig whimpers his adieu to Jezebel and Nero, who for some minutes accompany the course of the boat along the shore; and then finding we are really going, remain fixed with astonishment, gazing upon their departing friend. Soon, how soon, vanishes from their breasts every feeling of regret! Before we have turned the first headland we perceive them playfully biting each other about the ears and neck: and now Nero scampers off under the trees, in the direction of the house, and Jezebel (type of her sex!) hurries after him.

The breeze came rattling up the river, and the boat flew merrily before it. We had occasionally sailed to Perth in the passage-boats, and therefore knew something of the channel. Sand-spits frequently run far out into the river, and those who think only of steering a straight course, are very sure of running aground several times during the voyage.

The distance from Fremantle to Perth, by water, is about twelve miles, and it is about as many more from Perth to Guildford. After passing the ferry-reach, the river appeared about a quarter of a mile broad, having abrupt rocky banks on either side; far a-head was the wooded bottom of Freshwater Bay. Instead of coasting round this bay, we passed through a channel cut across the spit into Melville water. Here is a beautiful site for a house: a sloping lawn, covered with fine peppermint trees, which in form resemble the weeping willow, and a great variety of flowering shrubs, down to the water's edge. The view from the house (lately the seat of Alfred Waylen, Esq.) is exceedingly pleasing; on one hand is the fine sheet of Melville water, seven miles in extent, and three or four in breadth, surrounded by thick woods; in front is the graceful curve of Freshwater Bay; and on the opposite side of the house from Melville water, the river sweeps abruptly round through the deep and broad channel I have already mentioned towards the ferry-reach.

We passed up Melville water, and in about an hour and a quarter after starting came abreast of the town of Perth, which we left about three-quarters of a mile on our larboard side, and continued our passage up Perth water. We had now a difficult channel to pass through, where the river is extremely shoal; and in our inexperience, we soon got the boat aground. Jumping into the water, we succeeded in shoving her again into the channel, and passed by a small island called Harrison's Island. It was here that a French exploring party took refuge after they had come so far up the river in spite of many alarms. These men were some of the crew of Captain Perron, who was engaged in a survey of this part of the coast of Australia, for the French Government. During the night they were thrown into a state of agitation and alarm by hearing incessant noises in the thick woods on the main land, that were thought by some to be the bellowing of wild bulls; by many the howling of wolves; and by others the cries of savages. After a night spent in momentary expectation of attack and massacre, the Frenchmen got into their boats and hastened down the river again with the utmost expedition, and scarcely thought themselves quite safe until they were once more on board their ship.

This account of the French navigators was uppermost in the minds of the English settlers on their first arrival, and contributed greatly to the dread they felt at wandering a few yards from the settlement. In those days, an orderly scarcely durst take a message from the Governor to the Surveyor General's tent, within sight, unless accompanied by a couple of his fellows, with their muskets ready for action.

The borders of the river were in many parts, especially on the present town site of Perth, so entangled with thick brushwood, that enemies might be lying in swarms, close at hand, without the least fear of detection. When Sir James Stirling and his party first passed up the river in boats, they had the accounts of the French sailors fully in mind, and were very cautious how they landed. They passed the night in a state of preparation, if not of alarm, and were kept in constant vigilance by the same fearful noises.

The woods were now supposed to be filled with wild beasts, and it was not until some time had elapsed that people became convinced that the dreadful sounds which assailed their ears at night proceeded from myriads of frogs. These little creatures swarm in the samphire marshes near the river, and possess voices far surpassing anything known to their species in Europe.

I was once looking out for ducks or coots in a thicket of bulrushes higher than my head, when I was startled by hearing a loud "bomb!" at no great distance from me. Having no idea what kind of wild beast had made its lair in that dense thicket, I got ready to fire both barrels on the first appearance of danger. Again the same awful noise! It must be the snorting of a bison, or vast buffalo, seeking shelter from the sun—or it may proceed from some kind of water-dragon, I thought. I looked in every direction, but could see no living creature; and at last was about to retreat in the quietest manner possible, when I espied a little frog perched on the top of a reed, about a yard from my nose, and apparently looking full in my face, whilst, ever and anon he inflated his cheeks, and uttered the fearful sounds I had heard.

But besides the dread of wild beasts, the colonists were long in the greatest apprehension of losing themselves in the vast wilderness of forest by which they were on every side enclosed. The country being extremely level, up to the Darling range of hills, which is seen trending north and south about twelve or fourteen miles at the back of Perth, a man once in the woods has no object but the sun by which to direct his course. Every now and then he comes upon an impassable swamp, which throws him out of his track, and causes him infinite difficulty before he can get round it, and then he begins to doubt of his true direction. This is, certainly, an awkward predicament; and nothing is so easy as for inexperienced bushmen to lose their way. When once a man begins to doubt whether he is right, he loses all confidence in himself; he wanders first in one direction and then in another, in the hope of finding something to guide him; and fears lest every step should take him farther into the labyrinth of the forest-wilderness. I have myself been several times lost for a short period, and know how very unpleasant is the sensation. A common soldier, sent on a message from Perth to Fremantle, happened to get off the track. Becoming alarmed, he tried to recover it, but as it had made a bend, he walked as far as he thought its position ought to be, without success, and then fancied he must have mistaken the direction. He therefore diverged at right angles, and, after walking a short time, recollected that he *must* now be going in the wrong direction, as he had left the path originally on his left hand. Accordingly he turned back again, and walked so far without perceiving any signs of the track that he now fancied he must be going parallel with it. Had he gone on a few yards farther, all would have been right, but now he really took a parallel course, and after walking for some time longer, he again turned back, and walked in another direction. Now this man had the sea on one side of him, and the river on the other, at most not more than four miles apart; yet the dread of having walked back into the wilderness behind Perth overpowered his faculties, and he walked for hours in a circle of about half a mile in diameter. He might have considered that the Darling Hills were behind Perth, and must have brought him up, but reason does not always act freely at these times. At length, completely exhausted, he sat down at the foot of a tree, where he remained all night, expecting

death from starvation, from the natives, or some
unknown wild beasts.

The next day he walked again as long as his
strength would allow, but before night sank down
in the extremity of despair. It was not until the
third day of his misfortunes that he was tracked up
by a party sent in search of him, and guided by
friendly natives, who followed his many devious
steps with unerring eyes.

Another man, similarly lost in the interior, after
vainly trying to recover the road, determined to
make for the coast, which he knew lay to the
west. He was also confident that the sun regularly
set in that quarter, and therefore, he boldly determined to trust himself to the guidance of the sun,
making sure, that if he followed it far enough, it
must lead him to the coast at last. Accordingly, he
marched after the sun till night-fall, and then went
cheerfully to sleep, having supped upon some bread
and pork, which he carried with him. The next
morning, at sunrise, he started off in the direction
of his guide, perfectly unconscious that he was now
retracing his steps, and journeying eastward. All
day, however, he continued to follow the sun, and
when it set, wondered that he had not yet reached
the sea. At night, he finished his bread and pork,
and the next morning set off again on his long and

tedious journey; still, at night, there was no appearance of the ocean, and he fired off his gun at a black cockatoo, which he killed with his only charge of shot.

Upon this bird he lived for the next two days, and for two more he subsisted upon roots. He had now given up all hopes of discovering the sea, and had lain down to die, when he was found by his master and a party of natives, who had come in search of him.

It appeared that he was found upon almost the very spot on which he had first lost himself.

When once a man begins to believe that he is lost in the wilderness, he feels as helpless as one who is blind-folded at the game of blindman's buff, and who has been twirled round so often, that he has no idea whereabouts the door or the fire-place is situated. Those who are used to the bush steer their course with almost unerring precision by the sun, and a few known objects, but there are numbers who never acquire this power. The natives appear to know by instinct the direction of every spot they wish to reach; and many white men seem to possess the same faculty.

But I have almost forgotten that we are all this time sailing up the river in our whale-boat. It was a very beautiful sail, and we repeatedly passed cheerful-looking farm-houses on either bank—sometimes goodly mansions with park-like enclosures about them. In the afternoon we dined upon cold wild-duck; and as each man sipped his grog in his pannikin, we felt so exceedingly cheerful, that Simon and Melibœus favoured the public with " Away with melancholy!" and divers other agreeable ditties. The wind however died away, and evening set in as we passed Guildford. The banks of the river had now risen into steep cliffs, which threw a deep gloom over our course. We had furled the sails, and taken to the oars, and as we blindly poked our way, we began to think this kind of work was not quite so agreeable as it had at first appeared. Nothing was now to be seen but the outlines of the steep sides of the river on which occasional houses were visible, the light streaming through the windows, and making us fancy how comfortable every thing must be within, and how pleasant it would be to be sitting at supper in a cheerful room, instead of toiling at our oars with blistered hands, and without the prospect of a good bed at the end of the voyage.

Romance was gone; the sad reality of life remained. Still we pulled along, steering by turns, and doubting and wondering every hundred yards whether we had not gone past the place we sought. Sometimes we paused on our oars to debate the question, but still we continued to push on; till at

length we found ourselves close abreast of the
wooden building we were so anxiously looking out
for, and experienced a sensation of surprise as well
as of delight.

The boat was soon safely moored, and the door
of the building unlocked; and by the light of a
wax taper, which we had brought on purpose, we
found ourselves in a large empty room, without any
fire-place. A heap of dead wood was soon collected
at the entrance; and a glorious fire lighted up the
small enclosure which surrounded the building, and
sufficiently illuminated a considerable portion of the
room itself. The kettle being put on, we soon had
tea ready, and managed to get through our rations
of bread and pork, not forgetting to give little Fig
his supper, who sat very seriously before the fire,
wondering what it all meant.

Cigars, and brandy and water, having been duly
administered before bed-time, we next proceeded to
litter down coats and cloaks; and having made
ourselves as comfortable as circumstances would
admit of, stretched ourselves on the floor, with a few
sighs and thoughts of home, and slept until day-
break.

The first thing we did next morning was to
unload the boat; and then having breakfasted, and
secured the door on our effects, we started on our
homeward trip, and had the satisfaction of pulling

the whole distance to Perth, where we were obliged
to sleep the next night, as it was impossible for us
to get down Melville water in the teeth of a strong
sea-breeze.

  When we had to start again with another load of
goods, our hearts were much heavier than on the
first excursion.

CHAPTER VIII.

FARMS ON THE RIVER.

FIRST impressions endure the longest, and are recalled with most pleasure. Further acquaintance does not always give us a truer idea of the value of the object, as familiarity frequently makes us overlook as insignificant that which is constantly before us. It is not the object that is proved to be really less valuable as we become better acquainted with it, but our own views which change with our position. My first impressions on visiting the various farms, or rather gentlemen's residences, on the banks of the Swan, were extremely agreeable. I thought nothing could be more delightful than to live at one of those picturesque and lovely spots. If the romance of that first feeling be now faded from my heart, it is not because I have discovered that all which I then saw was an illusion, but because a more sober state of mind—that state into which the mind settles as the excitement of sudden change and unwonted novelty subsides—teaches that happiness is not local, and that it is no more likely to be found in the finest country residence than in the main street of a town.

At the first view we are apt to imagine that people who live in one of these pleasant retreats must needs be happier than ourselves, who possess nothing but a miserable shieling.

This is the delusion; and when with increasing knowledge, we recover from this, we cease to envy and to covet.

My first ride up the Swan was a most delightful one. No park in England could be more beautiful than the grounds around some of the dwellings.

The ride through the scattered village of Guildford, with a view of the rich and extensive flats of Woodbridge, the property of Sir James Stirling, and the frequent bends of the river, is a very agreeable one. The whole country of the middle and upper Swan resembles a vast English park. We passed the pretty country church of the Middle Swan, with its modest parsonage beside it, and then proceeded through wooded ravines along a pleasant drive to one of the most hospitable mansions in the colony. Extensive stables, barns and out-buildings occupied the back of the premises. As it was now too late in the evening to see much of the surrounding scenery, we entered the house of SAMUEL MOORE, Esq., and sat down to an excellent dinner. In the evening we had music—pianos are as common

in Western Australia as in England.   At night I
occupied a sofa in the parlour.   The excitement
and novelty of my present situation—so many
thousands of leagues removed from the spot on
which, only a few months before, I had deemed I
I was to spend my life—kept me wakeful ; and
about one o'clock I arose, and opening the French
window, stepped out into the verandah.   How
solemn was the scene before me, faintly lighted by
the moon !   In front of the house was a pretty
sloping garden, and below this stretched a broad
clearing, now waving with corn, amidst which rose
up a number of scattered, lofty, dead trees, which
had been purposely killed by ringing the bark.
How mournful they looked in that gloomy light !

The river bounded this clearing, and beyond the
river stretched its high bank, covered with forest
trees, the advanced lines, as it were, of the vast
wilderness which lay behind.   From out the
depths of those woods rose the occasional shrieks
of an owl, or other night bird, and at intervals
the long dismal howl of a wild dog—the only car-
nivorous animal indigenous in that country.   The
air was balmy, but there was something in the
mournful aspect of the scene that weighed upon the
spirits, and made one feel inexpressibly lonely in
the midst of that boundless wilderness of forest.

Time soon takes off the edge of novelty, and long

ago I have learned to feel perfectly at ease and cheerful, whilst lying in the midst of much deeper solitude, with no companions but my horse grazing near me, and the fire at my feet. There is no country in the world so safe for the traveller as Western Australia.

The next day we went over the farm of our host. His best land was on the flats at the river side, but his upland, by judicious cultivation, is made productive and valuable. A carriage-drive extends through the grounds and affords beautiful prospects of the river, and of the estates through which it runs; and on the other side, of the Darling Hills. The hedge-rows on this property are planted with olive, almond, and peach trees—an admirable policy, which ought to be adopted throughout Australia. In a few years—for the olive bears fruit much sooner here than in the south of Europe — a valuable traffic in olive-oil may be expected from this colony.

The ingenious gentleman who owns this property (which is, in point of soil, one of the worst farms on the Swan) continues annually to add to its value by his persevering system of improvement. He has had a steam-engine constructed on his own premises, and under his personal superintendence; and he grinds his own flour as well as that of his neighbours.

The neighbouring estate of W. L. Brockman, Esq., is a more valuable property, and equally attractive in possessing a well-cultivated farm, a beautiful situation, a comfortable residence, and an amiable family.

With similar energy and *savoir faire*, all the beautiful farms on this river might be made most enviable residences.

Whilst on the subject of farming, I may mention a reaping-machine which has been introduced into this colony from South Australia, where it was invented. It is only adapted to a very dry climate, but there it is most valuable. A pair of horses push a machine before them, which consists of a threshing-machine and a set of revolving combs, some six feet wide. These combs, in their revolutions, catch up the wheat, and tear off the ears from the stalks, throwing them back into the threshing-machine. A field of wheat is thus reaped and threshed as fast as the horses can walk over it. The straw is afterwards mown.

The roads are hard and good in this neighbourhood, and some of the settlers keep their open carriages.

I doubt whether I have conveyed to the reader a just idea of some of the pleasantest spots which are to be met with in this colony; but I would not have him (full of romantic thoughts and agricultural purposes) rush hastily into the mart and sell his substance in order to lead a life of tranquil retirement in this distant Eden. It requires a good deal of philosophy to make a contented settler. Most colonists leave England full of virtuous resolutions— with bosoms glowing with the ardent love of nature ; and fully persuaded that they need nothing to make them happy but a small farm, beautifully situated, with its cottage *ornée,* and its spreading vines, and a noble fig-tree, beneath which they are to sit in the cool of the evening, with their little ones around them. All this they may really possess ; and for some time they are in raptures at the novel feeling of being men of landed interest. This is always the first ambition of a colonist—to have some property which he may lawfully call his own. And, indeed, the human heart never expands with more satisfactory pride than in the breast of him whose territorial possessions have hitherto been confined to a few flower-pots in his parlour-window, but who now stands firmly beneath a lofty gum-tree, and looking round him, murmurs "This is mine!" It is, indeed, a very pleasant sensation, but, unfortunately, it is very short-lived.

Men do not come out to a colony to spend an income, but to make a living. When once their capital is laid out in the acquisition of a farm, and in the necessary purchase of stock, they have to raise money out of it to pay their labourers' wages, and find their households with tea, sugar, clothing, and "sundries." Many things may be grown upon your farm, but not everything. At first, the settler is satisfied with finding that he can sell sufficient produce to enable him to pay his way, provided he practise the utmost economy, and exhibit a reasonable degree of good management.

But soon there are extra expenses to be liquidated ; a long illness in his family brings him in debt to the doctor ; or his neighbour has injured him, and he has, thereupon, further injured himself by going to law and avenging the wrong. He now becomes discontented, and thinks he is as badly off as he was before he left England ; or, perhaps he may have sustained no losses, and is just able to live on his property without getting into debt ; he forgets, however, the principles on which he came out to settle ; he begins to complain that he is not making money. It is true he leads an easier life than he did in England ; he is not striving and struggling for existence as he was there, but he is making no money. His wife asks him daily, in the pleasantest connubial key, why he brought them all from England, to bury them there, and see nobody from morn till night ? What, she urges, is to become of their children ? Will Jonadab, their first-born, be a gentleman like his maternal ancestors ?—But how, indeed, should he, with the pursuits of a cow-boy and the hands of a scavenger? It is very well for one who cares nothing for genteel society, and whose bearish manners, in fact, unfit him for it, to lead such a life; but is *she* to endure this for ever, and see her daughters married to men who wear long beards and Blucher boots?

These incessant attacks at length overthrow the ennobling philosophy of the colonist. He knows not where to procure more than he already possesses, or he would gladly return to the country of his forefathers; but alas! he sees no prospect of gaining even a bare livelihood there. Without knowing, then, how or where to improve his condition, he deplores the penury of his lot, and sighs for wealth which he has no prospect of ever obtaining.

My own opinion has ever been that colonists, with few exceptions, must always be poor men. They may possess large estates and numerous herds; but the more numerous these herds, the less is their marketable value: for population and demand can never increase in equal ratio with the supply. A man, therefore, who possesses the elements of wealth, may still be poor in the article of money.

Nor will his estates produce him more income than his herds; for in most cases the only rent which his tenants can afford to pay is in kind. *The only real wealth to a colony is the incessant influx of immigration, combining capital and labour.*

There are some of us, happily, who still retain the ancient philosophy. We have not thought of pecuniary wealth, and are content to live easily, with those moderate blessings which attach to a beneficent climate and a simple mode of life.

So very little is required which money can buy, that men seem to be annoyed at the fact, and insist upon creating new wants.

A great deal of discontent and repining generally prevails in a colony. People who have lived miserably in England, who have long doubtfully hovered between suicide and highway robbery, determine at length to adopt the still more melancholy alternative of emigration. After bequeathing a few tender sighs to the country which they have hitherto regarded rather as a step-mother than a parent; and having pathetically solicited the sympathy of those who more readily bestow upon them a few pounds than a few tears, in the pious hope of never seeing them more, our emigrants betake themselves to the favoured land of their adoption, in the full and confident belief that they have nothing now to do, but live "like gentlemen," though without the means, or any other qualifications of that class. Their Faith is of that affecting and unlimited description, as to lead them to suppose that He who beneficently feeds the ravens will not neglect the rooks or the drones.

In a very short time, however, they find that they are no better off in the new than they were in the old country. The gum-trees do not produce bread, nor the banksias shoulders of mutton; and, consequently, their hopes have been miserably disappointed, and they loudly proclaim their wants and sorrows in the streets. There are unfortunately in all colonies—those *refugia peccatorum*—many emigrants of this class, idle and worthless, who have never done well, and never will succeed in any part of the world.

A colonial life is not for these men, and we recommend them to pass on to some other region as quickly as possible.

CHAPTER IX.

THE MORAL THERMOMETER OF COLONIES.

IN the chief town of every colony, there is always agreeable society to be found among the resident Government officers, and the other principal inhabitants. Many estimable individuals are to be met with in all communities; in that in which I have myself resided for some years, there are many for whom I entertain the highest regard. I hope, therefore, it will not be considered that, in the remarks which I am about to make, I am actuated by any ill or invidious feeling, or at all allude to individuals. Since I have undertaken the task of drawing sketches of colonial life, I must not endeavour to conceal any portion of the truth, nor tacitly allow erroneous conclusions to be drawn from my remarks.

I have already observed that a good and kindly feeling towards one another prevails in this colony among the settlers generally. But I must qualify this remark by adding—in all cases in which individual interests are not concerned. There is less perhaps of *the spirit of dealing* in this colony than in any other of the British empire. Ours is not a mercantile community, and the farm-settlers generally are young men of good birth and gentlemanly spirit. Still, even here, beyond all question, exists the same odious tendency (though less apparent) which prevails more or less in all colonies, to advance self-interest on every possible occasion, without being deterred by any scruples whatsoever.

When men become emigrants, they leave behind them their relations, friends, connexions, and all their old associations, and appear upon a new theatre of action, where they have no feelings to consult beyond their own personal wishes and interests.

They find themselves suddenly emancipated from all those restraints which formerly acted with a salutary influence upon their natural inclinations; and having no one near them whose opinion they regard, or whom they care to conciliate, they fall rapidly into the belief that they have no one to live for but themselves, and, consequently, make self the sole guide of all their actions, and sole god of their idolatry.

This spirit of *Yankeeism* is the prevailing spirit of colonies. It is the natural consequence of the isolated state in which men feel themselves to exist, when they have no longer those less selfish motives of action that influenced and regulated their conduct under other circumstances. The eye of a parent no longer watches over them with approbation or anxiety ; and what has a still more powerful influence upon their conduct, they are now beyond the observation of that circle of friends, relations, and acquaintance, to which they had been known from childhood ; which had constituted their world, and the censure or approbation of which determined their state of self-reproach or self-satisfaction. Few men may be trusted far who can say, " *I am not known here ;*" for these are always the people who care least what they do. Good and well-meaning persons will exclaim, "Colonists can have very little sense of religion, if they allow themselves to act at a distance differently from what they would do at home." Those who have more than a theoretical acquaintance with mankind, and who are used to look upon them in their undisguised selfishness, know well that their sense of religion is greatly dependent upon the circumstances in which men find themselves placed. We are not speaking of what such and such people would do and feel, but of what is really done and felt by thousands.

Besides, I have already premised that it is not every colonist who acts on these principles, but that such is the general tendency to act in a colony.

We can now understand the origin of that intense selfishness in the American character, which has never yet been cast aside, and which, in fact, is perpetuated by a republican form of government.

The high and nice sense of honour, the chivalrous generosity, the frank acknowledgment of superiority, and the ready devotion of self to the interests of others at the call of duty, constituted the brightest ornaments of the feudal system, and still glitter (though with feebler lustre) among the fragments of that system throughout civilized Europe.

The Spirit of Trade, which has shattered feudalism, has impaired the brightness of that principle which was the soul of feudalism. Nor has religion yet succeeded in supplying the loss. Religion, which is the bond between Man and his God, has less influence in regulating his dealings with his fellows than Honour, which is the bond between man and man.*

And when the principle of honour loses its purity, you may be sure that the principle of religion is already decayed or dead. Now the principle of honour being (so to speak) of human origin, depends greatly for existence upon the opinions of men; and when we are emancipated from all great

---

* In making this observation, I refer to the general conduct of the World; and am far from intending to say, that honour *ought* to have more influence with mankind than religion. The truly religious, a small but sacred band, " do justly, love mercy, and walk humbly with God."

regard for those opinions, it almost inevitably follows that our sense of honour becomes much impaired; and having no longer any fear of censure,
we no longer have any feeling of shame.

In a colony, then, is most apparent the accursed
Spirit of Trade—that insidious spirit which under-
mines the truth of the heart, which destroys its
most generous impulses, and sneers at every mani-
festation of disinterestedness. The first object of
a colonist is that of a petty shopkeeper,—to grasp
at every thing which is likely to benefit himself,
without regard to justice, religion, or honour. His
own interest is the only guide of his actions, and
becomes the very soul of his existence. He came
out to make a fortune, if possible, and he thinks
himself justified in using every means to this end.
Do not suppose that he is a downright villain who
would commit highway robbery. He would be
greatly shocked at such an imputation, for his conscience is still too timid for so flagrant a crime.
He merely follows the golden maxim of *caveat
emptor*, and, like the petty shopkeeper, thinks he is
justified in cheating those who are too stupid to
look after their own interests, and too ignorant or
too feeble to enforce their just dues.

When that nice sense of honour which rules the
conduct of the high-minded gentleman, and makes
him scorn to take advantage of the ignorance or

the necessities of another, ceases to influence, the
accursed spirit becomes dominant, and men look
with suspicion on all around them.

It has become the pride and the boast of colonists, as of horse-dealers, that they are sharp fellows;
that they have cut their eye-teeth, and are remarkably wide-awake. These honourable distinctions
are acknowledged by the simple-minded with alarm.
They feel like men involved among a mob, and
instinctively button up their pockets.

The moral thermometer in a colony is lamentably
low.

We do not, however, look upon this state of
things as irremediable, and without hope; on the
contrary, we doubt not but the Better Spirit will in
time resume its pre-eminence, and colonists will be
respected for their elevated sentiments and high
sense of honour, rather than for their acuteness in
driving a bargain. This evil, which is the natural
consequence of their present condition as isolated
atoms, unconnected together by those bonds of
mutual respect which confine men in older countries, will cease as society becomes re-organized,
and men feel themselves occupying in a colony the
same position, as regards obligations and duties,
that they would have filled in the parent state. As
they settle themselves more firmly in their places,
they will come to feel that respect which ever

attaches to the character of HOME; and conscious that example is necessary from men who occupy prominent positions, a higher tone will insensibly be assumed, and the Better Spirit again be diffused throughout all the ramifications of society. But to this end, it is most essential that every aid should be given that Government has the power to bestow. Religious instruction, and that good example which, we may assume, is ever afforded to society by the English clergy, are the principal instruments to be sought. In Western Australia there are at this time only six clergymen, who are scattered over a country many hundred miles in extent. Many districts are, unavoidably, entirely without the exhortations and offices of a minister. At King George's Sound, an important post, no clergyman is seen from one year to another. Human beings are born, married, and buried, without a minister to baptize, to teach, to bless, or to give consolation in their extremity. There is no bishop to consecrate, to watch over, or to reprove.*

This is a state of things that must be remedied, or moral improvements cannot be expected.

* By the munificence of Miss Burdett Coutts, a bishopric has been recently founded in South Australia; and the Western Colony is for the present to be included in the same diocese. But when it is remembered that there is no overland communication between the colonies, and the route by sea occupies about ten days, it must be evident that this provision is very inadequate to our wants.

The Roman Church has been more thoughtful
of her children in this colony, there being now
settled here a bishop, and about a dozen priests of
that persuasion—reason the more for the active
interference of a Protestant Government to protect the spiritual welfare of the Protestant community.

The next most important object is the education
of the youth of the colony. So soon as ever
Government can afford the grant of a few hundreds
a - year, free-schools ought to be established in
various districts. Such is usually the scarcity of
money in a colony, that parents cannot afford to
bestow even the commonest education upon their
children. Of course, I allude only to the general
condition of society; there are individuals who
educate their families in a judicious and sufficient
manner; but the great prevailing want is not the
less felt and deplored. Boys, the sons of men who
have themselves been well educated, are early made
to supply the place of labourers and servants.
Hardy and manly in appearance, they are naturally
rough and uncouth in manner, and unhappily possess no mental stores beyond those early principles
of gain which have grown with their growth. In
their anxiety that their sons should do well in the
world, the parent's first object is to impress upon
them the necessity of making the most of every
thing. Their early powers are exercised in selling

stores, sheep, cattle, or other produce, and they are applauded in proportion to the hard bargain which they have driven. If a man, threatened with law proceedings, is compelled to sell his whole crop of potatoes at a ruinous loss, our keen and knowing youngster glories in the opportunity of making a bargain by which he shall profit to the amount of a hundred per cent., though the seller return to his agitated family writhing with despair. The malleable intellect of our youth is annealed by the Demon of Gain upon the anvil of Self-interest.

National education is one of the first objects of a paternal government. The course of study ought ever to be adapted to the circumstances and position of the scholars. In the first years of a colony, the human mind peculiarly exhibits a downward tendency. Few men prove themselves in their new condition of life superior or equal to the character which they had formerly borne, as pious, learned, or humane. The circumstances which formerly so eminently conduced to the maintenance of piety, the cultivation of intellect, and the exercise of benevolence, no longer exist. Solitary and selfish from position, men of naturally generous temper and good disposition, feel their hearts contract and shrivel within them. Surrounded by a sordid and selfish crew, they find no objects for sympathy, no inducements for the increase or the

preservation of knowledge, no animating impulse to
lead them forward in a good cause. Struggling for
a time in the net which is around them, they at
length fall from the edge, down into the seething
cauldron, and become fused among the mass.

The tendency of colonization is to deteriorate. The
first object of Government should therefore be to
arrest this impulse, and remedy the evil so far
as may be accomplished. If the original settlers
degenerate in their moral condition, their children
sink still lower. When parents cease to feel the
influence of those high and pure principles in which
they were themselves brought up, they naturally
forget to inculcate them in the minds of their
offspring. What, then, are the guides that direct
these in their progress through life? What can they
be but Self-interest, relieved perhaps occasionally
by a few touches of Good-nature?

The young women inevitably grow up mere
creatures of impulse. Where are those high
qualities which are necessary to give them their
proper influence over the minds and actions of
the other sex? Where is that powerful sense of
the duties of their calling and position, that is
necessary to create confidence in the breast of the
lover or the husband? Where are those unswerv-
ing principles which alone can keep them, through
trial and temptation, in the right way?

Woman, alas! has lost her power, when she ceases to inspire veneration and command respect.

It is the interest of every colony, and the duty of every Government, to raise the moral character and condition of the people. The necessity of this must be forcibly present in the minds of those to whom the duties of legislation are intrusted; and as the most obvious means of improvement lie in the judicious instruction of the young generation, the attention of Government must soon be directed to this grand object.

CHAPTER X.

IT is most undeniably true, " that there is no place like England," for men who are in " easy circumstances," and who therefore think no more of direct or indirect taxation, and of those multitudinous burthens which highly-civilized life imposes, than a besom-maker's ass does of the load under which it daily journeys. But how many thousands are there (children of sad parents—Toil and Sorrow) who find their utmost efforts scarcely sufficient to keep them out of the debtor's prison ! Continual gloom fills the chambers of their hearts ; the sun bestows its cheering rays in vain ; and all the gay and beautiful influences of the bright world of Nature fail to inspirit him whose every energy is directed to the task of raising his family beyond the threatening grasp of Want. In his few moments of relaxation, when those whom he loves—for whom he is toiling unto death—hang around him with gentle fondness ; in those sweet moments, when love unutterable beams through the glistening eye, and tender solicitude watches the care-worn face, seeking to win one happy smile —even then, he dare not give himself up to joy. The thought is never absent from him that life perhaps is ebbing fast; the very labours to which his only hope of income is attached, are gradually wearing him down to the grave; and when he is no more, what shall be the lot of those whose beaming faces smile so sweetly? What struggles, what miseries are in store for the beloved wife and those young and innocent daughters whose hearts are full of him! No! he dare not give himself up to joy; he smiles in answer to their endearments —but it is rather a shadow than a sunbeam that passes across his countenance.

How many thousands are there in England so circumstanced, who curse the artificial state of society in which they are compelled to live! In their profession or trade they are bound to keep up a certain degree of appearance, or they are shunned by those whom it is their chief interest to conciliate. The great bug-bear ever present in the mind of an Englishman, is the dread of not being thought sufficiently "respectable." Professional men and tradesmen depend for their subsistence upon appearances. To be flashy is as bad as to be shabby; the great object is to appear

substantial. If you are rich, you have less temptation to be dishonest, and may consequently be
trusted. Every man, therefore, who depends upon
the opinion of others, is compelled to assume the
appearance of being comfortably circumstanced in
order to inspire confidence. Character is the life-
blood of Englishmen, but character alone will
seldom extricate a man from the slough of Poverty.
In our highly artificial state of society, something
more powerful than character alone is required to
place a man in the road to fortune—call it as you
please, tact or humbug.

This necessity for keeping up appearances in
order to move in that rank of life which his business requires him to occupy, is the heaviest tax
imposed upon the income of an Englishman. How
often does it draw from him all his profits, leaving
him to lament how little he is enabled to lay by
annually for his children! Many times, without
doubt, he wishes he durst retire to a cottage too
small to admit the visits of the heartless acquaintance who form his "fashionable" world. Does
their society afford him or his family any real
happiness? Is it not rather the cause of many
heart-burnings to him and to them? How much
happier he feels he should be, had he never looked
abroad for happiness, but sought it only around
his own hearth! To see his daughters elegantly

attired, would gratify him extremely, were it not for the unwelcome reminiscences of expense. But would they look less lovely to his eyes, or be less dear to his heart, when moving about him in the useful performance of domestic duties, clad in homely garments, and thinking more of him and home than of visiting and display?

How economically, and how happily too, might he live, were his own house his world, and his wife and children the only beings for whose opinion he cared! But, alas! these are the persons whose opinion is of least importance in his pursuit of fortune. He must do as the world does if he would secure its smiles, and is compelled to think less of happiness than of gain.

Is such a man happier, leading such a life, than he would be as a colonist? Here—ever blessed be the recollection!—there is no necessity for sacrificing peace of mind to appearance. The man whose conduct proves him to be of gentlemanly mould, is everywhere treated as an equal; and though his occupation and mode of living be ever so humble, he loses nothing in the consideration of his fellow-colonists. The half-pay officer, or gentleman farmer, who occasionally drives his own cart, or sows the seed which he has purchased in the market, is not thought less qualified to act as a magistrate, nor is less respected by the great and small in his neighbourhood. His cares are directed towards obtaining substantial comforts for his family, and not towards making a display in the eyes of the little world around him.

Conscious that he is respected only for his character as an upright man, and that as every one knows he is not wealthy, it would be ridiculous to affect the appearance of wealth, he wears the coarsest garments with more pleasure than the finest coat, and draws all his happiness from domestic sources. His sons and daughters equally indifferent to show—though the latter, at least, are always neatly dressed—are busied with their different duties, all tending to promote the general comfort.

Happy family!—how pleasantly the evenings pass in your society! Gladly would I ride many miles to spend such pleasant hours, and witness happiness so unpretending and real. How cheerful looks that large room, with its glorious fire of Jarra-wood and black-boys, (for it is the winter season,) and how lightly those young girls move about, arranging the tea-table, and preparing for the evening meal! The kind-hearted mother, relieved of all duties but that of superintendence, sits by the fire chatting cheerfully with the guest, whose eyes, nevertheless, wander round the room after a certain light and dancing shape; the host, a man of eld, but stalwart in appearance, full of hospitality and noble courtesy, appears in his easy slippers and an old and well-worn coat, which formerly had seen service in London ball-rooms. He discourses not only of the crops and colonial politics, but of literature, and the last news from England; for like many other colonists he receives the English papers, and patronizes the *Quarterly Review.* On the sofa lie the latest numbers of *Punch* and *the Illustrated London News*—some four months old, of course—for the ladies like fun and pictures, whilst their father laboriously wades through a three months' accumulation of the *Times.*

With what alacrity the old gentleman rises up and welcomes a traveller, who has unexpectedly arrived, and has just stabled his horse, and seen him fed before he made his appearance in the parlour! There is no beating about the bush for a bed, or an invitation to supper. Of the latter he is certain, and indifferent about the former; for having slept the last night under a tree, he feels sure of making himself comfortable on the sofa, or on the hearth-rug before the fire. And then the girls, who have no affectation or nonsense about them, crowd round the new-arrived, and ply him with questions about their young friends in other parts of the colony, and whether he was at the last ball at Government House, and what was most worn on that occasion—until the good man, laughing, breaks through the circle, declaring he will answer no more questions till he has had his supper, and, it may be, a glass of whisky-toddy screeching hot.

During the evening the girls sing, and happily they sing well; and they take most pleasure in those songs which papa likes best to hear. And the poor bachelor-guest, who looks on, feels his heart melting within him, and reviles himself for the destitution in which he lives at home. Suddenly, perhaps, horses at a gallop are heard to enter the yard; and soon afterwards two young fellows, fresh from the capital, come dashing into the room, full of spirits, and vowing they have gallopped over on purpose to ascertain whether the ladies were still living. Here is authority of undoubted value for everything relating to the ball at Government House; and the merits and appearance of every person who attended it are soon brought under discussion. This naturally inspires the young people with a desire to dance; so the table is pushed aside, and papa being squeezed nearly into the fire, mamma takes her place at the piano, and bursts off with the Annen Polka.

It may seem strange to you, dear reader, who have an idea that colonists are merely wild beasts, that snch things should be. But so it is; and though people may dance the Cellarius with more gravity in the saloons of St. James's, I question whether dancing be half the fun there that our light-hearted colonists seem to think it. There are no strangers in small colonies—it is always a family party dancing together; and, consequently, people are as merry as if it were Christmas-time all the year round.

Your fashionable people may pity them; but God help them, poor things! In their dark and degraded state they seem to enjoy themselves so much, that I should not like them to be put out of conceit with themselves, or made to repudiate whatever gives them innocent pleasure. Nor are they entirely insensible to the good opinion of great people; for when they learnt that the Polka was thought vulgar at Buckingham Palace, they had serious intentions of denying it admittance into the ball-rooms of Perth; and I sincerely believe it would speedily have pined away and died, like a maiden under the breath of slander, but for a confidently entertained hope that her Majesty would never hear of the offences of the people of Perth—and people will do all kinds of things when they can do them secretly. So the Polka continues to be danced in Western Australia; and the courage of the dancers has been much revived of late by hearing that it is still greatly in vogue at home,

notwithstanding the august censures said to have
been passed upon it.

A country life might always be a happy one,
were people possessed of the smallest competence,
and of properly regulated minds. There is as much
unhappiness, or at least discontent, in colonies
as elsewhere; but discontented colonists are the
greatest fools in the world, because they have themselves created the evils, and the remedies are generally in their own power. The grand object of
man's search is happiness, which he strives to
obtain by a thousand various ways. Wealth he
covets, because he fondly believes that it contains
the prize he seeks; but if happiness may be found
without wealth, of what value are riches? Money
is not so indispensable a necessary in a colony.
Very little indeed suffices to enable a proprietor on
the banks of the Swan, the Avon, or the Brunswick, to bring up his family in comfort, and to
perform all the rights of a generous hospitality. The
discontent which is so often felt in colonies arises
from two causes: first, it is the natural feeling of
those who emigrate late in life; who, although unsuccessful at home, have ever been fondly attached
to home associations, to the friends and connexions
with whom they have been bound up during many
years, and to the national belief that a man can
never be truly happy out of England. In addi-

tion to this, the emigrant of mature years has been so long accustomed to feel himself living in the very centre of intelligence, he has so long been accustomed to watch the progress of political action at home and on the continent, and to drink the fresh draughts of scientific discovery at the fountain-head, that now, when far removed from the busy and exciting scenes of the ever-moving panorama of European life, he feels lost in the wilderness—a fragment of drift-wood washed ashore and left far behind by the fast-progressing waves of Knowledge and Action.

The second cause of discontent is found in the non-acquisition of money. Every one goes out to a colony with the full conviction that he shall make a fortune in a few years, and then return to England and become a man of landed interest.

A man has to conquer his first disappointments before he can become a happy settler; he has to form new and more just ideas of his actual position. Generally, it is necessary that he should return to England once more before he can entirely appreciate the advantages open to him in a colony. He then fully perceives how much more difficult it is to obtain a bare subsistence in the old country. He finds that with the utmost economy he cannot supply the numerous wants of his family, and he longs for his old Australian dwelling again, and the easy, independent life which he was accustomed to lead, when his children used to run about in brown holland, and his wife looked becoming in printed cotton, and thought no beverage so good as the wine which she had assisted to make.

CHAPTER XI.

PERSECUTIONS.

SCEPTICISM is the offspring of ignorance. There are many people still living who doubt the existence of dragons; who go so far as to assert that such creatures never did exist upon the face of this earth, and never did torment and destroy the inhabitants thereof, and persecute forlorn maidens. They scoff at the records which have descended to our times, as fabulous legends, composed by idle monks; who were accustomed to write fictitious histories during the dark ages. They deny to historical ballads that authority which Mr. Macaulay attaches to them; and yet the principal fact in the biography of Andromeda (even before the times of the monks) may have been true; and the poor people of Wantley may really have been harassed by the celebrated dragon of that ilk. We speak seriously.

Geologists have ascertained beyond a doubt that winged monsters of the size described in ancient

legends did really inhabit this earth at some period
or other. Happily they no longer exist of the same
dimensions as formerly; like the descendants of
Anak, they have become *fined down*, as it were, in
the course of ages, until their proportions no longer
awaken personal fear, nor do their exploits engage
the attention of historians. Sometimes, however,
the ancient ferocity, the propensity for devastation,
still breaks forth, even in the diminutive descendants of this formidable race, and persecuted Man
feels himself driven to the brink of despair.

Soon after I had settled at Perth, in a small
house, with three quarters of an acre of ground
about it, I began to think of improving my little
territory. I thought it was a duty I owed to
society to set a good example, by bringing my property into a high state of cultivation.

I intended to "make the barren desert smile"—
to embower my dwelling in the midst of blossoming
peas, and aspiring kidney beans,—to draw around
me, as it were, a little luxuriant Eden, which should
be the admiration of a Sunday public, as they stood
riveted at the palings, unable to pass by without
a lengthened survey; whilst the envied possessor,
stooping behind his magnificent cabbages, would
listen to their unstudied bursts of rapture with jus-
tifiable pride. Glowing with horticultural fervour,
I rose early in the morning, and dug up the soil

with stern resolution, toiling with a Patagonian pick-axe at the great roots which ran in every direction, until I thought myself a perfect pattern of a settler. My man also exerted himself with equal energy and more steady endurance; and in process of time a considerable portion of ground was got ready for seed. In order that nothing might be wanting to insure the most unlimited success, I purchased a quantity of manure, and had it drawn upon the ground. Then it was that the Evil Genius, who (like the wicked Enchanter that always kept his eye upon Don Quixote,) hath ever dogged my steps, made his baleful presence manifest by the most rampant hostility. The day on which the manure arrived, I went out in my pleasure-boat upon Melville Water, accompanied by my man Hannibal, to manage the head-sheets. On our return, at dusk, we found the manure scattered all over the premises, as if it had been kicked about by a party of dancing demons.

The traces of talons were clearly discernible on the ground. I knew not what to make of it. I thought a dragon must have been rampaging about the premises. Well! the next day the man scratched the manure together again as well as he could, and we sowed a quantity of seed—peas, beans, and divers succulent vegetables. The following morning Hannibal rose late, having overslept himself, as he

alleged. I was awakened by his sudden appearance
at my bed-side, but no sooner sat up than I fell
back again, appalled by the ghastliness of his visage.

" The d—ls," said he, " have been again, and
have scrat up the earth far and wide; and (he
added, using a strong expression,) I'll be dashed if
there's a seed left ! "

Alas ! " 'twas but owre true." The ground
so neatly raked the evening before, which I had
returned again and again to look at with fond pride,
until it was obscured by darkness, was now torn up
and defaced throughout its length and breadth.

" Well ! " I exclaimed, as soon as I could speak,
" there *are* dragons in the world."

I could now enter into the feelings of the poor
husbandman of the dark ages, when he got up in
the morning, and found a dragon finishing the last
of his highly-prized dairy cows. If I could only
catch him at it ! I felt immediately a fit of blood-
thirstiness creep over me. I could have destroyed
a dozen dragons with pleasure, might I only come
within reach of them. Calmly, however, I ordered
Hannibal to sow the seeds again, and keep better
watch and ward in future.

It now became a serious question how my
property was to be protected. Am I to be subject
to these incursions without defence ? Is there no
safeguard in this country for a man's possessions ?

I finished breakfast hastily, and went to consult the chief magistrate. To my question as to how I ought to guard my garden and vegetables from the attacks of the insidious enemy, he replied by referring me to the 2 Wm. IV. No. 2, a local act, by which people whose property is trespassed upon, are allowed the privilege of impounding the trespassers.

Impound a dragon ! I thanked the worthy magistrate, "But," said I, " the creatures that destroy my substance have wings, and are not to be caught by men who have none."

" The law," replied his worship, " is decisive on the subject ; you must follow the law, whether you be able to follow the offender or not."

" But," said I again, "if the law gives me no protection—and merely to authorize me to impound a creature with wings, is a mockery unworthy of the dignity of the law—I may surely protect myself? I will have a file of men on guard, and fire on any creature that infringes upon the vested rights which I possess in my property. I will defend myself," said I, growing warm under the oppressive weight of the law, "and maintain my vested rights."

" No man," replied the worshipful justice, " as you know very well, has a right to defend himself, except with the weapons of the law. You will only get into scrapes if you fight with any other weapons."

Finding that I was kicking against the pricks, I made my bow, and went home again in a very ireful mood.

Hannibal had resown the beds, and was at work upon others. On seeing me, he stepped up to a fine Nuytsia floribunda, which ornaments my grounds, and taking up a double-barrelled gun that was leaning against it, gave a few significant slaps upon the breach, and, smiling complacently, winked his eye. I turned away and entered the house, filled with a kind of grim satisfaction, as thoughts of vengeance flitted through my brain. Too much disturbed to sit still, I paced up and down the room, listening eagerly for sounds which should announce the hour of slaughter and revenge.

The milk of human kindness had curdled in my breast; I felt that I could sympathize with the restless anxiety of Charles IX. on the memorable eve of St. Bartholomew. But the butchery of unarmed Huguenots was a different affair altogether from a war of extermination against invading dragons. I looked out of the windows every moment to see what Hannibal was about; but there he continued hoeing, and weeding, and raking, and looking as calm and amiable as the Duke when he awaited the proper moment to attack the French. Suddenly he paused; I watched him quietly drop his rake, and retire backwards behind a bush, where he remained crouching down, with the double-barrelled gun in his hands.

Unable to remain quiet any longer, I opened the window, and cried in a fierce whisper, "Kill! kill!" With his hand he motioned me to be quiet, so I withdrew and paced about the room with feverish anxiety. The discharge of both barrels made me drop into a chair. Murder had been committed! Vengeance was satisfied, and remorse arrived as usual. Remorse, the ill-favoured offspring of Fear!

"You will get yourself into scrapes," said the chief magistrate, "if you use any other weapon than the law." I reasoned with Conscience; I repeated the argument that I had a right to defend my property when the law failed to afford me protection. Dragons, said I, are *feræ naturæ;* the people of Perth, it would seem, are in the habit of keeping them as pets, and thus they come to be considered private property. But then, let the people of Perth destroy their own substance, and not mine. If they do not choose to have gardens of their own, they have no right to prevent the growth of my radishes. Because they do not like sack, shall we have no more cakes and ale? Because they can exist without cauliflowers, must

I renounce all hopes of having hyssop in my pottage?

What! am I to rise up early in the morning and sow the seeds of carefulness and labour, merely for the sustenance of other people's harpies?

To whom am I to look for redress, when I know not to whom the ruthless creatures belong? —Creatures that wander far and wide in search of food; that gain their precarious subsistence by plunder and rapine; and are intensely hostile to the labours and improvements of civilization. No wonder the poet looked upon them as hell-born, and called them a pest and a curse to society:—

> " ——— nec sævior ulla
> Pestis et ira Deum Stygiis sese extulit undis."

I had made these reflections, and received a good deal of comfort from them, when Hannibal appeared at the door with a pallid countenance.

"Two of them, Sir, are done for; one's a big un —eight pounds, if he weighs an 'unce. He's a handsome feller, that un; black feathers, and spurs to his heels six inches long. They'll make a houtcry about him, I expect."

"What have you done with the carcases?"

"Dragged 'em behind the bushes. 'Tan't legal to lift the bodies."

"Go on with your work, Hannibal, and don't appear at all fluttered or discomposed. Look as if nothing had happened. If any one calls, I am not at home."

An outcry *was* raised about the death of the dragon. He was the favourite of a young lady who was a pet of her papa's—(next to dragons, children are the most horrid nuisances).—An accursed dog (the d—l take all dogs! say I,) had found the body, and dragged it into the street, where it was recognised by the girl. The papa, furious at the sight of the favourite's tears, roamed and raged about the town in search of witnesses. Men of Belial are always to be found, especially in a colony, and Hannibal was openly accused of the murder.

The whole town was in a state of excitement. People seemed to think that a blow had been struck at the very roots of civil and religious liberty; and as every one had his favourite dragon, every one felt alarmed for its safety so long as Hannibal remained unpunished.

The ladies were especially bitter in their remarks and inuendoes.

I was told by *friends*, that more than one lady had observed, that an old bachelor like myself cared nothing about dragons, and therefore it was just like my selfishness to seek to deprive them of their innocent pleasures and amusements.

No one would listen to my plea of self-defence; no one regarded my losses; I was not looked upon

as a sufferer; and instead of sympathy received
only abuse.

A summons being issued against Hannibal, he
appeared before the tribunal of two of Her Majesty's
Justices of the Peace, accused of a grave misdemeanour.

As every one knew that I was the instigator of
the offence, I magnanimously avowed the fact, and
was requested to stand in the place of Hannibal.

In vain, however, did I use every argument to
justify the deed. The chief magistrate reminded
me that I had been fully advised to proceed only
according to law, under the Act, 2 Wm. IV. No. 2,
amended (*! !*) by 4 Wm. IV. No. 5 ; by either of
which I was fully authorized to seize and impound
all trespassers—a limit and license that included
dragons.

My defence was allowed to be a sensible and
rational one ; but the law was opposed to it, and
their worships were bound by oath to prefer the
law to common sense. (I doubted myself whether
dragons came within the Law, but the Justices
decided that they were poundable animals.) This
being the case, I was under the necessity of paying
the sum of ten shillings damages, and as many
more for costs and expenses incurred by the bailiff,
in travelling up and down his bailiwick in search of
the body of John Hannibal Muckthorne (whose

body was all the time sitting quietly in my kitchen) —rather than go to Fremantle gaol for a month, and help to draw stones about the streets in a large cart.

I need scarcely add, that I returned home a wiser and a sadder man. "Hannibal," said I, "the Spirit of the Age in this colony is opposed to territorial and to social improvement. My grounds must still remain a barren waste. Instead of embowering myself in fertility, as I had intended; instead of creating new beauties which should transfuse fresh charms into the minds of the peripatetics of Perth; I must continue to live in a desert, and shall doubtless soon subside into an ascetic recluse. Hannibal! turn the horses into the garden, and let them trample over the beds."

Thus have I reluctantly shown the reader that the dark ages still cast their shadows over the city of Perth;—the dawn of a high state of civilization is still wanting there, where man continues defenceless from the ravages of noxious monsters peculiar to an early and uncivilized era.*

* The laws which colonists make for themselves are often as absurd as any that the Imperial Parliament thinks proper to enact for them. To this day, the only legal remedy (except an action, and a shilling damages) against the winged and long-clawed nuisances that destroy the hopes and break the heart of the horticulturist, is to impound them.

CHAPTER XII.

MICHAEL BLAKE, THE IRISH SETTLER.*

MICHAEL BLAKE was a native of Skibbereen, a well-known barony in the " ould country." His parents lived in a hut, " quite handy " to the road, in the midst of a bit of turf-ground, where they managed to rear their annual crops of potatoes and their sprouts of children with as little trouble to themselves as possible. Michael, as he said himself, was the youngest of four, but there were five younger than he. As soon as he could walk, his mother clothed him in an old coat of his father's, the tails of which swept the ground far behind him, as he trotted over the cabin-floor with a stick in his

---

* A dry and humorous old man, who I cannot help suspecting coins a good many of his anecdotes, gave me this account of one of the early settlers, just as I record it. The fact of Blake's coming to this colony, solely because he had heard there was an estate in it called Skibbereen, (after the place of his nativity,) struck me as being something truly Irish and original. The man's whole history is given almost in the words of my informant, who professed to have received it pure from the fountain-head.

hand, to wallop his favourite companion, the long-legged and long-snouted sow, as she lay dreaming in the door-way. His father was an upright man, and dealt equal justice among his children, whom he *lathered* daily with the strictest impartiality. This was all the education they had any reason to expect, as the priest was always in a hurry when he called at their door, and had not time to dismount from his pony, from whose back he bestowed his blessing upon the tattered crowd of children as they pressed around, and gazed upon his Reverence with their wild grey eyes and open mouths. And their parents could not be expected to give any other education than they had themselves received.

Michael grew up, therefore, as might be expected, a hungry, dirty-faced, unbreeched, long-coated urchin. Although his parents had done no more for him than to usher him into a life of mud and misery, Nature had been more compassionate. She had bestowed upon him a restless imagination, apparently for the purpose of removing him from this scene of trouble as quickly as possible. It led him, at an early age, to explore the passes of a neighbouring bog, where he fell into a deep hole filled with water, and was just on the point of escaping from the cares of the world, when his eldest brother unfortunately came by, and fished him out.   Their father seized the opportunity, and lathered them both.

Michael next travelled in a northerly direction, and reached the high-road with another brother, who was sent out to beg.   Here they both sat upon a stone and cried for their breakfast, until a brilliant idea occurred to Michael, which dried his tears.   He made a dirt-pie, and presented it to his brother; and they both passed their time very pleasantly, until an English carriage appeared coming along the road.   Little Pat ran forward, begging and praying their honours to give him a halfpenny for the love of the Virgin, as he had been carefully instructed to do by his dear mother, whilst his father took measures to impress the lesson upon his mind and person.   Michael, on his part, made a vigorous effort to cross over to the other side, crying lustily, " Please Sir, a halfpenny ! " but his mother, in order to give him a good appearance in front, had buttoned the old coat wrong side before, and poor Mike, in his haste and hurry, happening to put one of his little feet into the remains of a pocket, unhappily tripped himself up, and rolled before the horses' feet.   The post-boy cleverly turned them aside as quickly as possible, but nothing could prevent the hind-wheel of the carriage from grazing one of Michael's shins, and making him squall out in the most dreadful manner.

A young lady and gentleman descended from the carriage, and showed the greatest compassion for the sufferer, whom they caused to be carried by a servant to his father's hovel, whither they accompanied him, and soon relieved the anxieties of his parents by a present of five golden guineas.

Some years elapsed, and things went on in the old way with the Blake family. Mike had sprouted out into a fine gossoon of a boy, and exercised his errant disposition by running after the gentlemen when they went out shooting, and helping the keepers to carry the game. One day, a gentleman who was shooting in the neighbourhood called at his father's cabin, and asked for the little boy whom he had run over in his carriage some seven years before. Mr. Blake, senior, after blessing his honour for his goodness, and wishing him long life and every earthly happiness, called to the young spalpeen to get out of that; and why was he not for coming when the gentleman was spaking to him? Mr. Blake hinted to his visitors that he should correct the manners of the youth at an early opportunity, and in the meantime Mike slyly approached, with a gun that he was carrying for the keeper in his hands, and received the compliments of the gentleman on his good looks.

The end of it was that the gentleman, who was an officer, took Mike into his service; and in process of time, when he joined his regiment, Michael became his constant attendant. Dying, however, unexpectedly, as most people do, the worthy Mr. Blake, junior, was left to his own resources; and finding nothing better to do, he accepted a shilling from a friendly serjeant, and entered Her Majesty's service as a full private.

In process of time he married a wife—a real jewel, from that "gem of the sea" so *dear* to poor old England—and accompanied his regiment to Van Dieman's Land, *en route* to India. He was well known and liked by the officers, having a peculiar talent for blarney; and nothing pleased him so much as a little conversation with a superior.

The regiment remained seven years in Van Dieman's Land, and then passed on to its destination, leaving a number of men, who had received their discharge, to become settlers in the colony. Among these was Mr. Michael Blake, who soon established himself on a block of land, and became a prosperous colonist. But times grew bad, ere he could retire with a fortune. His wife formed undesirable acquaintances, and Michael endeavoured to reclaim her by wholesome correction; but, unhappily, he bestowed so much attention upon her amendment that he entirely neglected himself, and before he was aware that he was falling into error, had become an habitual drunkard.

Everything now went wrong. Mike, hating

himself, began to hate everything about him; he hated the colony; he hated the magistrates, who now and then imposed a penalty upon him; he hated the laws, and discovered the difference between law and justice, without being able to find any traces of the latter. His fences fell into decay; his pigs and cattle committed trespasses, and the neighbours made him pay damages. It was the fault of the law, or rather of the lawyers, whom he condemned to the flames with dreadful imprecations.

Unable to pay the storekeeper for sugar and tea, judgment was given against him, and his last surviving cow was seized by the sheriff. He had the satisfaction of beating the officer nearly to death; but the cow was sold notwithstanding, and he took a month's exercise on the treadmill, whilst his wife spent the time with her friend the excise-officer, and drank to his better health and general improvement.

On being released, he complained to the Governor, and presented petitions to the Legislative Council against the unjust judges who ruled the land, and crushed the hearts out of the people.

Soon, however, softer feelings came over him; thoughts returned of home, so long forgotten in days of prosperity. He wondered whether his parents were alive, whom, forty years ago, he had left in the barony of Skibbereen, and had not heard of since.

He thought of the home of his boyhood; of
the antiquated cabin in which, at the will of
his father, he had so often " eaten stick;" of
the long-legged and long-snouted sow, that used
to grunt uneasily in her dreams before the fire;
of the potatoes and salt for breakfast and dinner,
of which he never got enough; of the puddle
before the door, in which he used to love to dabble
—all these visions of the past came back upon him
now in the time of his sorrows, and filled him with
a craving for the scenes of his youth.

Every one in trouble goes to the Governor, who
has consequently plentyof morning-callers. A few
words of sympathy from his Excellency are very
consoling, and serve the afflicted for a topic of
conversation for some time to come. " His Excellency, the last time I saw him, desired me
to write to my friends." " His Excellency particularly wishes me to make it up with Smith, or
I 'd never have forgiven him for seizing my cow."
" His Excellency swears that he can't spare me
from the colony, or nothing should make me stay
another day in it," &c. &c.

Mike presented himself at the Government-offices,
and after waiting a couple of hours, caught sight
of the Governor as he was passing out through
the ante-room.

" God bless your Honour, it's bould I am to be

stopping your Honour and Excellency this way, and you going out too with the business of the Nation upon your Honour's showlders."

" What do you want, my good friend, what do you want?"

" It's your Honour and Excellency that's the good friend to me and the poor, and many's the prayer that's offered up night and morning for your Excellency, by them that blesses the Good God and the Virgin for having sent your Honour to reign over us."—

" What is it, Mike, what is it? I'm in a hurry."

" And is it me that's hindering your Honour? sure and I'll walk wid ye to the world's end and talk all the same. Och, and it's the bad times that have come upon us all entirely—and the ould settlers feels it the most, as is likely. Faith and we'd all die off, out and out, if it wasn't for your Excellency thinking of us, and schaming to do us the good turn, when the Council (bad luck to 'em!) raises the duties."

" My horse is waiting; I really cannot stay."

" Arrah, and it's a fine baste that same, and the two of you looks well together, with the white cockatoo feathers, and the sword all gould and diamonds."

Here his Excellency showed signs of mounting

his horse, so Mike hastened to whisper confidentially,

"Governor, dear, my heart's broken entirely for the ould country, and the poor father and mother that's looking out for me night and morning these forty years, to give me their blessing; and the woman at home, the crathur, kills me day-by-day with her going on; and I'd like to see ould Ireland once before I die, and Skibbereen, which your Honour knows is the finest place under God Almighty's blessed canopy, and I can't die in pace till I see it —'deed I can't, Governor dear; and there's a Man-of-war, no less than the Shannon herself, going to sail for the Indies, where I'd get passed on by Colonel Maxwell (God bless him for the rale gintleman!) only, Governor dear, spake the good word for me to Captain Widdicombe, and I'll be took to Calcutty free for nothing; and it's not a tinpenny-piece that I have in the world, the blessed Virgin pity me!"—Here his Excellency, being mounted on horseback, felt himself in more independent circumstances, and told Mike that he must not think of leaving the colony without his wife, as it would be most improper conduct (the Government would have to support her), and that he himself had no interest with Captain Widdicombe—His Excellency's charger, being of an impatient temper, allowed no further time for parley, but cantered off with his rider, leaving Mike rather at fault.

The more numerous the difficulties that appeared in the way of Mike's return to Skibbereen, the more yearning became his desire to lay his bones there. Every day he appeared at the Government-offices, and waylaid the Colonial-Secretary, or the Attorney-General, or some other of the officials, entreating them to obtain a free passage for an old soldier, whose only desire on earth was to die among the bogs of Skibbereen.

He talked incessantly of that beautiful spot, and swore that he loved it better than the Garden of Eden. He pined after Skibbereen as the melancholy pelican pines for his desert home; but hope gradually seemed to leave him—all other friends had long since abandoned him, and he had fallen helplessly into the power of his arch-enemy the Rum - bottle, when a fellow - countryman arrived at Hobart Town from Western Australia. Mr. Denis Maguire listened patiently to Mike's pathetic lamentation over the lost Skibbereen, and then calmly replied, " Och, but it's little that I'd distract myself for a place like that in the ould country; sure isn't there Skibbereen near the Swan River, belonging to Mr. O'Driscoll, and isn't it a beautifuller place entirely than any other Skibbereen in the world ?" " What !" interrupted Mike,

"is there Skibbereen at the Swan River, and is it
Mr. O'Driscoll that's living there? Arrah! say that
again, my darling, if you plaze." Maguire repeated
the statement; on which Mike, starting up, began
to dance an Irish hornpipe; and then, stopping
short of a sudden, swore that he was the happiest
boy alive, and thanked the blessed Saints for all
their goodness to him.

The next day he managed to sell all the remains
of his property, and made a bargain with the
owner of a small coasting-vessel to convey him and
his wife (whom he was compelled to take with him)
to Swan River, where he arrived in due course of
time, and managed to locate himself at Skibbereen,
where he built a hut, cultivated several acres of
land, and became quite a reformed character.

Although his landlord, Mr. O'Driscoll, was his
countryman, Mike managed to blarney him so that
he did just what he liked, and never paid any rent
either in cash or in kind. His yearning desire had
been to live at Skibbereen, and now that he had
attained his object he was (wonderful to say) contented and happy.

He frequently came to Perth for the sake of a
little chat with the storekeepers and the gentry, and
as he was sure to blarney some one into giving him
a dinner, he always returned home light of heart
and unimpaired in pocket. But alas! poor Mike

was not destined to die in peace at Skibbereen. A large party of the natives had suddenly attacked the abode of a neighbouring settler, and put the owner to death. Michael Blake and two of his friends, without waiting for other assistance, hastened to the rescue, imperfectly armed. They were overpowered in an instant. Blake and one of his companions fell pierced with many spears, whilst the other, being on horseback, escaped, carrying with him four spears fixed in his body. Years afterwards, one of the natives who had assisted at the slaughter coolly related the particulars of the death of Michael Blake.

When he was lying on the ground, said this man, he turned round, and supporting himself on his arm, entreated for mercy in the most moving terms. The savages stood round him, looking on, and listening patiently to his address.

"Did you show him mercy?" asked my informant.

"No!" replied the savage, with calm indifference.

"What did you do?"

"We cut his tongue out."

"Wretch! what for?"

"He wongee (chattered) too much."

Poor Mike! his blarney could not save him; it had often before done him good service, but the savages valued it not.

CHAPTER XIII.

WILD CATTLE HUNTING.

HAVING received intelligence that a numerous herd of wild cattle had lately been seen grazing upon some extensive plains a day's journey south of Perth, I got up a party with the intention of hunting them.

Our preparations were made the day before starting on the expedition. A bullock-cart was loaded with fire-arms, kegs of brandy, various kinds of provisions, and cloaks and blankets. A couple of natives had been engaged to act as guides, and these, with their wives and families, spent the greater part of the day lounging about my premises, idly inspecting the arrangements, and sleeping in the sunshine, lazy as the pigs, which they surpassed in filth. In the afternoon, taking with them a supply of flour, they commenced their journey, intending to sleep upon the road, and leave us to overtake them on the following day.

At day-break the next morning we were in our

saddles, the bullock-cart having started during the night. The party consisted of three, who were all clad in blue hunting-shirts, and had polished horns hanging at their backs, filled with eau-de-vie, wine and water, or the simple fluid, according to the taste of the wearer. As we passed down the silent street at that early hour, one of the party, an officer, agreeably dispelled the slumbers of the peaceful inhabitants by a most able performance upon a key-bugle; the others gave vent to the exuberance of their spirits by loud "tally-ho's!" and cries of "hark away!" and other encouraging expressions addressed to imaginary dogs. Then we gave our able steeds the head, and dashed along with all those happy and exulting thoughts which bubble in the breast of youth hurrying to the chase. Is there any moment in life so dear to memory as those we have passed on horseback, in the fine air of morning, when we hurried along towards the haunt of cunning Reynard, and expected every in-stant to see him break cover? Less exciting by far is hunting in Australia, but still it is hunting, and we are on horseback, and eager as ever for a gallop. Passing over two well-built wooden bridges, connected by a causeway, we crossed the river, and took the road for the Canning.

Thick woods of banksia, wattle, and eucalypti, closed in the view on every side; but occasionally

we ascended a gentle slope, and then looking back
we could see a beautiful picture before us. In the
still air and misty light of the morning, Perth water
lay clear and tranquil amidst the vast forest by
which it is surrounded. The heights of Mount
Eliza looked down into the glittering mirror. On
the right bank were the white houses of the capital;
far to the left we caught glimpses of Melville water.
Except the occasional flights of wild ducks, and the
dark gusts which from time to time swept along
the waters, heralding the rising land-wind, all was
still and breathless. One could not help asking
oneself how long this scene had existed as we now
beheld it? Was it designed for thousands of years
to be viewed only by savages, mindless as the birds
or fishes that frequented its waters? Had it
always existed thus, or been growing during centu-
ries under the hand of Nature, until it should be
adapted to the habitation of civilized man? And
was that period now arrived, or were we premature
in seizing upon our inheritance before it was
thoroughly prepared for our reception? Many
times have we asked ourselves this last question.
This singular country appears to represent the
ancient character of the earth in one of the earlier
stages of formation. It represents that epoch when
animal life was first developed in the lowest order
of quadrupeds.

There are a few small exceptions, but it may be laid down as a general rule, that all the animals indigenous to this country are marsupial—from the kangaroo, the largest, down to the little field-mouse.

The animals not indigenous are Man, the wild cattle, and the wild dogs.   Many speculations have been hazarded as to the origin of the first: to me it appears there can be little doubt that the first tribes found their way hither from the eastern islands, having proceeded originally from India. The language of the natives bears more traces of the Hindu than of any other.   This, I believe, is the opinion of the Rev. J. Mitchell, M.A., of the Middle Swan, whose long residence in India, and intimate acquaintance with some of the languages of that country, give weight to his conjectures. Many of the words used by the natives of both countries are identical in sound, and express the same meaning.

I have also noticed that the Coolies of India and the natives of this colony manage to understand one another much sooner than is the case between the latter and the whites.

The wild cattle have long existed in the interior, as appears from their remains.   Both they and the wild dog have probably descended from animals cast ashore by shipwreck.   The indigenous tribes are those of the kangaroo, the opossum, and the

lizard. It is curious to observe how the distinguishing features of the first are manifested in a
great variety of animals, of all sizes from the kangaroo downwards—the long hind, and short fore
legs, the three toes on the former, the rat-like head,
the warm pouch, betokening the immature partu-
rition. The opossums also are marsupial. All
these animals seem to belong to an early age of the
geological world. Many of the plants speak the
same language—especially the Zamia. The rocks,
too, of this portion of New Holland are all primary,
except the limestone and sandstone near the coast.
Is this country, then, a portion of the world that
has remained in the same state for thousands, or
hundreds of thousands, of years; or is it of comparatively recent formation, exhibiting that condition
which at one period belonged to the whole surface
of the earth? The latter, of course, must be the
case; and if so, we cannot help thinking that
further changes must take place in its geological
character before it shall be permanently occupied
by civilized man. At present, however, it must be
admitted there is no sign of volcanic action going
on to effect these changes. Our conjectures are
purely speculative, and will probably meet with no
sympathy from the reader, but we throw them out
because the subject is full of wonder and mystery;
and those who have brought personal observation

to bear upon it, best know it to be so. As we wander through the lacustrine valleys which abound here; valleys once the beds of rivers, but now broad swamps choked up with lofty reeds—we feel as though we were in the land and the age of the Saurians.

The whole country swarms with lizards, some of which, to the northward, grow to the size of five feet; but the most common are the *Iguana*, or *Guana*, a creature some ten or twelve inches long, with a flat head, very wide mouth, and only the stump of a tail. They are perfectly harmless, and subsist upon frogs and insects. One variety of this species, found in the district of King George's Sound, was brought to my notice by my brother. It is usually found in a tuft of grass, where it lies completely hidden except its tongue, which is thrust upwards, and bears an exact resemblance to the petal of a flower, crimson and pink. Flies seem to delight in resting upon this deceptive flower, which being covered with an adhesive mucous substance, takes them prisoner, and proves their destruction.

We have now had a long canter, which has brought us to the neighbourhood of the Canning River. The country hereabouts resembles a wild English park. The trees are all of the eucalypti species, large and dispersed; the surface of the ground is level, affording a view of the Darling

Hills, which appear to be close at hand. Crossing the river by a rustic bridge, we ascended the opposite bank, whilst our trumpeter blew a charge that was intended to announce our approach at a farmhouse close at hand. As we rode up to the door, the proprietor, attended by three stalwart sons, hastened to greet us. He was a gentleman who had passed a good portion of his life on the Continent, but having a large family to bring up had resolved to seek his fortune in the Southern hemisphere. Breakfast was already set out for us in a large room which served as the baronial hall of the mansion; whilst our horses, partaking of the prodigal hospitality of the farmer colonist, were tethered in various parts of a fine field of clover.

Breakfast is a famous meal after an early morning ride, and people have then not only good appetites but good spirits. Half-a-dozen kangaroo-dogs, attracted by the clatter of knives and the tempting savour that arose from the large dish of sheep's fry, crowded round the open door, whilst they seemed to feel keenly the selfishness of those who appropriated the whole of the feast to themselves. Every now and then arose a howl of anguish from this group, as one of the young men would arrive with fresh supplies of coffee or fried bacon, and kicked a clear passage for himself into the room. One only of the canine race was allowed to approach the table—the venerable Tip, who having formerly, in times of scarcity, earned his master five pounds a-week by catching kangaroos for the market of Fremantle, was now entitled to sit at his right hand, where a few morsels were occasionally bestowed upon him, which he received with becoming gravity and decorum.

Breakfast finished, we saddled our horses and proceeded on our way, accompanied by one of the sons of our host. We pushed along towards the foot of the hills, over a sandy country covered with scrub, and trees of various magnitudes.

The birds that we saw were chiefly fly-catchers and parroquets; and occasionally the wild turkey, or bustard, sailing along in the distance, made us sigh for a nearer acquaintance.

After a cheerful ride of several hours, having the hills on our left hand, we crossed a few small plains; and understanding from our guide, Tom H——, that we were now at our destination, we began to look about us for our bullock - cart, whose track we had noticed from time to time as we came along. Our "cooeys" were answered by voices not far distant; and following the sound, we soon came within view of a column of smoke curling lightly above the trees; and on arriving at the spot whence it arose, we found our man, assisted by the natives, busily engaged in erecting a kind of hut, or rather skreen of boughs, for our night quarters. The bullocks were feeding quietly at a short distance; the cart was conveniently placed for being unpacked; and a group of three native women and their children, squatted round a fire of their own, about a hundred yards from ours, and busily occupied in baking flour-dampers, signalled our approach by shrill cries of welcome, without rising from their places.

Our horses were soon relieved of their saddles, and each man leading his own steed by the long tether-rope which had been carefully coiled round its neck, took it to a neighbouring pool to drink, and then proceeded in search of the best pasture. Our animals having been attended to, our next thought was of ourselves; and every one took his bundle of blankets and cloaks out of the cart, and unrolled it beneath the sloping skreen of boughs, and prepared his bed according to his particular taste or experience; testing the accommodation from time to time by flinging himself upon his couch, and ascertaining the different vents by which the wind would be likely to prove annoying during the night. These were next stopped up by handfuls of xanthorea leaves, or by strips of bark from the paper-tree.

The lodging being pronounced perfect, and the sun being level with the horizon, we hastened the

Lieut. A. H. Fry 8.th Reg.t del.

THE BIVOUAC.

E. Radclyffe, sc.

preparation for our meal; and hampers and boxes soon gave forth their stores of cold fowls, tongues, hams, and meat-pies. Sausages are excellent things in bush-campaigns; and as every man toasts his own on the point of a long stick, a high degree of nervous excitement is felt by each, lest he should lose his savoury morsel in the fire.

The kettle soon boiled, and as we ate our tea-dinner, the sun went down, and night quickly swallowed up the short twilight, leaving us to depend entirely on our fire, which presented a goodly pile that shot forth cheerful flames, making the scenery around us bright with light. The ground for the space of many yards glittered beneath the flickering rays; the bowls of the tall trees seemed whiter than usual; even the brown cheeks of the natives looked less dark, as they chattered and laughed over their supper. Cold grog, or hot brandy-and-water, was leisurely sipped by those who lay on their couches in the full tranquillity of after-dinner ease; and as digestion proceeded, songs and catches awakened the echoes of the woods.

Tired at last, we sank to sleep, having first, however, visited our horses and changed their tether. During the night I woke up. All around were fast asleep in different postures; some rolling about uneasily in their dreams; others still as the

dead.   I heaped fresh logs upon the fire, which
blazed forth anew.   The natives were all huddled
under their wigwams, which are about the size
and shape of an open umbrella resting on its edge.
The night was dark throughout the forest, and
overhead; the little circle of light within which I
stood, seemed like a magician's ring, sacred and
safe from evil spirits that filled the air around.
It was as the speck of Time amid the ocean of
Eternity—as Hope, bright and solitary in the
midst of unfathomable darkness.   There I felt safe
and secure—but without—who might tell what
spirits roamed abroad, melancholy and malignant?
Peering into that dark boundary of forest, the eye
vainly endeavoured to pierce the gloom.   Fancy
peopled its confines with flitting shapes, and beheld
a grinning hobgoblin in the grotesque stump of
many a half-burnt tree, on which the light momen-
tarily flickered.   The ear listened eagerly for sounds
in the distant solitude; and one almost expected to
hear shrieks of laughter or of terror borne upon
the night-wind from the recesses of the hills.   Evil
spirits seem peculiarly the companions of heathen
savages.   A wild, desert, and desolate region, traversed only in the day-time, and rarely even then,
by straggling barbarians whose hearts have never
known a single gentle emotion, seems naturally to
be the haunt of the Spirits of Evil.

Chingi, the terror of our natives, is often seen by them, as they lie cowering under their kangaroo skins, and huddled together in the extremity of fear, stalking giant-like and gloomy along the summits of the hills, whilst the moon shrinks timidly behind her curtain of clouds.

On that night, however, there was no moon, and Chingi was not visible to me, nor did any sound break in upon the silence of the forest, save that of our horses eating their food, and giving an occasional snort as the sand affected their nostrils. Anxious to behold any spirits that might please to be visible, I walked to the spot occupied by my quadruped, with the intention of changing his quarters; but finding him comfortably stretched in repose, I left him to dream of his own distant manger and two quarterns of oats, and returned to my couch. The appearance of the bivouac, to one viewing it from the surrounding darkness, was very picturesque. Every object was lighted up by the cheerful blaze—the cart with its packages in or about it, the sleepers in their blue or red woollen shirts, under the sloping roof, their guns leaning against the uprights, their shot-belts and pouches hanging in front—the kangaroo-dogs lying round the fire, and as near to it as possible—the surrounding trees and shrubs glittering with a silvery light, their evergreen foliage rustling at the breath

of the soft land-breeze—altogether formed a striking and peculiar scene.

Next morning we were up before the sun, and
having breakfasted, proceeded on horseback in
search of the herd of wild cattle, which we knew,
from the reports of natives, to be somewhere in
the neighbourhood. We rode down an extensive
plain, covered plentifully with grass, and presenting
numerous clumps of trees, which afforded shelter
to bronze-winged pigeons and immense flights of
white cockatoos. The latter screamed fearfully as
we drew nigh, but did not remain long enough to
allow us the chance of a shot. Many tracks of the
cattle were visible, traversing these plains in every
direction ; but, on reaching a small pool, we found
such recent traces as led us to believe the animals
could not be far distant. Remaining stationary
for a few moments, we allowed the two natives
who accompanied us to ascertain the direction in
which the herd had wandered, and their signs soon
led us to follow in profound silence. The natives
walked rapidly ahead ; the tracks were very apparent, and we were all in high glee, and growing
extremely excited. The sun shone brightly, but as
it was in the month of May, the air was mild
and pleasant, without being hot. After proceeding
along the plains for several miles we came to a
thick jungle, through which the cattle had formed

a path. The interior presented a rocky area of considerable extent. Fragments of rock lay jostled together, among which trees and shrubs appeared, and here and there an open space afforded room for the herbage which had tempted the cattle into this rough scene. In parts where grass refused to grow, beautiful purple flowers raised their heads in clusters—and ever in the most rugged and barren spots the gayest flowers are found to bloom. How grateful do we feel to Nature for bestowing such charms upon the wild desert! cheering our spirits with a sense of the beautiful, that else would droop and despond as we journeyed through the lone and dreary waste.

Although we sometimes proceeded over a surface of bare rock, and at others over large and loose stones, where no foot-print was visible to the eye of a white man, the natives never failed to discover the traces which they sought with unerring sagacity. After a ride of nearly two hours we observed one of the natives making signs to us to halt. "There they are!" passed in eager whispers from one to the other. Before us was a belt of wood, through which we could perceive about a dozen cattle grazing on a broad plain.

Already they had a suspicion of danger, and began to look around them. One of the natives, with my double-barrelled gun loaded with heavy ball, was creeping towards them through the grass upon his hands and knees, whilst we cautiously drew up at the side of the wood.

The herd consisted of a huge mouse-coloured bull, with an enormous hunch on his shoulders, and about a dozen cows, with a few calves. The bull came slowly towards us, muttering low bellows, and shaking his fierce head and ponderous neck, on which grew a short, black mane. From some unexplained cause or other the native fired his gun before the animal was within range, and the bull, being a beast of discretion, stopped short, as though extremely surprised, and, after a little hesitation, turned round and rejoined his female friends. The whole herd then began to trot off at a slow pace across the plain, which was there about a mile broad. We were now all eagerness for the pursuit; and Tom H——, the most experienced of the party, calling on us to follow him, dashed off at right angles from the herd, and outside the belt of wood, in the belief that he would be able to head the animals by a little manœuvring; but at the instant he started the old bull turned short on his course, and made across the plain in a new direction. I happened to be the last of our party, and was the only one who perceived this new disposition of the enemy. Anxious to be the first in the *melée*, I allowed my friends to gallop off, and dashed myself through the wood directly in pursuit of the herd.   Thinking there was no time to lose, I waited not for my gun, but resolved to trust to the pistols in my holsters.

The cattle, who had begun their retreat at a steady trot, increased their speed as they saw me gallopping up to them.   I was afraid of their crossing the plain, and escaping in the thick forest beyond, and so pushed my good horse to his utmost speed.   He seemed to be as much excited as myself, and in a few minutes I headed the herd, and tried to turn them back; but they would not deviate from their course, and would have rushed through a regiment of foot, had it been in their way: I therefore avoided the old bull, who came charging along at the head of the phalanx, and found myself in the midst of the herd.   It was a moment of delightful excitement; some skill was required to avoid the hurtling forest of horns, but I turned round and gallopped with the mass; and having perfect confidence in my horse and horsemanship, I felt that I could pick out any of the animals I pleased.   My gun, however, was wanting to bring the huge bull to his bearings.   He looked so enormous as I gallopped alongside of him, that I despaired of making any impression with a pistol, and resolved to limit my ambition to the slaughter of one of the cows.   We were now across the plain, the bull had entered the forest, and the others were in the act of doing the same, when I rode against the outside cow, in the hope of turning her away from the thick cover, and keeping her in the open plain.   She would not, however, turn aside, and I fired my first pistol at her eye, and though I only grazed her cheek, succeeded in separating her from her companions, and turning her up the long plain.   At this moment four kangaroo-dogs, (a cross between a greyhound and a blood-hound, bold, powerful, and swift,) that had followed me in the chase, but had only gallopped alongside of the cattle, finding me seriously engaged with one of the num-ber, made a simultaneous dash at the unfortunate cow, and endeavoured to impede her career by barking, and biting at her nostrils, dew-lap, and flanks.

It was a fine sight to see these four noble hounds chasing away on either side of the animal, whilst she, every now and then, stooped low her head and made a dash at them, without pausing in her career.   Away she went at a slapping pace, keep-ing me on the gallop.   Fearful of hurting the dogs, I refrained from firing for some time, but at length got a chance, and aimed a ball behind her shoulders, but it struck her ribs, and penetrated no deeper than the skin.   Loading as I rode along, I deli-vered another ball with better success, and she began to abate her speed. The rest of the party now came up, cheering and hallooing, but the game had dashed into a swamp in which the reeds and shrubs were high enough to conceal horses and huntsmen; nevertheless, we pushed through, and found her on the bank of a muddy pool, where she stood at bay, whilst the dogs barked cautiously before her. She was covered with sweat, blood, and dirt, and perfectly furious; and the moment we approached she made a rush, trampling over several of the dogs; and darting madly against the nearest horseman, caught his charger on the flank, and steed and rider rolled together on the ground. The furious assailant stumbled over her prostrate foes, and was saluted with a discharge of fire-arms, which, however, did not prevent her from rushing against me in return for a ball in the shoulder, but I eluded the assault, and the animal fell exhausted to the ground.

All this may sound savage enough to those who read in cold blood, but it was very exciting at the time; and MAN, when a hunter, becomes for the moment ruthless and blood-thirsty. This was a very severe chase; the animal had run full five miles over a rough country at such a pace as to cover our horses with foam, and they now stood thoroughly blown, and shaking in every limb.

We returned to our home after a short rest,

taking the tail with us as a trophy. A party
was despatched in the evening with the cart, and
a large portion of the carcase was brought in and
skilfully salted by the experienced hand of Tom H.

This evening passed away as pleasantly as the
last, and as we were all rather fatigued, we retired
early, and slept until awakened by the sun.

A native arrived early in the morning with
intelligence that a herd of wild cattle was now
grazing in a ravine of the hills about four miles
distant. As we could not well follow them on
horseback in that locality, we started off on foot
armed with our rifles. The morning as usual was
brilliant, but not too warm, and we walked along
in high spirits. We had not proceeded far through
the woods when one of the natives, who was in
advance, stopped short on a sudden, and we all
instinctively did the same. Stealing back to us,
he took my rifle out of my hands without any
ceremony, and telling us to remain perfectly still,
crept slowly forward, stooping nearly to the ground.
We now perceived a small plain about two hundred
yards a-head of us, on which were six wild turkeys
leisurely feeding and walking about.

The native had dived among the scrub, and we
lost all signs of him. It soon, however, became
evident that the turkeys suspected danger; they
erected their tall brown and grey necks, and looked

about them like alarmed sentinels. "They're off!" cried we—but just as they were preparing to run, which they do with great rapidity, one of them was seen to flutter his wings and tumble over, whilst the crack of the rifle proclaimed the triumph of Migo. We rushed through the brushwood, elated as schoolboys who have shot their first throstle with a horse-pistol, and found the bustard flapping out its last breath in the hands of the native, whose dark visage gleamed with triumphant pride.

Resuming our march, we passed over the side of a hill covered with inferior Jarra trees, and soon entered the ravine in which we expected to find the cattle. They were not visible; so we crossed the valley, and passed up the other side for about half-a-mile, when we entered another valley, some distance up which we perceived a herd of cattle quietly grazing, or lying ruminating in the confidence of perfect security. We endeavoured to creep towards them as quietly as possible, but their senses of smelling and hearing were so acute that they became acquainted with their danger too soon for us, and trotted gently up the valley before we could reach them. We now dispersed in the hope of heading them. Attaching myself to Migo, who considered my rifle the most likely to prove successful, as he had killed the bustard with it, we walked for half an hour across the hill-side without seeing anything of our game.   A rifle-shot and a loud shout prepared us for something, and in an another minute we heard the crashing of branches and the tread of feet, and soon beheld half-a-dozen cows and two or three calves making their way up the hill at a short distance from us.

"What for you no get behind tree?" said the native in an angry whisper, and giving me a push that prevented my staring idly any longer, and sent me into a proper position.

"Oh! why will they go in that direction? Why will they not come within range?   I will give every-thing I have on earth for one good point-blank shot!"

And sure enough a bouncing bull-calf, turning aside from a thick clump of trees, came within about a hundred yards of me apparently wild with fright, and not knowing which way to run. Just as he was turning off again, I fired, and he fell upon his knees, struck in the shoulder.

Migo was upon him in an instant, and felled him to the earth with a blow of his stone-hammer. I shouted the pæan of victory, and was answered by a loud "cooey" from the valley and the voice of my friend Mr. B. calling out, "I have killed a splendid cow and dispersed the herd.   The bull and several cows are gone down the valley towards the plains."

All the party, with the exception of Tom H., were soon assembled round the body of B.'s cow, which was black and fine-limbed. She was evidently in milk, and there was little doubt that the calf slain by me had belonged to her.

Every one now asked what had become of Tom, whose assistance was absolutely necessary in cutting up the carcases. B. had heard his rifle down the valley, and we now began to "cooey" for him. In a few moments we heard a faint "cooey" in reply, and started in that direction. After walking for about ten minutes towards the opening of the valley we heard distinctly, and at no great distance, the bellowing of a bull. Proceeding cautiously, with our rifles all ready, we soon arrived at the spot, and there beheld a huge bull tearing up the ground with his feet and horns, and bellowing in the most savage manner. A shout of joy directed our attention among the boughs of a low banksia tree, where our unfortunate friend Tom sat painfully perched, only just out of reach of danger. The animal below every now and then fell upon his knees, crushing and smashing something which we had great difficulty in recognising as poor Tom's rifle.

"He is badly wounded," cried Tom, "pitch into him, and don't be afraid!"

Without waiting for this exhortation, we let fly

a volley, which brought the animal down upon his
knees ; and after a few staggering efforts to run at
us, he sank to rise no more; whilst his first assailant, Tom, slipped down from his perch, and limped
towards the remains of his rifle, execrating the
dying bull in a furious manner, and even venting
his wrath in a kick. As Tom wore a red shirt that
only reached to his hips, he had no chance of con-
cealing an enormous rent in his nether garment,
through which protruded the remains of a shirt,
which at the best of times was probably far from
presenting the appearance of virgin purity, but now
was stained with blood. As people in Tom's plight,
when not seriously hurt, are usually more laughed
at than pitied, the chagrin of our friend enhanced
. the interest with which we listened to his story.

Knowing that there was no escape for the herd
of cattle up the valleys, as they terminated in steep
rocks, and that therefore they would either cross
over the side of the hill, or return down the first
valley towards the plains, Tom hung back, leaving
the rest of the party to head them. After some
time had elapsed, he distinguished the bull and
several cows trotting along the hill - side ; and
hastening to meet them, he posted himself behind
a tree, close to which he saw they would soon pass.

Anxious, however, to get a view of the game, he
stepped out from his ambush just as the bull had

approached within fifty yards. Each saw the other at the same moment. The bull stopped short, and Tom felt rather queer. He did not like to fire at the vast head of the animal, lest the ball should glance off without effect. The bull, instead of turning aside, began to bellow and tear up the ground with his hoofs. The cows stood still, and stared at Tom, who began to think the state of his affairs looked gloomy; but he knew that his best policy was to remain stock-still; so he looked at the bull and the cows, and the bull and the cows looked at Tom. At length the bull had sufficiently nerved his resolution, and began to advance, tearing up the ground and bellowing as he came on. Tom took aim between the shoulder-blade and the neck, and fired; the enemy staggered, and roared with fury, rushing like a whirlwind upon Tom, who took to his heels, and began dodging round the trees. But the bull was in earnest; and savage with rage as a thousand lions, he tore round the trees more quickly even than Tom, carrying his head close to the ground, and his tail straight out behind, whilst his eyes, Tom said, glared with such fury, that our poor friend's heart froze up within him. Luckily he espied a banksia tree which seemed easy to ascend; but just as he reached it the bull was upon him. The bull roared, and Tom, roaring almost as loudly, made a spring at the tree, but slipped down again just upon the horns of the animal. The next hoist, however, rent his garments, and lacerated a portion of his person which he had always considered especially sacred; but as the thrust heaved him upwards at the same time, and gave a fresh impulse to his agility, he succeeded in scrambling upon a bough that kept him just out of danger. No one may describe the pangs of despair by which he was assailed when he beheld the utter destruction of his only rifle. He threw his cap in the face of the bull, but he only lost his cap as well as his rifle by this rash and inconsiderate action, which was the highest proof he could have given of the extremity of his distress.

Poor Tom! he had often been made a butt of, but had never been so butted before.

The cup went merrily round that evening, and many and jovial were the songs that were sung, and witty and pleasant were the jokes that passed freely at the expense of the unfortunate *tauricide*, who, bereft of his rifle, and dilapidated in reputation and pantaloons, was heartily glad to be able to hide his sorrows in sleep.

CHAPTER XIV.

WOODMAN'S POINT.*

THERE is a pleasant ride along the shore from
Fremantle to a little bay about seven miles distant,
one side of which, covered with lofty trees, runs far
into the sea, and is called Woodman's Point. The
sea in this part appears to be only a few miles
broad; Garden-island forming the opposite shore,
the southern extremity of which seems almost to
join Cape Perron, and thus presents the appearance
of a vast bay. Not long ago, the blackened remains
of a small house, or hovel, were to be seen on the
verge of the wood, facing towards Cape Perron.
Around it might be distinguished the traces of a
garden of considerable extent ; a few stunted vines
still continued annually to put forth the appearance
of verdure, which served only to tempt the appetite of the stray cattle that wandered down to this
solitary spot. A large bed of geraniums had ex-

* This is a more sentimental story than that of Michael
Blake, but I owe them both to the same authority.

tended itself across the path which used to lead to
the door of the house; and their varied and beautiful flowers, rejoicing in this congenial climate,
gave additional melancholy to the scene.   It was
evident those plants had been reared, and tended,
and prized for their beauty; they had once been
carefully cultured, pruned, and watered—now they
were left to bloom or to die, as accident permitted.
Near to this bed of geraniums, but apart and solitary, untouched even by weeds, of which there were
only few in that sandy soil, grew an English rose-
tree.   Its long, unpruned boughs straggled wildly
on the ground.   It looked the picture of desolation
and despair.   A few imperfect flowers occasionally
peeped forth, but knew only a short and precarious
existence, for the shrub being no longer sheltered
behind the house, was now exposed to the daily
violence of the sea-breeze.

This widowed rose, deprived of the hand which
had tended it so carefully, and of the heart which
its beauty had gladdened, seemed now in its careless desolation awaiting the hour when it should
die.   It really looked, with its drooping boughs,
its torn blossoms, and its brown leaves, rustling
and sighing to the breeze, like a sentient being
mourning without hope.   Those who have never
lived in exile from their native land, can have no
idea of the feelings with which a lonely colonist,

long separated from all the associations of home, would regard a solitary plant which so peculiarly calls up home memories. Pardon us, good reader, this appearance of sentiment; you who will read these lines in Old England—that land which we must ever think of with pardonable emotion—will evince but little sympathy with us, who necessarily feel some fond regard for the Mother from whom we are parted, and are naturally drawn towards the inanimate things by which we are reminded of her. There is in this colony of Western Australia a single daisy root; and never was the most costly hot-house plant in England so highly prized as this humble little exile. The fortunate possessor pays it far more attention than he bestows upon any of the gorgeous flowers that bloom about it; and those who visit his garden of rare plants find nothing there that fills them with so profound a feeling of interest as the meek and lowly flower which recalls to their memories the pleasant pastures of Old England.

But to return to the ruins of Woodman's Point. This plot of land, now so neglected and forlorn, was once the blooming garden of a very singular old man, who owed his support to the vegetables which it produced, and to the fish that he caught from the little cobble which danced at anchor in the bay, whenever the weather permitted the fisherman to exercise his art. No one knew his history, but his conversation and deportment told you that he was of gentle birth, and had been well educated. His manners were particularly amiable and retiring, and every one who visited the solitary old man came away impressed with a melancholy interest in his fate.

He always welcomed a visitor with gentle pleasure, and seemed glad of the opportunity of showing his crops of vegetables and the flowers in which he delighted.

The rose-tree never failed to arrest his steps for a moment. He had brought it himself from England as a cutting, and there was evidently some history attached to it; but he never shared his confidence with any one; and the history of the rose-tree, like his own, was never revealed.

There was only one point on which he betrayed any feeling of pride—and that was his name. No one else would perhaps have been so proud of it, but he himself ever seemed to regard it with veneration.

He called himself Anthony Elisha Simson; and never failed to make you observe that his patronymic was spelt without a "*p*."

Nothing irritated him so much as to receive a note addressed, "A. E. Simpson, Esq."

The Simsons, he would assure you, were an

old family in the northern counties of England, and traced back their genealogy to the Conquest; whereas the Simpsons were of quite a different, and doubtless inferior origin. Nothing more than this did he ever relate concerning his family or his personal history.

He arrived in the colony a few years after its foundation, without any other effects than what were contained in a portmanteau and carpet-bag, and with only a few sovereigns in his purse. Without associating himself with any one, he early fixed upon the spot where he afterwards built his house, and established his permanent abode. Here he began to make his garden, and did not disdain to earn a few shillings occasionally by cutting firewood for a man who supplied Fremantle with that necessary article. It was this occupation that caused the settlers, who knew nothing more of him, to give him the title of " The Woodman"—a name which soon attached to the locality.

After he had been some time in the colony, Mr. Simson began to express great impatience for the arrival of letters from England. Whenever a vessel arrived at the port, he would put on his old shooting-coat, and walk along the shore to Fremantle, where, after having inquired in vain at the post-office, he would purchase a pound of tea, and then return home again.

Years went by. Every time that a vessel arrived, poor Simson would hurry to Fremantle. He would watch, with eyes of ill-repressed eagerness, the mail carried to the post-office in boxes and large sacks. Surely amid that multitude of letters there must be one for him! Patiently would he wait for hours at the window, whilst the postmaster and his assistants sorted the letters; and when he had received the usual answer to his inquiry, he would return to his abode with downcast looks.

As time passed on he grew more fretful and impatient. Receiving no intelligence from England, he seemed to be anxious to return thither. He would drop expressions which led his visitors (generally government officers who called upon him in their rides) to believe he would depart from the colony were he rich enough to pay his passage, or were he not restrained by some other powerful motive.

His mind ran altogether upon the Old Country, and it was with reluctance that he planted the vegetables and cured the fish which were essential to his support.

For many hours during the day he used to be seen standing fixed as a sentinel on the low rock which formed the extremity of the ridge called after himself—the Woodman's Point—and looking *homewards*.

Doubtless, thought was busy within him—the thought of all he had left or acted there. None had written to him ; none remembered or perhaps wished to remember him. But home was in his heart, even whilst he felt there was no longer a home for him. A restless anxiety preyed upon his mind, and he grew thin and feeble; but still whenever a sail was seen coming round the north end of Rottnest, and approaching the port, he would seize his staff, and set out upon his long journey to Fremantle to inquire if there were, at last, a letter awaiting him.

May we imagine the growing despair in the heart of this poor old exile, as life seemed ebbing away, and yet there came no news, no hope to him from home? Frequently he wrote himself, but always to the same address—that of a broker, it was supposed, in Throgmorton-street. But no answer was ever returned. Had he no children—no friends ?

Naturally weak-minded, he had now grown almost imbecile; but his manners were still so gentle, and every thing about him seemed to betoken so amiable and so resigned a spirit, that those who visited him could scarcely part again without tears. As he grew more feeble in body, he became more anxious to receive a letter from home; he expected that every one who

approached his dwelling was the bearer of the
intelligence so long hoped for in vain; and he
would hasten to greet him at the gate with eager
looks and flushed cheeks—again only to be disappointed.

At length it was with difficulty that he tottered
to the Point, to look for a vessel which might
bring him news. Although no ship had arrived
since he last sent to the post-office, he would urge
his visitor, though with hesitating earnestness, to
be so good as to call there on his return, and
ascertain if by chance a letter were not awaiting
him. He said he felt that his hour was approaching, but he could not bear to think of setting out
on that long journey without having once heard
from home. Sometimes he muttered, as it were to
himself, that treachery had been practised against
him, and he would go and expose it; but he never
allowed himself to indulge long in this strain.
Sometimes he would try to raise money enough by
drawing bills to pay his passage, but no one would
advance anything upon them.

Daily he became more feeble, and men began to
talk of sending him a nurse. The last visitor who
beheld him alive, found him seated in the chair
which he had himself constructed, and appearing
less depressed than usual. He said he expected
soon to receive news from home, and smiled with

child-like glee. His friend helped him to walk as far as the rose-tree, which was then putting forth its buds. " Promise," said the old man, laying his trembling hand upon the other's arm, " promise that when I am gone you will come and see them in full blow? Promise! you will make me happy."

The next day they sent a lad from Fremantle to attend upon him. The boy found him seated in his chair. He was dead. A mound of earth at the foot of a mahogany-tree, still marks the spot where he was buried. Those *friends* at home who neglected or repulsed him when living, may by chance meet with this record from the hand of a stranger—but it will not move them; nor need it now.

CHAPTER XV.

HOW THE LAWS OF ENGLAND AFFECT THE NATIVES.

The native population of our colony are said to be a much more peaceable and harmless race than those of any other part of Australia. In the early days of the settlement they caused a good deal of trouble, and were very destructive to the pigs and sheep of the colonists; but a little well-timed severity, and a steadily pursued system of government, soon reduced them into well-conducted subjects of the British Crown. There appears, however, to be little hope of civilizing them, and teaching them European arts and habits. Those of mature age, though indolent, and seldom inclined to be useful in the smallest degree, are peaceful in their habits; and when in want of a little flour will exert themselves to earn it, by carrying letters, shooting wild ducks with a gun lent to them, driving home cattle, or any other easy pursuit; but they appear to be incapable of elevation above their original condition. Considerable pains have been bestowed (especially by the Wesleyans) upon the native children, many of whom are educated in schools at Perth, Fremantle, and other places, in the hope of making them eventually useful servants to the settlers. Most of these, however, betake themselves to the bush, and resume their hereditary pursuits, just at the age when it is hoped they will become useful. Very frequently they die at that age of mesenteric disorders; and very few indeed become permanently civilized in their habits.

Nothing could be more anomalous and perplexing than the position of the Aborigines as British subjects. Our brave and conscientious Britons, whilst taking possession of their territory, have been most careful and anxious to make it universally known, that Australia is not a conquered country; and successive Secretaries of State, who write to their governors in a tone like that in which men of sour tempers address their maladroit domestics, have repeatedly commanded that it must never be forgotten "that our possession of this territory *is based on a right of occupancy.*"

A "right of occupancy!" Amiable sophistry! Why not say boldly at once, the right of power? We have seized upon the country, and shot down the inhabitants, until the survivors have found it expedient to submit to our rule. We have acted exactly as Julius Cæsar did when he took possession

of Britain. But Cæsar was not so hypocritical as
to pretend any moral *right* to possession. On what
grounds can we possibly claim a *right* to the occupancy of the land? We are told, because civilized
people are justified in extending themselves over
uncivilized countries. According to this doctrine,
were there a nation in the world superior to ourselves in the arts of life, and of a different religious
faith, it would be equally entitled (had it the physical power) to the possession of Old England under
the " right of occupancy;" for the sole purpose of
our moral and social improvement, and to make us
participants in the supposed truths of a new creed.

We have a right to our Australian possessions;
but it is the right of Conquest, and we hold them
with the grasp of Power. Unless we proceed on
this foundation, our conduct towards the native
population can be considered only as a monstrous
absurdity. However Secretaries of State may
choose to phrase the matter, we can have no other
right of occupancy. We resolve to found a colony
in a country, the inhabitants of which are not strong
enough to prevent our so doing, though they evince
their repugnance by a thousand acts of hostility.

We build houses and cultivate the soil, and for
our own protection we find it necessary to declare
the native population subject to our laws.

This would be an easy and simple matter were it

the case of conquerors dictating to the conquered;
but our Secretaries of State, exhibiting an interesting display of conscientiousness and timidity,
shrink from the responsibility of having sanctioned
a conquest over a nation of miserable savages,
protected by the oracles at Exeter Hall, and reject
with sharp cries of anger the scurrilous imputation.
Instead, therefore, of being in possession by right of
arms, we modestly appropriate the land to ourselves, whilst making the most civil assurances that
we take not this liberty as conquerors, but merely
in order to gratify a praiseworthy desire of occupying the country.   We then declare ourselves seised
in fee by right of occupancy.   But now comes the
difficulty.   What right have we to impose laws
upon people whom we profess not to have conquered, and who have never annexed themselves or
their country to the British Empire by any written
or even verbal treaty?

And if this people and country be not subject to
our rule by conquest, and have never consented or
desired (but the contrary) to accept of our code of
laws, and to submit themselves to our authority,
are they really within the jurisdiction of the laws
of England—*especially for offences committed inter
se?*

Such is the anomalous position in which the
native inhabitants are placed through the tender

consciences of our rulers at home. A member of
a tribe has been speared by one of another tribe,
who happens to be patronized by a farm-settler,
and is occasionally useful in hunting-up stray cattle.
The friends of the dead man proceed to punish the
assassin according to their own hereditary laws;
they surprise him suddenly, and spear him. The
farmer writes an account of the fact to the Protector of Natives at Perth; and this energetic
individual, rising hastily from dinner, calls for his
horse, and endowing himself with a blue woollen
shirt, and a pair of dragoon spurs, with a blanket
tied round his waist, fearlessly commits himself to
the forest, and repairs to the scene of slaughter.

He learns from the mouth of the farm-settler,
that the facts are really what he had been already
apprised of by letter; and then, having left word
that the offender may be caught as soon as possible,
and forwarded to Fremantle gaol, he hastens back
again to his anxious family; and the next morning
delivers a suitable report to his Excellency the
Governor of all that he has performed. In course
of time the native is apprehended—betrayed by a
friend for a pound of flour—and brought to the bar
of justice. His natural defence would be that he
certainly slew an enemy, as he is accused of having
done, but then it was a meritorious and necessary
act; he glories in it; his own laws required that he

should slay the murderer of his relative; and his own laws, therefore, accuse him not. What are English customs, prejudices, or laws to him? He is not a British subject, for he is not the inhabitant of a conquered country (as English governors tell him), nor has he, or any of his tribe or complexion, consented or wished to be placed under the protection of our laws. Why, then, should he be violently dragged from the arms of his *wilgied* squaws, and his little pot-bellied piccaninnies, and required to plead for his life in the midst of a large room filled with frowning white faces? Much obliged is he to the judge, who kindly tells him, through the interpreter, that he is not bound to convict himself, and need not acknowledge anything that may operate to his disadvantage in the minds of the jury.

The unfortunate savage disregards the friendly caution, and heeds it not; he maintains, stoutly, that he *gidgied* Womera through the back, because Womera had *gidgied* Domera through the belly. He enters into minute details to the gentlemen of the jury of the manner in which these slaughters were effected, and describes the extent and direction of the wounds, and every other interesting particular that occurs to him. The gentlemen of the jury, after duly considering the case, return (of necessity) a verdict of "Wilful murder," and the judge pronounces sentence of death—which is afterwards

commuted by the Governor to transportation for
life to the Isle of Rottnest.

Now if our laws had been imposed upon this
people as a conquered nation, or if they had annexed
themselves and their country to our rule and empire
by anything like a treaty, all these proceedings
would be right and proper.   But as it is, we are
two nations occupying the same land, and we have
no more right to try them by our laws for offences
committed *inter se*, than they have to seize and spear
an Englishman, according to their law, because he
has laid himself open to an action of *crim. con.* at
the suit of his next-door neighbour.

Look at the question in another point of view.
Is jurisdiction a necessary incident of sovereignty ?
Do a people become subject to our laws by the very
act of planting the British standard on the top of a
hill ?   If so, they have been subject to them from
the days of Captain Cook; and the despatches
of Her Majesty's Secretaries of State, declaring that
the natives should be considered amenable to our
laws for all offences which they might commit among
themselves, were very useless compositions.   We
claim the sovereignty, yet we disclaim having obtained it by conquest; we acknowledge that it was
not by treaty; we should be very sorry to allow
that it was by fraud; and how, in the name of
wonder, then, can we defend our claim ? Secretaries

of State have discovered the means, and tell us that Her Majesty's claim to possession and sovereignty is " based on a right of occupancy." Jurisdiction, however, is not the necessary incident of territorial sovereignty, unless that sovereignty were acquired by conquest or treaty. We question, indeed, whether it is the necessary consequence even of conquest— the laws of the conqueror must first be expressly imposed. The old Saxon laws prevailed among the people of England after the Conquest, until the Norman forms were expressly introduced.

It is well known in colonies, that the laws propounded in certain despatches are more powerful, and more regarded and reverenced, than any others, human or divine. A kind of moral gun-cotton, they drive through the most stupendous difficulties, and rend rocks that appeared to be insuperable barriers in the eyes of common sense or common justice. Judges are compelled to yield to their authority, and do violence to their own consciences whilst they help to lay the healing unction to those of their lawgivers.

The most convenient and the most sensible proceeding, on the part of our rulers at home, would be to consider this country in the light of a recent conquest. Instead of declaring, as now, that the natives are to be treated in every way as British subjects—thus making them amenable to the English law in all its complexity, whilst their own laws and habits are so entirely opposite in character—it would be better to pass a few simple ordinances, in the nature of military law, which would be intelligible to the natives themselves, and which would avoid the difficulty of applying the cumbrous machinery of our criminal code to the government of savages who can never be made to comprehend its valuable properties. It is most essential that the natives who commit offences against the persons or property of the whites should be brought to punishment. At the same time it is most difficult to establish the guilt of the party accused, according to the strict rules of legal evidence. The only witnesses, probably, were natives, who understand not the nature of an oath, and who lie like the Prince of Darkness whenever they have wit enough to perceive it is their interest to do so. In general, the only chance of obtaining a *legal* conviction is through the confession of the prisoner; and as it is most desirable that he should be convicted, when there is no moral doubt of his guilt, as his acquittal would be looked upon as a triumph by his fellows, and make them more daring in their opposition to the law, very little delicacy is used in obtaining that confession.

Were the prisoner defended by counsel, who did his duty to his client, without regard to the interests of the public, the guilty person would escape in almost every instance. As it is, the law is outraged, and a trial by jury made an occasion of mockery and gross absurdity, in order to obtain a conviction which is necessary to the welfare of the white population. Nothing would be more easy than to legislate for the proper government of the Aborigines; but you must begin *de novo*, and throw aside with scorn the morbid sentimentality that refuses to look upon those as a conquered people, whom, nevertheless, it subjects to the heavy thraldom of laws which they are not yet fitted to endure.

CHAPTER XVI.

REMARKS ON THE PHYSICAL ORGANIZATION OF THE NATIVES.

THE native inhabitants of Western Australia are only superior in the scale of human beings to the Bosjemans of Southern Africa. Their intellectual capacity appears to be very small, and their physical structure is extremely feeble. In some respects the Australian peculiarly assimilates to two of the five varieties of the human race. In the form of his face and the texture of his hair he resembles the Malay; in the narrow forehead, the prominent cheek-bones, and the knees turned in, he approaches towards the Ethiopian.* There is a remarkable difference between the jaws and teeth of the Australian and those of any other existing race. The incisores are thick and round, not, as usual, flat-

* The observations in this chapter were contributed by Henry Landor, Esq., Colonial Surgeon on the Gold Coast, who resided five years among the natives of Western Australia, and is intimately acquainted with all their habits and peculiarities.

tened into edges, but resembling truncated cones; the cuspidati are not pointed, but broad and flat on the masticating surface, like the neighbouring bicuspides. This may be attributable to mechanical attrition, depending on the nature of the food which the teeth are employed in masticating. The upper does not overlap the under jaw, but the teeth meet at their surfaces. This peculiarity of teeth has been noticed by Blumenbach as a characteristic of the Egyptian mummy; but he thinks the nature of the food not sufficient to account for it, and imagines it to depend on a natural variety. He observes, that "although it seemed most easy to account for this appearance by attributing it to the nature of the food used by the Egyptians, yet the generality of its occurrence in Egyptian mummies, and its absence in other races, are remarkable; and it affords some probability that the peculiarity depends upon a natural variety."* A constant uniformity in the structure and arrangement of the teeth is an important particular in the identification of species; and if any human race were found to deviate materially in its dentition from the rest of

---

* In a former chapter (XIII.) I have expressed an opinion that the natives are descended from the old inhabitants of India, which I think is exceedingly probable. It is interesting to remember, that the ancient Egyptians are supposed to have originally come from the same country.

mankind, the fact would give rise to a strong suspicion of a real specific diversity. I have examined
the teeth of infants and children, and found them
in every respect similar to those of Europeans of
similar ages. Moreover, the process of degradation
may be traced in natives of different ages up to the
teeth worn to the level of the gums in the old man.
I therefore consider it the effect of attrition; but it
becomes an interesting question to determine what
may be the nature of the food which produced the
same character in the ancient Egyptian and the
modern Australian.   Did the fathers of science live
on barks and roots, like the wretched Australian?
Although attrition may cause this singular appearance of the teeth, the real question is, why
does the lower jaw so perfectly and exactly meet
its fellow?   And is this confined to these two ex-
amples?

There is no fixed law determining invariably the
human stature, although there is a standard, as in
other animals, from which deviations are not very
considerable in either direction.   Some varieties
exceed, others fall short of, the ordinary stature in
a small degree. The source of these deviations is
in the breed; they are quite independent of external influences.

In all the five human varieties, some nations are
conspicuous for height and strength, others for

lower stature and inferior muscular power; but in no case is the peculiarity confined to any particular temperature, climate, or mode of life. The Australians, in general, are of a moderate stature, with slender limbs, thin arms, and long taper fingers. Although in general stature there is nothing to distinguish one variety of man from another, yet in the comparative length of the different parts of the human frame there are striking differences. In the highest and most intellectual variety (the Caucasian) the arm (*os humeri*) exceeds the fore-arm in length by two or three inches—in none less than two inches. In monkeys the fore-arm and arm are of the same length, and in some monkeys the fore-arm is the longer. In the Negro, the *ulna*, the longest bone of the fore-arm, is nearly of the same length as the *os humeri*, the latter being from one to two inches longer. In a Negro in the lunatic asylum of Liverpool (says Mr. White) the ulna was twelve and a half inches, and the humerus only thirteen and a half. In the Australian, the ulna in some I have measured was ten and a half, nine, ten, eleven and a half; the humerus was in those individuals respectively eleven and a half, ten and a half, eleven and a half, twelve and a half. Thus, in none of the measurements did the humerus exceed the ulna two inches, which in the Caucasian variety is the lowest number. In all the black races the arm is

longer in proportion to the stature than in the
white. The length of the leg of the Australian
averages thirty-six inches; in one man it was only
thirty-three and a half, and the tibia of that man
measured sixteen and a half, leaving only seventeen
to the femur—a very remarkable disproportion.

Thus in the proportion of their limbs, the Australian ranks far below the European; nay, even
below the Negro, and approaches far nearer to the
simiæ than any of the other races of mankind.
Perron, in his voyage, made an estimate of the
average strength of the arms and loins of the
Australian, and of some French and English; this
is the result in French measures :—

	ARMS.	LOINS.
	Kilogrammes.	*Myriagrammes.*
Australian	50.8	. . . 10.2
Natives of Timor . .	58.7	. . . 11.6
French	69.2	. . . 15.2
English	71.4	. . . 16.3

Thus in whatever manner the capacity of the
race is tested, its inferiority is strikingly exhibited.
We shall find, when examining the skull, that the
coronal suture falls on the temporal instead of the
sphenoid bone, which is one of the strongest marks
of the simiæ, and does not occur in other human
skulls.

I have no desire to place the Australian lower in
the scale of intelligence than he is fairly entitled to

rank, but I cannot shut my eyes to facts; and if his organization is in conformity with his inferiority, there he must rank, in spite of the wishes of his warmest friends.   At the same time I agree with the most enthusiastic philanthropist that no attempt should be left untried to amend his condition, and bestow upon him the blessings which Providence has lavished upon us; but I cannot help fearing the result will be disappointment. A fair comparative experiment, says Mr. Lawrence, has been made of the white and dark races of North America; and no trial in natural philosophy has had a more unequivocal result. The native races have not advanced a single step in 300 years; neither example nor persuasion has induced them, except in very small numbers and in few instances, to exchange the precarious supply of hunting and fishing for agriculture and the arts of settled life.

The colour of the skin is chocolate, and resembles the Malay, although perhaps a little darker. The colour of the skin is, of course, greatly dependent upon the nature òf the climate and the constant exposure of the surface of the body to the sun; the parts under the arms are of a brighter colour than those more exposed. We find in human races, as in vegetation, that every successive level alters its character; thus indicating that the state of the temperature of high regions assimilates to high latitudes. If, therefore, complexions depend upon climate and external conditions, we should expect to find them varying in reference to elevation of surface; and if they should be actually found to undergo such variations, this will be a strong argument in favour of the supposition that these external characters do in fact depend upon local conditions. The Swiss in the high mountains above the plains of Lombardy have sandy or brown hair. What a contrast presents itself to the traveller in the Milanese, where the peasants have black hair and almost Oriental features! The Basques, of the tracts approaching the Pyrenees, says Colonel Napier, are a strikingly different people from the inhabitants of the low parts around, whether Spaniards or Biscayans. They are finely made, tall men, with aquiline noses, fair complexions, light eyes, and flaxen hair; instead of the swarthy complexion, black hair, and dark eyes of the Castilian. And in Africa what striking differences of complexion exist between the Negro of the plains and of the mountains, even whilst the osteology is the same, therefore I pass over the hair and skin of the Australian as parts too much subjected to the influence of climate to afford means of legitimate deduction. It is the general opinion that these natives are not a long-lived race. The poverty of their

food may account for this, together with the want
of shelter from the vicissitudes of the climate.
The care taken by civilized man to preserve health
is, by increasing susceptibility, the indirect cause
of disease; the more rigid is the observance of
regimen, the more pernicious will be the slightest
aberration from it; but a total disregard of all the
comforts of regular food, and efficient shelter, the
habit of cramming the stomach when food is plentiful, and of enduring long abstinence when it
cannot be procured, has a far more baneful effect
upon the human constitution than all the excesses of
the white man.   As man recedes from one hastener
of destruction, he inevitably approaches another:

> " Gross riot treasures up a wealthy fund
> Of plagues, but more immedicable ills
> Attend the lean extreme."

I have observed that the natives mix the gum of
certain trees with the bark, and masticate both
together. This is attributed to the difficulty of masticating the gum alone; but I am persuaded that it
has another cause also, and that it arises from that
experience of the necessity of an additional stimulus to the digestive organ which has taught the
Esquimaux and Ottomacs to add sawdust or clay
to their train-oil. It arises from the fact that
(paradoxical as it may appear) an animal may be
starved by giving it continually too simple and too

nutritious food; aliment in such a state of condensation does not impart the necessary stimulus, which requires to be partly mechanical and partly chemical, and to be exerted at once on the irritability of the capillaries of the stomach to promote its secretions, and on the muscular fibres to promote its contractions.

I shall now point out the difference between the Australian skull and those of some other races, without giving a description of skulls in general, which would unnecessarily lengthen these observations. "Of all the peculiarities in the form of the bony fabric, those of the skull are the most striking and distinguishing. It is in the head that we find the varieties most strongly characteristic of the different races. The characters of the countenance, and the shape of the features depend chiefly on the conformation of the bones of the head."

The Australian skull belongs to that variety called the prognathous, or narrow elongated variety; yet it is not so striking an example of this variety as the Negro skull. If the skull be held in the hand so that the observer look upon the vertex, the first point he remarks is the extreme narrowness of the frontal bone, and a slight bulging where the parietal and occipital bones unite. He also sees distinctly through the zygomatic arches on both sides, which in the European skull is impossible, as the lateral portions of the frontal bone are more developed. The summit of the head rises in a longitudinal ridge in the direction of the sagittal suture; so that from the sagittal suture to that portion of the cranium where the diameter is greatest the head slopes like the roof of a house. The forehead is generally flat; the upper jaw rather prominent; the frontal sinuses large; the occipital bone is flat, and there is a remarkable receding of the bone from the posterior insertion of the *occipito-frontalis* muscle to the *foramen magnum*. It is a peculiar character of the Australian skull to have a very singular depression at the junction of the nasal bones with the nasal processes of the frontal bone. This may be seen in an engraving in Dr. Pritchard's work. I have before described the teeth, and mentioned the remarkable junction of the temporal and parietal bones at the coronal suture, and consequently the complete separation of the sphenoid from the parietal, which in European skulls meet for the space of nearly half an inch. Professor Owen has observed this conformation in six out of seven skulls of young chimpanzees, and Professor Mayo has also noticed it in the skulls he has examined. But although this is a peculiarity found in this race alone, it is not constant. I have a skull in which the sphenoid touches the parietal on one side, whilst on the other they are separated a sixth of an inch; and in the engraving, before referred to, the bones are slightly separated, but by no means to the extent that they are in European skulls. The super and infra orbital foramina are very large, and the orbits are broad, with the orbital ridge sharp and prominent. All the foramina for the transmission of the sensiferous nerves are large, the auditory particularly so; while the foramen, through which the carotid artery enters the skull, is small. The mastoid processes are large, which might be expected, as their hearing is acute. The styloid process is small; in monkeys it is wanting. The position of the *foramen magnum*, as in all savage tribes, is more behind the middle transverse diameter than in Europeans; but this arises in a great measure, though not entirely, from the prominence of the alveolar processes of the upper jaw. Owing to constant exposure to all seasons, the skulls of savages are of greater density, and weigh heavier than those of Europeans:—

		Avoirdupois.	
		lb.	oz.
Skull of a	Greek	1	11½
„	Negro	2	0
„	Mulatto . . .	2	10
„	Chinese . . .	1	7½
„	Gipsy	2	0
„	Australian . .	1	12½

Upon an examination of the foregoing points of diversity, it is unquestionable that the Australian skull is inferior in development to the European, and the capacity of the cranium of much less.

CHAPTER XVII.

SKETCHES OF LIFE AMONG THE NATIVES.

THE Natives have very few traditions, and most of those which they relate resemble the disconnected phantasies of a dream rather than the record of a series of facts.

They have some indistinct ideas about Chingi, the Evil Spirit, but no notion whatever of a Supreme God. When first the English arrived, many of the Aborigines considered them to be the spirits of their deceased relatives; and some of them fancied they could trace the features of former friends in the lineaments of individuals among the whites. One of these natives, still living, has more than once told me that his late uncle is now a certain eloquent and popular member of the Legislative Council. The nephew and resuscitated uncle occasionally meet, when the former never fails to claim the relationship, which the latter good-humouredly acknowledges; and the relatives separate with mutual expressions of politeness and good-will.

One of their most remarkable and most intelligible traditions was recorded some time ago in the *Perth Inquirer*, by Mr. ARMSTRONG, Interpreter to the Natives.

It is as follows :—

" The natives assert that they have been told from age to age, that when man first began to exist, there were two beings, male and female, named Wal-lyne-up (the father) and Doronop (the mother); that they had a son called Bin-dir-woor, who received a deadly wound, which they carefully endeavoured to heal, but without success; whereupon it was declared by Wal-lyne-up, that all who came after him should also die in like manner. Could the wound have been healed in this case, being the first, the natives think death would have had no power over them. The place where the scene occurred, and where Bin-dir-woor was buried, the natives imagine to have been on the southern plains, between Clarence and the Murray; and the instrument used is said to have been a spear thrown by some unknown being, and directed by some supernatural power. The tradition goes on to state that Bin - dir - woor, the son, although deprived of life and buried in his grave, did not remain there, but arose and went to the west;

to the unknown land of spirits across the sea.
The parents followed after their son, but (as the
natives suppose) were unable to prevail upon him
to return, and they have remained with him ever
since."

The following is one of their fables : — The
kangaroo was originally blind, and could only
walk or crawl. The frog seeing it so much at
the mercy of its enemies, took compassion on
it, and anointed the sightless eyeballs of the
kangaroo with its saliva, and told it to hop
as he did. The kangaroo did so, and is now
become the most difficult animal in the world to
catch.

Besides Chingi, the evil spirit who haunts the
woods, there is another in the shape of an immense serpent, called Waugul, that inhabits solitary
pools. Snakes that frequent both water and land,
of great size—twenty feet long, according to some
authorities—have been occasionally seen, and give
a colour to this belief of the natives. One day,
whilst bivouacking at a lonely and romantic spot,
in a valley of rocks, situated some forty miles north
of Perth, called the *Dooda-mya*, or the Abode
of Dogs, I desired a native to lead my horse to
a pool, and let him drink. The man, however,
declined with terror, refusing to go near the pool,
which was inhabited by the Waugul. I therefore

had to take my horse myself to the spot, whilst the native stood aloof, fully expecting that the Waugul would seize him by the nose and pull him under water.

The natives are polygamists. Each male is entitled to all the females who are related to him in a certain degree. A newly-born child is therefore the betrothed spouse of a man who may be thirty years of age, and who claims her from her parents so soon as she is marriageable—when she is twelve years old, or earlier. Some men have, consequently, four or six wives of various ages, whilst others have none at all. The latter are therefore continually engaged in stealing the wives of other people.

This causes incessant wars among the tribes. When the legitimate husband recovers his wife, he does not restore her to the full enjoyment of domestic happiness, until he has punished her for eloping. This he does by thrusting a spear through the fleshy part of her leg or thigh.

The natives are very good-natured to one another; sharing their provisions and kangaroo-skin cloaks without grudging. The head of a family takes the half-baked duck, opossum, or wild-dog, from the fire, and after tearing it in pieces with his teeth, throws the fragments into the sand for his wives and children to pick up. They are very fond of rice and sugar; and bake dampers from flour, making them on a corner of their cloaks.

Fish and other things are frequently baked in the bark of the paper-tree.

The following observations have been sent to me by my youngest brother: "Every tribe possesses a certain tract of country which is called after the name of the tribe—as Mœnaing Budja— the Mœnai-men's ground. They are not always very particular about trespassing on their neighbour's territory. Many of the colonists say that each tribe has its chief or king; but among all whom I have seen, I never could discover that they paid any particular respect to one individual, though they appear to reverence old age; and I have frequently seen a party of young men, alternately carrying an old grey-headed patriarch during their excursions from one encampment to another.

"They have no religion whatever, but they believe in some kind of an evil spirit. I have often tried to discover, but could never clearly understand, whether they believe in only one all-powerful evil spirit, or whether it is merely the spirits of their departed friends that they fear: or, (as I am inclined to believe) they fear both; and for these reasons:—wherever there is a large encampment of

natives, each family has its own private fire and
hut, but you will always perceive another fire
about one hundred yards from the camp, which
apparently belongs to no one; but which the old
hags take care shall never go out during the
night; for they will frequently get up and re-
plenish that fire, when they are too lazy to fetch
fuel for their own. They call that Chingi's fire;
and they believe if he comes in the night he will
sit quietly by his own fire and leave them undis-
turbed. That they likewise believe in the reappearance of departed spirits, may be easily proved
by the manner and the formalities with which they
bury their dead. In the first place they cut off the
hair and beard; they then break his finger-joints
and tie the thumb and fore-finger of the right hand
together; so that if he rise again, he may not have
the power to use a spear and revenge himself.
They then break his spears, throwing-stick, and all
his other implements of war, and throw them into
the grave, over which they build a hut; and a fire
is kept lighted for a certain length of time. It is
likewise customary for his wife or nearest relation,
if at any future period they should happen to pass
near the grave, to repair the hut, rekindle the fire,
and utter a long rigmarole to the departed, to induce
him to lie still, and not come back and torment
them. Nothing will induce a stranger to go near

a new grave, or to mention the name of the
departed for a long time after his death. They
always speak of him as So-and-so's brother, or
father. If the deceased be the father of a family;
it is the duty of his eldest son, or nearest relation,
to avenge his death by killing one of the next, or
any other tribe; and this often leads to furious
battles or cold-blooded murders; for they are by
no means particular whether it be man, woman, or
child who is the victim; and it is generally the
poor women who suffer on these occasions: the
men being too cowardly, unless under the influence of very strong passion, to attack those of
equal strength with themselves. The women do all
the work, such as building huts, carrying water,
digging up roots, and procuring grubs out of the
wattle and grass-trees. I have seen a poor unfortunate woman marching twenty miles a-day, with
(at least) a hundred pounds'-weight on her back,
including the child and all their effects; whilst the
husband has been too lazy to carry even his cloak.
A hunting excursion with a large party of natives
is capital sport. They choose, if possible, a valley,
at one end of which they station ten or twenty of
the most expert spearmen; with whom, if you
want any fun, you must station yourself, taking
care to remain concealed. All the juveniles of the
party then start off, and make a circuit of many

Lieut. A. H. Irby, 51st Reg. dal.

E. Radclyffe sc.

SPEARING KANGAROOS.

miles in extent, shouting and hallooing the whole
time. They form a semicircle, and drive all the
kangaroos before them down the valley, to the
spot where the old hunters are placed. Then
comes the tug of war, the crashing of bushes,
the flying of spears, and the thump, thump of the
kangaroos, as they come tearing along, sometimes
in hundreds, from the old grey grandfather of six
feet high, to the little piccanniny of twelve inches,
who has tumbled out of his mother's pouch; and
numbers fall victims to the ruthless arms of the
hunters. The evening terminates with a grand
feast and a corrobery."

Each tribe has its doctor, or wise man, who is
supposed to have supernatural powers of healing
wounds, and is the oracle of the tribe. One of
these fellows described to me the mode of his
initiation. He said his father, himself a wise man,
took him one night to the edge of a steep hill,
where he left him lying wrapped in his kangaroo-
skin cloak. He was very much frightened, but
durst not stir. During the night Chingi came and
tried to throw him down the hill, and to strangle
him, but did not succeed. Chingi was like something very black. He afterwards came again, and
told him a great many secrets; and thus it was
that my informant became a doctor and a wise
man. I think I have heard of people obtaining

the power of second sight in the Isle of Skye by lying on a rock all night, wrapped in a bull's hide, and receiving a visit from the devil. The similarity between these initiatory processes struck me forcibly.

CHAPTER XVIII.

THE MODEL-KINGDOM.

A WELL-GOVERNED colony is the Model of a great kingdom. As in the case of other models, every part of the machinery by which it is moved is placed at once before the eye of the spectator. In a great empire, the springs of action are concealed; the public behold only the results, and can scarcely guess how those results were brought about. In a colony, every one stands so close to the little machine of Government, that he can readily discern how it is made to work, and therefore takes a more lively interest in the working of it. The model has its representative of a sovereign; its Ministers, who comprise the Executive Council with the Colonial Secretary as Premier; its Parliament, the Legislative Assembly; its Bishop of London, who is represented by the Colonial Chaplain, *the* dignitary of the Church in those parts. In the Legislative Assembly there are the Government party, consisting of the Colonial Secre-

tary and the Attorney General, who prove their
loyalty and devotion by adhering to His Excellency
the Governor on every division, and (according to
general belief) would rather vote against their own
measures than against the representative of their
Queen.   Then there is the popular party, consisting
of *the* popular member, who speaks at random
on either side of the debate, but invariably votes
against the Government, in order to maintain invio-
late the integrity of his principles.   We have also the
Judge, or Lord Chancellor, the great Law officer of
the Crown, who sits silently watching the progress
of a Bill, as it steals gently forward towards the
close of the second reading; and then suddenly
pounces upon it, to the consternation of his Excellency, and the delight of the popular member, and
tears it in pieces with his sharp legal teeth, whilst
he shows that it is in its scope and tendency
contrary to the Law of England in that case
provided, and is besides impossible to be carried
out in the present circumstances of the Colony.
The Model Nation has its national debt of one
thousand pounds, due to the Commissariat chest;
and this burthen of the State costs his Excellency
many a sleepless night, spent in vain conjectures
as to the best mode of relieving the financial
embarrassments.

It is pleasant to learn from the model, how Govern-

ment patronage is disposed of in the Parent
country. Kindly motives, however, which never
appear in the arrangements of the latter, are
always conspicuous in a colony. A public work is
sometimes created for the sole purpose of saving an
unfortunate mechanic from the horrors of idleness;
and a debt due to the State is occasionally discharged by three months' washing of a Privy
Councillor's shirts.

Then we have the exact fac-simile of a Royal
Court, with its levees and drawing-rooms, where
his Excellency displays the utmost extent of his
affability, and his lady of her queenly airs. There
may be seen, in all its original freshness and vigour,
the smiling hatred of rival ladies, followed by their
respective trains of admirers; whilst the full-blown
dames of Members of Council elbow their way,
with all the charming confidence of rank, towards
the vicinity of her who is the cynosure of all eyes.
The early levees of the first Governor of Western
Australia were held in a dry swamp, near the
centre of the present town of Perth. His Excellency, graciously bowing beneath the shade of a
banksia tree, received with affability those who
were introduced to him, as they stumbled into his
presence over tangled brushwood, and with difficulty avoided the only humiliation that is scorned
by English courtiers—that of the person.

Ladies, in struggling through the thorny brake, had sometimes to labour under the double embarrassment of a ragged reputation and dress. To appear before the Presence, under such circumstances, with a smiling countenance, proved the triumph of feminine art, and of course excited general admiration. But this was in the early days of the settlement. We have now a handsome Government-house, where ladies who attend drawing-rooms incur no danger of any kind.

From the financial difficulties of a small colony you may form some idea of the troubles of the Chancellor of the Exchequer at home. And yet there is less financial talent required to raise five hundred thousand pounds in England than five hundred in an impoverished colony. In the former country only a few voices, comparatively, are raised in expostulation; and no one cares about them, if Mr. Hume could be gagged, and the other patriots in the Commons. But in a colony! threaten to raise the price of sugar by the imposition of another half-penny per pound, and the whole land will be heaved as though by an earthquake. Not only will the newspapers pour forth a terrific storm of denunciations against a treacherous Government, but every individual of the public will take up the matter as a personal injury, and roar out his protest against so monstrous a political crime. Those

who called most loudly for the erection of a necessary bridge, will be most indignant when asked
next year to contribute towards its cost.

The Governor of a colony should not only be a
good financier, but, if he would avoid the bitter
pangs of repentance, must possess great firmness
in resisting the innumerable calls upon the Government purse.

His Excellency may lay his account to being
daily vituperated for not consenting to the con-
struction of this or that national work, but he will
be still more taken to task when the melancholy
duty of paying for it becomes imperative, and is
found to be unavoidable.

It is the general belief, that in a colony we are
altogether out of the world ; but it has always
appeared to me, that within the narrow confines of
one of those epitomes of a kingdom we may see
more of the world than when standing on the outer
edge of society in England.

A man thinks himself in the midst of the world
in Great Britain, because he reads the newspapers
and knows what is passing and being enacted
around him. But the same newspapers are read
with equal diligence in a colony, and the same
knowledge is acquired there, though some three
months later. To read the newspapers, and to
hang, close as a burr, upon the skirts of society, is

not to be in the world. The world is, in truth, the heart of Man ; and he knows most of the World who knows most of his species. And where, alas ! may this knowledge, so painful and so humiliating, be better acquired than in a colony ? There we have the human heart laid open before us without veil or disguise : there we see it in all its coarseness, its selfishness, its brutality.

How many fine natures, cultivated, delicate, and generous, have gone forth from their native land, full of high resolves, only to perish in the mephitic atmosphere of a colony !

There we find whatever there is of good and bad in human nature brought immediately before our eyes. It is a school of moral anatomy, in which we study subjects whose outer covering has been removed, and where the inner machinery (fearful to see !) is left exposed.

A knowledge of the world ! if we gain it not in a colony, it must ever remain a sealed book to us.

We shall leave but a bad impression on the mind of the reader in concluding this short chapter with these sombre observations ; but we would not leave him without hope. Time will remedy all this. Some moral evils correct themselves ; as the water of the Nile becomes pure again after it has gone putrid.

CHAPTER XIX.

TRIALS OF A GOVERNOR.

EXCEPT the waiter at a commercial inn, no man has so much upon his hands, or so many faults to answer for, as the Governor of a colony. If public affairs go wrong, every voice is raised, requiring him immediately to rectify them; and as every one has a particular plan of his own, the Governor is expected instantly to adopt them all. Nor has he public calamities only to answer for; the private misfortunes of individuals are, without hesitation, laid at his door. He is expected to do something, and not a little, for all who are in trouble; he has to devise expedients for those whose own wits are at fault: it is among his duties to console, to cheer, to advise, to redress, to remedy; and, above all, to enrich.

As men set up a block of wood in a field to become a rubbing-post for asses; as bachelors take

to themselves wives, and elderly spinsters individuals
of the feline race, in order to have something on
which to vent their occasional ill-humours, so is a
Governor set up in a colony, that the settlers may
have a proper object or mark set apart, on which
they may satisfactorily discharge their wrongs,
sorrows, wants, troubles, distractions, follies, and
unreasonable expectations. A Governor is the
safety-valve of a colony; withdraw this legitimate
object of abuse, and the whole community would
be at loggerheads. A state of anarchy would be
the immediate consequence, and broil and bloodshed would prevail throughout the land. Sometimes a Governor forgets the purpose for which he
was sent out from home, and placed on high in a
colony, as a rubbing-post; he sometimes lapses
into the error of fancying himself a colonial Solon,
and strives to distinguish his reign by the enact-
ment of laws, which only increase the natural irritability of the settlers, and cause him to be more
rubbed against than ever. On these occasions he
is not always entitled to much sympathy; but when
private parties come crowding round him to have
the consequence of their follies averted, or merely
in a state of discontented irritation, to have their
backs scratched, his poor Excellency is much to be
compassionated.

Almost every morning a long-eared crowd as-

sembles around the Government-offices, where the
rubbing-post is set up, and one after another
they are admitted to find what relief they may from
this cheap luxury. It is pleasant to observe that
they almost all come out again with smiling countenances. For a moment, the sense of pain or
discontent has been alleviated by the gentle application.

Sometimes an honest farmer has ridden fifty
miles in order to have the pleasure of complaining
to his Excellency of the mal-administration of the
post-office department, evidenced by the non-deli-
very of a letter, which, after a vast deal of investigation and inquiry, turns out never to have been
posted. Sometimes a man comes for advice as to
the propriety of going to law with his neighbour
about a bull which had taken the liberty to eat
some of his turnips. One man wishes to have
his Excellency's opinion upon a disease which has
lately broken out among his pigs ; another has
mysteriously carried a piece of iron-stone in his
pocket for a hundred miles, and claims the reward
for the discovery of a coal-mine; a third has a
plan to propose for fertilizing the sand-plains around
Perth, by manuring them with sperm oil. Some
are desirous that their sons should be made Government clerks, and insist upon their right to all
vacant appointments on the plea of being " old

settlers." Others have suggestions to make, the
neglect of which would prove ruinous to the colony :
general misery is only to be averted by the repeal
of the duty on tobacco : no more ships need be
expected (this is after a gale and wreck,) unless a
break-water be constructed, which may be done for
ninety-five thousand pounds, and there was a surplus revenue last year over the expenditure of
thirteen shillings and sixpence, the local government being also indebted to the Commissariat chest
in the sum of nine hundred pounds odd. Some
complain of roads and bridges being in a defective
state, and wonder why two thousand pounds extra
per annum are not laid out upon them ; these are
succeeded by a deputation from the inhabitants of
Rockingham, requesting, as a matter of right, that
half that sum may be applied in ornamenting their
principal square with a botanical garden. Then
the Governor has to attend to complaints against
public officers. The Commissioner of the Civil
Court has proved himself to be an unjust judge
by deciding for the defendant contrary to the truth,
as proved by the plaintiff; or the Commissioner of
the Court of Requests has received a bribe of three-
and-fourpence, and refused to listen to the com-
plainant's story. The magistrates have granted a
spirit license to a notorious character, and denied
one to the applicant, an unimpeachable house-

holder. The Post-Master General has embezzled a letter, or the Colonial Secretary has neglected to reply to one.

All these things, and a thousand others, the Governor is expected to listen to, inquire about, remedy, or profit by.

One day, I remember, I went myself to complain of the absurdity of an Act of Council which I thought might be advantageously amended by the aid of a little light which had lately dawned upon me.

Among those who haunted the ante-room, waiting for admittance to the rubbing-post, was a tall Irish woman, who had seen better days, but was now reduced to much distress, and was besides not altogether right in her intellects.

She was in the frequent habit of attending there, for the purpose of complaining against the Advocate General, who never paid her proper attention when she went to lay her grievances before him. This woman was the terror of the Government officers. She never allowed her victim to escape when once she had begun her story;—in vain might he try to edge away towards the door—if he were not to be retained by the fascination of her voice, she would seize him by the coat with a grasp of iron, and a fly might as well try to escape from a pot-bellied spider. Whenever she appeared, no public officer was ever to be found. A general epidemic seemed to have fallen upon the offices, and exterminated all the inhabitants. The Colonial Secretary would rush out to luncheon, deaf as an adder to the cries of female distress that rang in the troubled air behind him. The Advocate General, hearing the well-known voice inquiring for him in no friendly key, would hurry away through an opposite door, and dive into the woods adjoining Government-house, and there gnaw his nails, in perturbation of spirit until he thought the evil was overpast. His Excellency himself would sooner have seen the Asiatic cholera walk into the room than Miss Maria Martin, and invariably turned paler than his writing-paper, and shuddered with a sudden ague. She had so many wrongs to complain of, which no human power could redress, and she required so much to be done for her, and insisted upon having reiterated promises to that effect, that no wonder she excited the utmost terror in the minds of all whom she approached. She was, moreover, a huge, brawny, fierce-looking creature, and though upwards of fifty years of age, had the strength of an Irish porter. She was reported on one occasion to have taken a gentleman of high reputation, and unimpeachable morals, by the collar of his coat, and pinned him up against the wall, until he had promised to speak for her to the

Governor; and when he subsequently accused her of this violence, she retorted by saying that it was in self-defence, as he had attempted improper liberties. The fear of such an unscrupulous and cruel accusation made Government officers, especially the married ones, extremely shy of granting a *téte-à-téte* conversation to Miss Martin; and as no one was, of course, more correct in his conduct than his Excellency the Governor, no wonder that he should feel extremely nervous whenever he was surprised into an interview with this interesting spinster.

When I found her in the ante-room I naturally recoiled, and tried to back out again, smiling blandly all the time, as one does when a violent-looking dog comes up, and begins sniffing about your legs. Miss Martin, however, was used to these manœuvres, and suddenly getting between me and the door, intercepted my retreat, and insisted on telling me, for the twentieth time, how villanously the Advocate General had deceived her. Escape was impossible; I groaned and sweated with anguish, but listen I must, and had to suffer martyrdom for an hour, when the Governor's door opened, and he himself looked out. On seeing the Gorgon he tried to withdraw, but she pounced like a tigress through the door-way, and slamming

the door after her, secured an audience with his
Excellency, which she took care should not be a
short one. I could remain no longer, and therefore owe the rest of the story to public report.
After an hour's *téte-à-téte*, his Excellency's voice
grew more imperative. The clerks, highly interested, conceived that he was insisting upon her
withdrawing. It is supposed that he could not
possibly escape himself, as she of course cut off all
communication with either the door or the bell-
rope. The lady's voice also waxed higher; at
length it rose into a storm. Nothing more was
heard of the poor Governor beyond a faint, moaning
sound; whether he was deprecating the tempest,
or being actually strangled, became a matter of
grave speculation. Some asserted that they heard
his kicks upon the floor, others could only hear
convulsive sobs; then all fancied they could distinguish the sounds of a struggle. The officials
debated whether it would be proper or indelicate
to look in upon the interview; but it became so
evident that a scuffle was going on, that the private secretary's anxiety overcame all other considerations. The door was opened just as his Excellency, escaping from the grasp of the mad woman,
had made a vault at the railing which ran across
the farther end of the Council Room (to keep back

the public on certain days), in hopes of effecting his escape by the door beyond. Nothing could have been better conceived than this design ; but unhappily the lady had caught hold of his coat-tail to arrest his flight, and therefore instead of vaulting clear over the rails, as he had anticipated, his Excellency was drawn back in his leap, and found himself seated astride upon the barrier, with a desperate woman tugging at his tail, and trying to pull him back into the arena. Nothing, we believe, has ever exceeded the ludicrous misery displayed in his Excellency's visage on finding himself in this perilous situation. But seeing the private secretary and a mob of clerks, with their pens in their hands, hastening to his rescue, he made a desperate effort, and cast himself off on the other side ; and finally succeeded in rushing out of the room, having only one tail hanging to his coat, with which he escaped into an adjoining apartment, and was received into the arms of the Surveyor General in a state of extreme exhaustion.

Such are some of the troubles and afflictions incident to the unenviable office of Governor of a colony. Those innocent country gentlemen who have expended the better part of their property on contested elections, and now weary heaven and Her Majesty's Principal Secretaries of State for colonial appointments, little know what they invoke upon themselves. In my opinion Sancho Panza had a sinecure, compared with theirs, in his Governorship of the island of Barrataria.*

* Our love of the ludicrous frequently makes us delighted to find even the most estimable characters in a ridiculous position. The above anecdote is perhaps exaggerated, but it is here recorded as a moral warning to those who yearn like Sancho Panza for a government, and not from a desire to cast ridicule upon one who was universally respected and esteemed, for the quiet decorum of his life, his high principles, his strict impartiality, and the conscientious discharge of all the duties of his office.

CHAPTER XX.

MR. SAILS, MY GROOM.—OVER THE HILLS.—A SHEEP STATION.

Soon after I was settled in my residence at Perth I purchased a couple of young mares unbroke, recently imported from the Cape of Good Hope. They were the offspring of an Arab horse and Cape mare, and one of them, a chestnut, was almost the handsomest creature I ever beheld. They cost me thirty guineas each; but since that period the value of horses is greatly diminished.

I was very much pleased with this purchase, which recalled the memories of boyhood and a long-tailed pony, whenever I found myself feeding or grooming my stud—which I often thought proper to do, as my establishment, though at that time numerous, did not comprise a well-educated groom.

Besides my own man, I had two runaway sailors from the ship in which we had come out, quartered upon me. They expressed so flattering a regard for me, as the only person whom they knew in this part of the world, and were so ready to dig

the garden and plant potatoes, or do any other
little matter to make themselves useful, that I had
not the heart to refuse them a nook in the kitchen,
or a share of our daily meals. I now called their
services into activity by making them assist at the
breaking in of my mares; and whilst I held the
lunging-rein, Mr. Sails would exert himself till he
became as black as a sweep with dust and perspiration, by running round and round in the rear of
the animal, urging her forward with loud cries and
objurgations, accompanied with furious crackings
of his whip. These sailors never did anything
quietly. If told to give the horses some hay, they
would both start up from their stools by the
kitchen fire, as if in a state of frantic excitement;
thrust their pipes into the leathern belt which held
up their trousers, and jostling each other through
the doorway like a brace of young dogs, tear round
the house to the stable, or rather shed, as though
possessed by a legion of devils. Then, unable to
use a fork, they would seize as much hay as they
could clasp in their arms, and littering it all about
the premises, rush to the stalls, where they suddenly grew exceedingly cautious; for in fact, they
felt much greater dread of these horses than they
would have done of a ground shark. Then it
was all, " Soh! my little feller! Soh! my pretty
little lass! — Avast there — (*in a low tone*) you

lubber, or I'll rope's end you—none of that!"
This was whenever the mare, pleased at the sight
of the hay, looked round and whinnied.   Unless I
superintended the operation myself, the hay would
be thrown under the horse's feet, whilst the men
took to their heels at the same moment, and then
turned round to see whether the animals could
reach their fodder.   If they could, these worthy
grooms would come cheerfully to me and tell me
that the horses were eating their allowance; but if
not, they filled their pipes, and took a turn out of
the way, trusting the hay would all be trampled
into the litter before I happened to see it.   Whenever I was present, I made them get upon the
manger and put the hay into the rack, (I never
could teach them to use a fork,) but it was with
fear and trembling that they did this.   One day,
Sails was standing on the manger, with the hay in
his arms, when the mare, trying to get a mouthful,
happened to rub her nose against the hinder portion
of his person.   Sails roared aloud, and let the hay
fall upon the mare's head and neck.

" What's the matter, man ?" said I.

" By Gad, sir," cried Sails, looking round with
a face of terror, and scrambling down, " he's tuk a
bite out of my starn !"

After the horses had been well lunged it became
necessary to mount them.   In vain, however, I

tried to persuade Sails or his comrade Dick to get
upon their backs. I therefore mounted first myself,
and after a deal of plunging and knocking about
was dismounted again, with the mare, who had
thrown herself down, actually kneeling upon my
body. All this time, Sails stood helplessly looking
on open-mouthed, holding the lunging-rein in his
hands; and I had to call to him to "pull her off"
before he made any attempt to give assistance.
This accident effectually prevented my gallant
grooms from trusting themselves on horseback;
but they proved more useful in breaking in the
animals to draw the light cart. One would ride
whilst the other drove, and their nautical phrases,
and seaman-like style of steering the craft, as they
called it, excited the admiration of the neighbourhood. But they never could bring themselves to
like the employment of tending horses; and finding
that I insisted upon their making themselves
useful in this way, they at last gave me up, and
volunteered as part of the crew of a vessel about to
sail for Sincapore.

Long after this period I drove the dog-cart over
the hills to York races. My brother had come
down to Perth, and we went together, taking with
us our friend the amiable and talented editor of one
of the Perth journals. Attaching another horse to
an outrigger, we drove unicorn, or a team of three.

It was a splendid October morning, (the commencement of summer,) and we rattled over the long and handsome wooden bridges that cross the two streams of the Swan, at a spanking pace, whilst the worthy editor, exulting in his temporary emancipation from office, made the wooded banks of the river ring again with the joyous notes of his key-bugle.

Half an hour carried us over five miles of road, and brought us to Mangonah, the beautifully situated dwelling of R. W. Nash, Esq., barrister at law, the most active-minded and public-spirited man in the colony. After a short delay, to laugh at one of our friend's last coined and most facetious anecdotes, and also to visit his botanical garden, we rattled off again to Guildford; a scattered hamlet that was made acquainted with our approach by loud strains from the editor's bugle. Here, however, we paused not, but proceeded along a hard and good road towards Green Mount, the first hill which we had to ascend. Green Mount, six miles from Guildford, is famous for a desperate skirmish which took place some years ago between a large body of natives and Messrs. Bland and Souper, at the head of a party escorting provisions from Perth to the infant settlement at York. Whilst slowly ascending the hill, a thick flight of spears fell among the party, wounding several of them. No enemy was visible, and the greatest consternation prevailed among the men, who hastened to shelter themselves under the carts. This induced the natives to rush out of their ambush, when they were received with a shower of balls; and at length driven back, after losing a good many men. Mr. Souper had several spears sticking in his body, and others of the English were severely wounded, but none mortally.

The natives are very tenacious of life, and so are all the birds and animals indigenous to the country.

The natives often have spears thrust completely through their bodies, and without any serious injury, receive wounds that would prove mortal to the whites. A vagabond who had speared one of those noble rams of ours, of whom honourable mention has been already made, was shot by our shepherd whilst in the act of decamping with the carcase. The ball passed completely through his lungs, and would have made an end of any white man; but the native recovered in the course of a few days, and walked a hundred miles heavily ironed, to take his trial for sheep-stealing at the Quarter Sessions.

From Guildford to the foot of Green Mount, the country presents a vast plain of cold clayey soil, unfit for cultivation, and though covered with scrub, affording very little useful herbage.

On ascending the hill, we come upon what is generally called the iron-stone range, which extends nearly to York, a distance of forty miles. These extensive hills (about fifteen hundred feet above the level of the sea) are composed almost entirely of granite rocks, with occasional tracts of quartz; and the surface is generally strewn over with a hard loose rubble.

Although the sides and summits of the hills present scarcely any appearance of soil, vast forests of large Jarra trees, and other varieties of the eucalyptus, extend in every direction; and flowers the most beautiful relieve the sombre appearance of the ground. Some few of the valleys afford a few acres of alluvial soil; and in the first of these, called Mahogany Creek, six miles from Green Mount, we found a comfortable way-side house, with good out-buildings, and other accommodations; and here we halted to lunch, and bait our horses.

Many other individuals, bent upon the same journey as ourselves, were lounging and smoking before the house, or partaking of the refreshments. Most were travelling on horseback; some in gigs, and some in light spring-carts. A famous round of cold beef, with bottled ale and porter, proved extremely agreeable after our drive.

In the afternoon we proceeded fifteen miles

farther, to the half-way house, where on my first arrival in the colony I had been initiated into the art of cooking a saddle of kangaroo, and serving it up with mint-sauce. The road, through a dense forest of evergreen trees, is excessively dreary, and the quarters for the night were never very satisfactory; but the traveller might always look forward to a comfortable sitting-room, kangaroo steaks and pork, with plenty of fresh eggs and good bread. Since that time the house has been given up by the energetic landlord; and the Local Government is partly responsible for the loss of this accommodation, in consequence of having insisted upon a heavy license being annually taken out. In good times, when the farm-settlers of the York and Northam districts brought their wool and other produce down this road to the capital, they invariably spent a merry evening at the half-way house; but since money has become scarcer in the colony, they have been compelled to avoid this place of entertainment, and kindle instead a fire by the road-side, where they spend their evenings in solitary meditation, to the advantage doubtless of their minds and purses. In the morning, full of philosophical thoughts and fried rashers of pork, they calmly yoke their bullocks to the wain, un-afflicted by those pangs which were often the only acknowledgment rendered to the hospitality of Mr.

Smith—pangs of mental remorse and a bilious stomach. And yet the worthy host never suffered a guest whom he respected to depart without administering to him what he called "a doctor"—of which, about five o'clock in the morning, the poor man usually felt himself much in need; and at that hour, as Aurora entered at the window, would mine host (equally rosy-cheeked) enter by the door, and deliver his matutinal salutation. This "doctor," a character universally esteemed by travellers in those parts, was a tumbler of milk fresh from the cow, tinctured with brandy.

The glory had not departed from the half-way house at the period to which I refer; and as we drove up to the door, amid the liveliest strains of the editorial bugle, our jovial host welcomed us with his heartiest greeting. This spot is truly an oasis in the desert, affording a few acres of tolerable land, and some excellent garden-ground which, in the season, produces abundance of grapes, peaches, apples, figs, and various kinds of vegetables. A deep brook runs at the bottom of the garden which is very well watered; and on its margin, in the midst of a green plot, protected by palings from rude encroachment, is the quiet grave of one of Mr. Smith's children. How different looks the solitary grave of the desert from the crowded churchyards of England! How much more home it comes to the heart! Across the brook is a large barley-field, and down the valley are several other inclosures; all around, beyond these, is the dark, melancholy, illimitable forest. At one end of the house, which is of goodly size, stands a huge erection of wood, resembling a gallows, from which are suspended the bodies of three kangaroos. Not far from this, a group of natives—men, women, and children—are squatted round a small fire, eating baked opossums, and chattering, and uttering shrill screams of laughter, with all their might. Half a dozen large kangaroo dogs are hanging about this group with wistful eyes, but evidently without any expectations of obtaining a morsel.

The house, being filled with people on their way to the races, resounded all the evening with jokes and merriment; and when the well-disposed retired to bed, and flattered themselves they were just sinking into repose, a mob of their evil-minded friends, headed by an Irish barrister and the usually sedate Crown Solicitor, beat down the door, and pulled them forth again. Then were the four walls of the room (which contained four beds) made witnesses to a scene exhibiting all the horrors of war. Dreadful was the conflict: bolsters and carpet-bags were wielded with fierce animosity; pillows and rolled-up blankets flew about the room like cannon-shot; and long was the contest doubt-

ful, until the despair of the besieged at length overcame the impetuosity of the assailants, and succeeded in driving them from the apartment.

The half-way house was often so crowded that
some of the guests had to sleep upon the dining-
table, the sofas, and the floor. At early dawn it
was usually cleared of its visitors, who would push
on to breakfast at Mahogany Creek; or, if going
to York, at St. Ronan's Well, distant some fifteen
miles. It was here that we breakfasted, sitting
upon the grass, whilst with our camp-kettle we
boiled our chocolate, and enjoyed our morning
meal exceedingly.

York is a scattered hamlet of good farm-houses.
The country is highly interesting. A lofty hill, or
mountain, called Mount Bakewell, confines the
view on one side, and below it is the river Avon, a
broad stream in winter, but in summer consisting
only of deep pools in various parts of its course.
The neighbourhood is beautifully wooded, and has
the appearance of a park. In the centre of the
hamlet a modest-looking, white-washed church
" rears its meek fane." Nothing could be more
peaceful and serene than the whole aspect of the
place.

At my brother's farm, comprising 4,000 acres,
the property of R. H. Bland, Esq., Protector of
Natives, we found a hearty reception, and a very

pleasant dwelling-house. For several days it was
filled with young men who had come from various
parts of the colony to attend the races.

These gentlemen were most of them young men
of good family, and well educated, who having
only a small patrimony, and having been brought
up to no trade or profession, had come out to a
colony in the hope of acquiring landed estates, and
of founding in this part of the world a family of
their own. In the meantime they had to drive
their teams, shear their sheep, thresh their corn,
and exhibit their skill in husbandry; whilst their
houses were as ill arranged and uncomfortable as
could be expected from the superintendence of
bachelors who thought more of their stables than
of the appearance of their rooms. They care more
about good horses than good cooks, and in most
cases prefer doing without kitchen stuff rather than
be troubled with a garden.

Freedom of discourse and ease of manner characterize the social meetings of our bachelor aris-
tocracy " over the hills."

Dinner is only to be obtained by dint of incessant shouting to the slave (frequently an Indian
Coolie) who presides in the detached kitchen, and
brings in the viands as fast as he " dishes up."
The roast mutton gradually cools upon the table
while Mooto is deliberately forking the potatoes

out of the pot, and muttering curses against his master, who stands at the parlour-door, swearing he will wring his ears off if he does not despatch. In order to moderate the anguish of stomach experienced by the guests, the host endeavours to fill up the time by sending the sherry round. The dinner is at length placed upon the table, and Mooto scuffles out of the room whilst his master is busy carving, lest he should be compelled to wait, an occupation less agreeable than that to which he returns, and which engages most of his time— sitting on an upturned box before the fire, and smoking his pipe. Here, piously thanking Vishnou and Brama for such good tobacco, he puffs away, heedless of the shouts of his suzerain, who has just discovered there are only eight plates for twelve people. One of the guests volunteers a foray into Mooto's territory, chiefly for the sake of relieving his own feelings by making that worthy acquainted with the opinion he entertains of him, and returns to his seat with cold plates and a tranquillized mind.

When the villain lacquey has smoked his pipe, he brings in the cheese, and clears away. No unnecessary feelings of delicacy restrain the guests from reviling him *seriatim* as he removes the platters; and he retires to his own den and the enjoyment of a pound of boiled rice with undis-

turbed equanimity, leaving the others to boil the
kettle and concoct egg-flip, which, together with
wine, brandy, cigars, and pipes, enables the party
to get through the afternoon. Some remain at the
table, drinking out of wine-glasses, tumblers, or
pannikins (every vessel which the house contains
being put in requisition), and talking loudly about
their horses, or making bets for the next day's
races ; others having thrown off their coats, and
flung their persons upon a sofa, with their feet on
a window-sill, puff away in meditative silence, only
joining occasionally in the conversation; whilst two
or three walk up and down the verandah, in solemn
consultation as to the best mode of hedging, having
unhappily backed a colt for the Margaux Cup that
turns out to be a dunghill.

I trust my good friends over the hills will not
think I am making an ungrateful return for much
hospitality by this rough and imperfect sketch.
Heaven knows they are a worthy, kind-hearted,
hospitable set of good fellows as ever drew a cork
or made egg-flip ; but I must say some of the
bachelor establishments are rather in a rude and
primitive state at present.

Those houses which are fortunate enough to possess a presiding genius in the gentle and attractive
form of Woman are very differently ordered. English neatness and English comforts pervade the

establishment, and the manners and customs of well-regulated society are never forgotten.

It is a pleasant sight in the evening to watch the cattle driven into the stock-yard by the native boy, who has been with them all day in the bush. Some of the old cows go steadily enough in the right direction, but others, and especially the young heifers, are continually bunting one another, and trying to push their next neighbours into the ditch. Several, tempted by a pleasant field of barley, have leapt over a broken rail, and are eating and trampling down all before them. But soon they are perceived by the dusky herdsman, who incontinently shrieks like one possessed by demons, and rushing after the stray kine with a bough hastily picked up, chases and belabours them up and down the field (the gate of which he has never thought of opening), until he has done as much mischief as possible to the crop. Somebody then opens the gate for him, and the cattle are at length secured in the yard.

Next arrives a flock of two thousand sheep, driven by white shepherds. On coming to the entrance of the fold-yard, they stop and hesitate, refusing to enter. All is uncertainty and confusion, the rearmost urged forward by the shouts of the men and the barking of the dogs, who run from side to side, thrusting their noses into the soft white fleeces, press into the mass; great is the scuffle, the rush, and the pattering of feet over the loose pebbles of the yard.   At length, a hardy and determined ram in the vanguard gives a leap of ten feet through the open gateway, and the others hustle through after him, every one leaping as he had done, and all congratulating themselves on having thus cleverly eluded the designs of some unseen enemy.

I do not intend to give an account of the races, though they afforded more amusement probably than is common at Epsom or Ascot.   Every one knew everybody and everybody's horse; and as the horses were generally ridden by gentlemen, there was no doubt of fair play.   There was an accident, as usual, in the hurdle-race; but not being fatal, it did not interrupt the sports.   Large groups of the natives, sitting on the ground, or standing leaning on their spears, gave increased effect to the picturesque scenery.   Some clumps of forest-trees still occupied the centre of the course, and through these you caught glimpses of coloured jackets and jockey-caps as they flashed by.   The green side of Mount Bakewell was spotted with sheep, and above them frowned a forest of dark trees.

A loaf of bread stuck upon a spear was a mark and a prize for native dexterity.   The dusky savages forming a line in front, and clustering eagerly upon one another behind, took their turns to throw at the coveted target; and every time that a spear left the *womera*, or throwing-stick, and missed the mark, a shrill yell burst simultaneously from the mass, relieving the excitement which had been pent up in every breast. But when a successful spear struck down the loaf, trebly wild and shrill was the yell that rent the air.

The York and Northam districts afford a vast quantity of land suitable for all kinds of grain. The sheep and cattle runs are excellent, but they are now fully stocked, and new settlers must direct their steps to the southward, the Dale and Hotham districts affording scope and verge enough for many a flock and herd. Our own sheep were generally kept at a squatting station on the Hotham, some sixty or seventy miles south of York. Thither, after the races, we drove to inspect the flock. There was no road, and only an endless succession of trees, and of gently rising and falling country. How my brother and his men used to manage to hit upon the site of the location is more than I can conjecture. People accustomed to the bush seem to acquire, like the natives, the faculty of knowing exactly the direction, position, and distance of the spot they want to reach.

On the way, we fell in with one of those extraordinary nests constructed by that singular bird called by the natives the Now. Mr. Gould's description of a similar bird in New South Wales, the Brush Turkey (*Talegalla Lathami*) does not exactly tally with that which we should give of the Now. His description is as follows :—"For some weeks previous to laying its eggs, the Brush Turkey collects together an immense mass of vegetable matter, varying from two to four cart-loads, with which it forms a pyramidal heap; in this heap it plants its eggs about eighteen inches deep, and from nine to twelve inches apart. The eggs are always placed with the large ends upwards, being carefully covered, and are then left to hatch by the heat engendered by the decomposition of the surrounding matter. The heaps are formed by the labours of several pairs of birds. The eggs are white, about three inches and three quarters long by two and a half in diameter, and have an excellent flavour."

Of this bird, Professor Owen observes, "On comparing the osteology of the *Talegalla* with that of other birds, it exhibits all the essential modifications which characterize the gallinaceous tribe; and among the Rasores, it most nearly resembles the genera Penelope and Crax."

The Now of Western Australia does not build its nest of vegetable substances, but collects together an immense heap of earth, sand, and small stones, into the form of a broad cone, four or five feet high in the centre, and about ten feet across. Directly in the centre it either leaves or subsequently hollows out a hole large enough to admit itself, into which it descends and deposits its eggs. The powerful summer sun heats the earth sufficiently to hatch the eggs, and the young birds come forth active and able to provide for themselves. Not the least astonishing part to me is, how they manage to scramble out of that deep hole. The natives declare that the hen frequently visits the nest, and watches the progress of incubation, and then when the young ones are hatched, they get upon her back, and she scrambles out with her family about her.

This bird is about the size of a pheasant, has long legs, and a very deep breast-bone. It runs fast. Each nest is supposed to be built by a single bird, but it is believed that other birds may occupy them in succeeding seasons.

In the afternoon of the second day after leaving York, we descended into a broad valley, abounding with grass and scattered gum-trees. A large flock of sheep were being driven towards the bottom of the valley, where we could discern signs of human habitation.

On arriving, we found a hut built of piles or stakes interwoven with boughs, before the door of

which was a fire with a large pot upon it, from
which a powerful steam arose that was evidently
very grateful to a group of natives seated around.
Two families seemed to compose this group, consisting of a couple of men, four women, and five
or six children of various ages. As we drew nigh,
the whole party, without rising, uttered a wild
scream of welcome, accompanied by that loud
laughter which always seems to escape so readily
from this light-hearted and empty-headed people.

On descending from the vehicle, and looking in
at the hut door, we perceived, lying in his shirt-
sleeves on a couch composed of grass-tree tops
covered with blankets and a rug made of opossum
skins, the illustrious Meliboeus himself, with a
short black pipe in his mouth, and a handsome
edition of " Lalla Rookh " in his hand. Perceiving us, he jumped up, and expressing his loud
surprise, welcomed us to this rustic Castle of
Indolence.

When a large flock of sheep is sent into the
bush, and a squatting station is formed, the shepherds take the sheep out to pasture every morning,
and bring them home at night, whilst one of the
party always remains at the station to protect the
provisions from being stolen by the natives. This
person is called the hut-keeper. His duty is to
boil the pork, or kangaroo flesh, and provide sup-

per, &c., for the shepherds on their return at night.
Melibœus, who superintended this station, undertook the duties of cooking and guarding the hut
whenever he did not feel disposed to go out
kangaroo-hunting, or shooting wild turkeys or
cockatoos. In all things, sports or labours, the
natives were his daily assistants, and in return for
their services were rewarded with the fore-quarters
of the kangaroos killed, and occasionally with a
pound or two of flour. There were some noble
dogs at this station, descendants of Jezebel and
Nero; and my brother had a young kangaroo,
which hopped in and out with the utmost confidence, coming up to any one who happened to be
eating, and insisting upon having pieces of bread
given to it. Full of fun and spirits, it would sport
about as playfully as a kitten; and it was very
amusing to see how it would tease the dogs, pulling them about with its sharp claws, and trying
to roll them over on the ground. The dogs, who
were in the daily habit of killing kangaroos, never
attempted to bite Minny, who sometimes teased
them so heartily, that they would put their tails
between their legs and fairly run away.

The great enemies of the sheep in the Australian
colonies are the wild-dogs. At York, and in the
other settled districts, they are very troublesome,
and require the shepherd to keep a constant look-

out. We were therefore much surprised to learn
that although wild dogs abounded near this squatting station, they never attempted to touch our
flocks. A sheep was to them a new animal; they
had yet to learn the value of mutton. A cowardly
race, they are easily intimidated, and as they have
not the art of jumping or clambering over a fence,
a low sheep-fold will keep them out, provided they
cannot force their way under the palings or hurdles.
They cannot bark, and utter only a melancholy
howl. The bitch generally litters in a hollow tree,
and produces four or five puppies at a birth.

The production of wool—the careful acquisition
of a good flock of well-bred sheep, and the
attainment of the highest degree of perfection in
preparing the fleeces for the English market—
appears to us to be the proper ambition of an
emigrant to the Australian colonies. When ill-
health compelled my steps hither, it was the intention of myself and brothers to invest our
capital entirely in sheep; and retiring into the
bush for some six or seven years, gradually accumulate a large flock, the produce of which would
soon have afforded a handsome income. It has
never, however, appeared to be the object of either
the Home Government or the Local Government
of any colony (though unquestionably the interest
of both) to encourage emigration. Settlers have

invariably every possible difficulty thrown in their way. On arriving in this colony, we found to our astonishment that squatting was illegal, and that we would not be allowed, as we had designed, to carry our goods into the interior and form a station upon Government land. No license could at that time be obtained, and if we bought the smallest section allowed to be sold, which was 640 acres, for as many pounds, it was ten to one but we should soon find the district in which it was situated insufficient for the run of a large flock, and should have to change our quarters again. The consequence was, that we were compelled to abandon our project: my brothers took a farm at a high rent, and wasted their capital upon objects that could never bring in a good return; whilst I *(infelix!)*, instead of listening to the gentle bleatings of sheep, and ministering to the early comforts of innocent lambs, have been compelled to hearken to the angry altercations of plaintiff and defendant, and decide upon the amount of damages due to injured innocence when the pot had insulted the kettle.

Now, however, limited licenses are granted to persons wishing to go as squatters upon Government land; and even before these were issued, we were *obliged* to send our sheep upon Crown lands, and form a station, for want of room in the settled districts.

Sheep flocks constitute doubtlessly one of the most profitable investments for the employment of capital, notwithstanding the many obstacles and discouragements still thrown by both governments in the way of the wool-grower. They yield a very large return *to those who attend to them in person,* and who confine their attention entirely to that pursuit, growing only corn enough for their own consumption.

CHAPTER XXI.

EXTRACTS FROM THE LOG OF A HUT-KEEPER.

May 10*th*.—Felt rather lonely to-day, in the midst of this endless solitude. Sat before the hut-door thinking of Zimmerman and his Reflections. Also thought of Brasenose, Oxford, and my narrow escape from Euclid and Greek plays. *Davus sum, non Œdipus.* Set to work, and cooked a kangaroo stew for the three shepherds.

June 4*th*.—We have removed the sheep from the Dale to the Avon. We go wandering about with our flocks and baggage like the Israelites of old, from one patch of good grass to another. I wonder how long it will be before we make our fortunes?

28*th*.—K. arrived from York with a supply of flour, pork, tea and sugar. Brings no news from England, or anywhere else. Where the deuce are all the ships gone to, that we get no letters? Moved the station to Corbeding.

29*th*.—K. returned to York with his bullock-cart. No chance of my being relieved at present.

Went out by myself kangarooing. The pup, Hector, out of Jezebel, will make a splendid dog. First kangaroo fought like a devil; Hector, fearing nothing, dashed at him, and got a severe wound in the throat; but returned to the charge, after looking on for a few moments. Crossed an immense grassy plain, eight or nine miles wide, without a tree upon it. Had to carry a kangaroo more than five miles on my back. Wished it at Hanover, and twice abandoned it, but returned for it again, being so much in want of fresh meat.

30*th*.—Spent the day in dreary solitude in the hut. All my books have been read, re-read, and re-re-read.

July 1*st*.—Went out with the dogs, and caught three kangaroos. Passed over some splendid country—wish it were peopled with white humans. How pleasant to have been able to call at a cottage, and get a draught of home-brewed! On the contrary, could not find even a pond, or a pint of water, and was nearly worried to death by sand-flies.

2*d*.—Some scabby sheep having got among our flock, have played the deuce with it. The scab has regularly broke out. I had rather it were the plague or Asiatic cholera, and cleared them all off (my own sheep are fortunately at York). Dressing lambs all morning—beastly work. In the afternoon went

out with the sheep, and left James to mind the hut.
Sand-flies infernal.

3*d, Sunday*.—Stayed in the hut all day. Smoked
sheep-tobacco,* all my Turkish being finished. Felt
pious, and wrote a short sermon, choosing the text
at random—Jeremiah ii. 7 : "And I brought you
into a plentiful country, to eat the fruit thereof and
the goodness thereof." Read it at night to the
shepherds. James said it was "slap-up."

4*th*.—Went out kangarooing. Killed an immense
fellow : when standing on his hind legs fighting
with me and the dogs, he was a foot higher than
myself. He ran at me, and nearly gave me a desperate dig with his claw, which tore my only good
hunting-shirt miserably. Smashed his skull for it.

5*th and* 6*th*.—Dressing sheep all day. Our
[band of] York natives, whom we have hitherto
kept with us, are all gone home again, leaving me
and my three men, with only two guns, among
a suspicious and treacherous tribe that cannot
understand a word we say to them. Wish my
brothers would come and look after their own sheep.
It would do E.'s health more good than sitting in
Court, hearing a set of fools jabber. Sand-flies
eat us alive here, and the mosquitoes polish our
bones.

* Coarse pig-tail, used as a decoction for dressing the
diseased sheep.

7th.—Muston and myself dressed fifty sheep to-day. John out with part of the flock.

8th.—Heavy rain last night. Cannot go on dressing. Did nothing all day.

9th.—Stayed in the hut doing nothing.

10*th, Sunday.*—Ditto.

11*th.*—Tired of doing nothing. Dressed sheep most of the day. Muston out kangarooing; caught three.

12*th.*—Cooking. Made a " sea-pie," which was generally admired.

August 1*st.*—The Doctor arrived from York, driving tandem in E.'s trap. He has brought me a parcel of books just come from England. Blessings on my dear sister for remembering me. I thought myself forgotten by all the world. Sisters (Heaven for ever bless them !) are the only people that never forget. News from home ! How many thoughts come flooding upon me !

2*d.*—Last night, I confess, I cried myself to sleep, like a great big baby. I am very comfortable and contented so long as I receive no letter from home ; and yet I am such a fool as to wish for them ; and when they come I am made miserable for a week afterwards. Somehow, they make me feel my loneliness more. I feel deserted, forgotten by all but *one.* She says she is constantly wishing for me in her rides. They seem to enjoy themselves more at home than they used to do, now that we are gone—always picknicking, boating, or forming riding parties. "Fairy" continues the favourite—I always thought she was a good hack. "Light-foot," whom I lamed hunting, was obliged to be sold. It seems to be a sore subject with the Governor. I wonder how Juno has turned out; she was a splendid-looking whelp. I wish they'd enter more into particulars when they write. It's ridiculous my asking questions, as it will be more than a year before answers can arrive. They ought to write about *every thing*. I cannot bear to think to-day of anything but home.

3*d*.—The Doctor gone back to York—sulky about the sheep being so bad. Why does he not send us more tobacco and turpentine? Says we smoke it all. The Doctor is an ——. Promises to send K. next week with mercurial ointment; it is therefore useless to waste any more tobacco on the sheep—the stock is low enough as it is.

4*th*.—Lay all day on my couch, reading "Rose d'Albret." Wish I had her here. One wants somebody to sympathize with so desperately in the bush.

5*th*.—Ditto, ditto.

6*th*.—Reading *Punch* all morning. In the afternoon made a damper, baked it, and eat it in company with the others. "Pit a cake, pat a cake, baker's man!" &c.

16th.—Dressing sheep all day with mercurial ointment. Wish this job was over. Dreadful work bending one's back all day, and rooting amongst the wool for the diseased places.

18th.—Went out with the dogs, and killed two kangaroos. It rained tremendously all the time, and I wished the kangaroos at the ———. The natives happened to be hunting in a large party, driving the game before them; and as I stood in the midst of a large plain which they had surrounded on three sides, multitudes of kangaroos—I believe I might say thousands—of all sizes, came rushing past me. The dogs were quite bewildered, and remained at my side aghast; and it was several minutes before they recovered themselves enough to give chase. The natives took no notice of me. In the evening fifty of them came about the hut. We took care to show our guns, and I shot a green parrot, sixty yards off, just to show them what we could do. They were quite peaceable, and danced a corrobery at night.

20th.—I dressed twenty-five sheep this morning myself. In the afternoon William came from York with six hundred more sheep (mine among them), which were found to be scabby. More work ! This is really too bad, thrusting all this cursed business upon me. He had been four days coming, and had not lost a single sheep.

21st.—Went out kangarooing, quite disgusted. Wandered a long distance, and had to carry a large buck several miles. Could scarcely find my way back, but at length got home (! !) quite knocked up, and more and more disgusted with human nature and every thing.

22d.—The Doctor is enjoying himself at York, and E. lives on the fat of the land at Perth, whilst I have never tasted anything but salt pork and kangaroo for many months, and have nothing to drink but tea. I have almost forgotten the taste of a potato. We have nothing here but kangaroo and pork, and unleavened bread, called damper. I wish I could exchange our bill of fare occasionally with that French fellow who complained of having " toujours perdrix." He would be the loser, I take it. I could eat even *perdrix aux choux*—a villanous dish formerly—but we have no more cabbages than partridges to thank God for. I have long been obliged to leave off saying " grace after meat ;" it really became an impious mockery, and was also impolitic and uneconomical, as my stomach used to turn against it. I consulted John this morning about killing a sheep, as none of them seemed inclined to die naturally. John caught at the idea with great quickness. He really is an intelligent fellow ; and both he and the other poor devils are so patient and unrepining, that the Doctor is little

better than a beast not to order them some mutton
occasionally. I consider it absolutely necessary for
their health. We fixed upon one of E.'s sheep, as
it looked the fattest ; and he being the richest, and
never coming himself to look at his flock, will not
care about a few sheep more or less. I'd kill one of
my own, but they are such a seedy lot. No one is
answerable for the murder of this sheep but myself,
as I hereby confess that I killed it with my own
hand, and afterwards held a coroner's inquest on the
body, directing a verdict of " Visitation of Providence " to be recorded in the accounts relating to
the flock. We had the liver for supper. Excellent !
never tasted anything half so good.

23*d*.—Dined on sheep's head and trotters. (Tea
to drink, *toujours*.)

24*th*.—Saddle of mutton.

25*th*.—Leg.

26*th*.—Shoulder.

27*th*.—Leg.

28*th*.—Shoulder.

29*th*.—Finished the sheep, and polished the
bones.

[The rest of the Journal runs on much in the
same way. This specimen will probably be enough
for the reader.]

CHAPTER XXII.

PELICAN SHOOTING.—GALES.—WRESTLING WITH DEATH.

THE large estuary of the Swan affords ample scope for boating or sailing in small pleasure-yachts.

Perth water, on the northern bank of which the capital is built, extends from two to three miles in length, and about the same distance in its broadest part, its form being that of a half moon. It is connected with Melville water by an opening of a quarter of a mile across. Melville water is some six miles long, and from three to four broad; a splendid bay, called Freshwater Bay, developes itself at the western extremity of this fine sheet of water; and the river, or estuary, here makes a turn at right angles, and pursues its course towards the sea between high precipitous rocks of marine limestone, which are from six to seven hundred yards apart.

My pleasure-boat has enabled me to pass many agreeable hours upon this estuary.

At first, especially, it was exceedingly pleasant to make expeditions for the purpose of exploring the different bays and inlets, which abounded with ducks, swans, and pelicans.

My youngest brother and myself would frequently rise at a good hour, and having supplied our little vessel with a stock of provisions, and a few bottles of ale or other drinkables, hoist the sails, and bear away upon a cruise. The warm dry air, tempered by the sea - breeze, made boating exceedingly pleasant; and as we often touched at gardens situated at the mouth of the Canning, or on the shores of Melville water, and procured a basket of grapes, or peaches and melons, we managed to lunch luxuriously, having first cast anchor and bathed.

Many readers must have felt the excitement experienced by young sportsmen when they have the luck to fall in with some bird or animal not previously known to them. Every one remembers the delight with which, when a boy, he shot his first wood-pigeon, or lay in ambush behind a hedge for an old crow.

When first we beheld a group of huge tall birds, standing lazily in the sunshine upon a sand-spit which ran far into Melville water, we could scarcely believe our eyes that these were really live pelicans; and it was not only with intense interest, but with feelings of self-reproach, that we drew nigh with hostile intentions to birds which in the days of our boyhood, when visiting Mr. Wombwell's menagerie, had filled us with awe and reverence, as creatures that were wont to evince the depth of parental devotion by feeding their young with their own blood.

Our first overt act of hostility against the pelicans was unsuccessful. The sea - breeze was blowing strong, and we had to beat out against it close-hauled; just as we made the last board, and were bearing down upon the enemy, the huge, heavy birds, awaking from their siesta "with a start," raised their heads and looked about them. Then the foremost began to flap his long wings, and lift himself on tip-toe, whilst the others followed his example; and soon they were all heavily skimming along the surface of the water, trying to launch themselves fairly into the upward air; and having at length succeeded, they rose higher and higher in wide gyrations. The leader seemed resolved to hide himself in the distant blue of the cloudless heavens; and upward—up, up, up—they continued to mount, going round, and round, and round, in lessening circles—whilst the spectator gazed in wonder at the slowly diminishing specks, that were almost lost in ether; and at length, moving slowly towards the east—the unknown, mysterious wilder-

ness—they altogether faded away. We have heard
of eagles soaring into the sun, but I doubt whether
even they could soar much higher, or look much
grander, than the noble pelican of the desert.

The sheets were eased off, the long boom of the
graceful sliding-gunter (a kind of latteen) sail,
stretched far over the gun-wale of the boat, which
slipped along easily and rapidly through the water,
the rolling waves heaving up her stern, and sending
her forward with a gentle impulse. We were
opening the broad mouth of the Canning, when
Melibœus pointed out two other pelicans fishing
in-shore on the lee-bow. Gently we edged away
towards them; Melibœus standing before the mast
with his double-barrel ready, and motioning to me
how to steer, as the main-sail hid the birds from my
view.

They perceived us, and began to swim along
shore at a rapid rate; the water was shoaling fast,
and we greatly feared they would escape, but still
we held on. The majestic birds rose slowly from
the water, one following the other, and made towards
the Canning. " I'll let fly at them," cried Melibœus, in an intense whisper, "luff up!—hard-a-
lee!" The helm was jammed down, and the sheet
hauled in; the boat luffed into the wind, and
became stationary, only bobbing upon the waves,
whilst her sails shivered and rattled in the breeze.

Melibœus fired—and the hindmost bird declined gradually towards the water; its long wings became fixed and motionless at their widest stretch, and slowly it sank down upon its heaving death-bed. Loud shouted the sportsman; and momentary envy filled the heart of him who steered.

Away goes the boat before the freshening breeze, and soon it dashes past the body of the pelican, which is seized by the ready Melibœus, and with great difficulty hauled on board. A shot had penetrated to its brain and killed it instantaneously. The wind up the Canning was nearly abeam, and we dashed through the deep and narrow passage called Hell's Gates, and held on till we came to the foot of a steep and rounded hill, Mount Henry. The river here turns at right angles, sweeping round the base of the hill, and leaving a broad and deep bay called Bull's Creek, to the southward. This is a famous spot for ducks and swans, and many a pleasant bivouac have I formed near it, waiting for early morn when the birds are busy feeding. As we rounded Mount Henry, we observed a large slate-coloured bird lazily flying across the river ahead of us. The Canning is here about four hundred yards broad, widening occasionally to a quarter of a mile. The wind was now right aft, and we soon came upon the line of the bird, which appeared to be a crested crane. The boom was topped-up in a moment, the jib-sheet let fly, and the boat's nose ran crashing through the sedges which in this part fringed the bank. The crane had alighted on the very summit of a straight and lofty tree, and there she sat, unconscious of the danger at hand.

Too much excited to care for any obstacles, and with eyes ever fixed upon the game, I tore my way through brambles, thickets, water and mud, until with no little difficulty I arrived at ground free from underwood. The bird was still sitting patiently on her lofty perch, and my heart beat anxiously with hope that I should be able to creep within shot. What a moment of interest! It is still vivid in the memory, with all its doubts and fears and wildly-beating hopes. The crane seemed preparing to fly. Death! I felt nearly distracted with apprehension. The interest and excitement became intense. I crept from tree to tree, and whenever I thought I was observed, stood motionless. My eye-balls became dry and hard with incessant gazing. I feared to wink lest she should be gone. She extended her wings! I bounded forward. She was just off, and barely within reach, as I fired; a single number two shot struck her pinion, and down she tumbled to the ground with a glorious wallop.

A loud shout from Melibœus, who had sat in the

boat scarcely daring to breathe, proclaimed the presence of a witness to my triumph.

Since then I have shot cranes without emotion or much feeling of interest.

Boating, as an amusement, ought only to be followed during the summer months, from the 1st of October to the 1st of April. In the winter season there are extremely violent gales of wind from the north-west, that sometimes last for three days together. Their arrival is generally foretold by the rapid falling of the barometer; and at Perth it is almost always preceded by the rising of the estuary. A singular storm visited the district of Australind in the night of the 17th June, 1842. It crossed the Leschenault estuary, and entered the forest, making a lane through the trees from three to four hundred yards wide. In this lane, which extended for many miles, nothing was left standing but the stumps of trees; whilst the trees on either side of the lane stood up like a wall and were perfectly uninjured. The storm in its course, which was in a direct line from N.W. to S.E. levelled the trees in the valleys as well as those on the hills. Its effects were not like those of a whirlwind, when trees appear twisted round, and scattered in every direction; in this lane the young healthy trees, which were generally broken off about two or three yards from the ground, all lay in the same direction.

Twice have I nearly paid dearly for my rashness in boating. My boat was once capsized in a moment in a squall, and Hannibal and myself were soused in the water before we knew what had happened. I caught hold of the bilge of the boat, and nearly drowned myself with laughing at the Son of Amilcar, who was splashing about, shrieking with terror, and swallowing quarts of salt-water, as his open mouth popped every moment under a wave. In vain I called to him to come to me, and lay hold of the boat; he could neither see nor hear, and would have soon joined his illustrious namesake in the Elysian fields, had I not managed to throw the bight of a rope round his neck, and towed him within reach, when I held him up by the collar of his jacket (ducking him under water occasionally to make him cease from howling) until we were rescued by a fishing-boat.

One day, the 11th April, 1843, feeling disposed to take my book on the water and enjoy the calm air, I embarked by myself—a most unusual occurrence, as I scarcely ever went out alone. What little wind there was blew down the estuary, but only gently ruffled the waters; and my boat glided noiselessly before it. A couple of hours took me to the farther extremity of Melville water, and here it fell calm. I now began to feel uncomfortable, for the air was close, and dark clouds appeared rising in the north-west. The wind began to blow in gusts; a sudden puff, curling the waters, would strike the boat and make her heel over until her gunwale kissed the wave, as with a sudden start she rushed forward under the impulse of the blast. I was now making homeward. The heavens became black with angry clouds; the wind first sighed and moaned like a reluctant Spirit driven forth to fulfil its task of evil, feeling something of remorse at crimes foreshadowed and inevitable; and then working itself into fury, as though it would stifle thought, and crush out the germ of pity, the Wind in its might and rage rushed roaring over the waters, making the foam fly before it, and tearing up the face of the estuary into rugged lines of wild tumultuous waves. The little bark vainly strove to keep her head to the storm, which bore her down until the water poured over the gunwale.

It was about six o'clock in the evening, and darkness, hurried on prematurely by the tempest, spread suddenly around. The waves, as if trying to leap beyond the reach of some internal agony, rolled high above my head, as the " Fair Maid of Perth" sank hopelessly in the deep channel, with rocking mast and shivering sails. But not yet submerged, she rose again, and fronted the storm, struggling desperately to reach the northern shore, which was not far distant. But the skies grew blacker still; the storm became a hurricane; the wind roared so loud that no voice of human agony or despair might be heard above its tremendous fury; the waves grew higher and mightier, and became rushing hills of water, overwhelming, irresistible. To me, quailing in my frail bark, in all the consciousness of helplessness and ruin, it seemed as though the winds and the waves were really sentient beings combining to overwhelm me, and increasing their efforts the more I struggled.

This is no fiction that I am relating, but a reality that happened to myself, and which it would be impossible to exaggerate. Never shall I forget the last tremendous wave that came down upon me, impelled by a maddening gust which whirled tearing along through the wild air, and scooping its deep passage through the waters. In vain was the jib-sheet let fly; in vain did I luff into the wind. I could not quit the helm, and therefore was unable to lower the sail which in that hurricane could not have been got in easily, and in the meantime the boat, breaking off from the wind, would have been swamped. I was so near the shore that I hoped still to reach it, the wind being abeam, in the course of a few minutes. But nothing could withstand the last wave and

blast. The boat lurched, and broke off. Hurled
on her beam-ends, the boom was in the water;
the waves rushed over the side; she struggled
bravely, and tried to right herself; but after staggering forwards a few seconds, the weight of the
in-rushing water bore her down, and she slowly
fell over on her side. The sensation was by no
means pleasant. I felt her going, without being
able to prevent it. I glanced around for aid or
hope; but there was neither. I could see nothing
but waves, and hear nothing but the roaring blast.
The shore was close to me, but the high waves, and
the darkness of the hurricane, prevented my discern-
ing even the tops of the trees. As the boat capsized, I kicked off my shoes and threw off my
coat and waistcoat, and seizing the main-sheet,
let myself down in the water, trying to find
bottom, but there was none within reach.

I struck out towards the shore, but the ablest
swimmer that ever swam could have made no progress against that sea, and I could scarcely swim
at all.

I scrambled back to the boat, which now lay on
her side, level with the surface. On getting upon
her, you may conceive—but no! you cannot—the
horror of the moment, as I felt her gradually go
down—sink, sinking beneath me. All now seemed
over. My time had arrived; my last moment was

come. I collected my thoughts, and prepared for it.

I did not feel so much terror as I should have anticipated in such a scene. Death seemed inevitable, and I nerved myself, and prayed. All the past did *not* press upon me at this moment, in this death-struggle, as some readers may imagine. I thought not of my sins, nor of my friends, nor of time misspent and work left undone—my whole mind was absorbed in the sense of DEATH and FUTURITY. The glances, rather than the thoughts which shot across my soul, seemed like revealings of immortality. My sensations were mixed of horror and hope; the *change* from the old to the new Life seemed beginning within me. It might have been excess of terror, but I did not feel terrified. I felt that all was over, and there was no room for the anguish that arises from doubt. All struggling was vain, and though in tumult and horror, I yet felt resigned. The World of Time was past, and new being was at hand.

Such is the memory which I must ever bear of the hour when (yet vigorous and full of Life) I was held in the arms of Death.

The boat went down. The waves rushed over me; the enemy held me by the throat, and seemed to press me into the opening grave. Even as the light faded from my eyes, and the Spirit waited for that quick, sharp touch of the dart which should free it from the bonds of mortal life, I perceived the stem of the boat rising slowly out of the waves, whilst the stern was borne down by my weight.

Instinctively I swam forward, and got upon another part of the boat. Down it went again; and as the water dashed against my face, I saw the stern now rising up, whilst the stem plunged down into the depths below. I scrambled amidships; the sea and the wind struck her, and she rolled heavily over, righting herself for a moment, with her mast and sail erect; but soon she lay on her larboard side, deep in the water. I had been washed off her, but clung to the main-sheet, and so got back again. I now held on to the side with one hand, whilst I managed to strip off all my clothes except my shirt and flannel waistcoat, first taking my knife out of my pocket. With this I tried to cut away the stays which held the mast in its place, hoping that it would then fall out, and relieve the boat of the sails which weighed her down so low in the water. Most fortunately I had not sand-ballast, in tarred bags, as most of our pleasure-boats had, but water-ballast in breakers, which now proved no additional burthen to the boat. It was also fortunate that she was built partly of deal, and had only her lower streaks of jarra wood, which does not float.

The blade of the knife, which was only a pen-knife, soon broke, and I was obliged to give up the attempt to remove the sails. Still the hurricane blew on, wild and terrible as ever; the spray washed over me like rain; the waves dashed me repeatedly from the boat, which was whirled and tossed about in a strange manner; sometimes rolling completely over, sometimes going down head, and sometimes stern foremost, I had to scramble from part to part, and exercise a good deal of agility in saving myself from being struck by the gunwale, or by the boom and sail, as they rose from the water and fell back again.

And now I could see but small prospect of being eventually saved. The only chance was that the boat would drift, in the course of time, across the estuary, here nearly four miles broad. Then I tried, and for a long time vainly, to ascertain whether she drifted at all. The anchor, with about five-and-twenty feet of cable, had doubtless fallen out, and the boat was probably stationary. Night had set in, and it was too dark to distinguish even the shore with its forest of trees. These gales sometimes continue three days, and I knew it would be impossible to exist many hours immersed in water. I dreaded lest I should become benumbed and unable to hold on to the boat.

In order to keep up circulation as much as possible, I shouted aloud, and rubbed my breast and thighs with my disengaged hand.

Some dark object was on the water near me. It moved; it came quickly towards me. I could just discern that it was a whale-boat containing several men. It had no sails or oars, yet it flew before the blast. I shouted and screamed as it went by, not twenty yards from me; and the men turned their heads and waved their arms, and doubtless answered, but the gale roared with un-abated fury, the waves intercepted them from my sight, and I could not hear their voices.*

The moon had now risen, and the clouds were partially dispersed, so that I could at length distinguish the woods on the weather-shore; and I could see the weary waste of waters over which I must drift before I could possibly be saved.

Sometimes the wind blew with lessened violence, and I could sit upon the submerged bilge of the boat, and consider my state and prospects. After long observation, I felt assured that the boat did really drift, but it was very slowly; and I feared that as we approached the other shore, her anchor must

* These men were about a mile and a half astern of me, when the hurricane began, and tried to pull in shore; but just as they thought to have reached it, one of their oars broke, and being now helpless, they were obliged to scud before the wind. By good fortune they were carried up the Canning, where they remained all night.

inevitably bring her up in twenty-five feet water, and that nothing could save me from perishing of cold. It never occurred to me during this memorable night, that when I set sail in the afternoon I had shortened the cable to about five feet in length, in order the more easily to trip the anchor. This was one of the circumstances, providentially ordered, that tended to save my life.

Some miles down the estuary I could distinguish a light in the house at Point Walter, high placed on a steep bank ; there two of my friends were at that moment carousing, whilst I was being buffetted by waves and tempest, and fearing that the saturated sails and heavy wood at length would sink the unfortunate boat to the bottom. I yet could scarely hope to escape ; my mind was still made up to die, and I tranquilly awaited the event.

The moon had now made half of her journey across the heavens ; the wind had moderated, and I redoubled my exertions to keep off the cold by shouting and rubbing myself. My flannel-shirt was another instrument of safety to me. It felt warm to my body though the waves poured continually over it.

The outline of the forest on the lee side of the estuary was now distinguishable, and hope would have been rife within me but for the expectation of finding myself anchored fast at a fatal distance from the shore.

Every thing appeared so indistinct in the gloom of the night, that I could not guess how far I was from land; and it was with surprise, as well as delight and gratitude, that I felt the boat bump against the sand. Oh that first bump, which told me of safety and deliverance after five hours of incessant peril! Shall I ever forget the thrill of delight which it gave me? I could scarcely credit my senses, and put down my benumbed feet with doubt; but they rested on the sand—real, hard, blessed *terra firma!* and without delay I waded through the water to the beach.

The wind had now fallen, and it began to rain.

I was on the edge of a thick wilderness of forest, without any house within reach—the nearest was some miles distant, and to reach it in the dark, and without shoes, through swamps and thickets, was almost impossible.

The Canning River was about half-a-mile from me, and on the farther side of it was a settler's house; but though I might reach the bank of the river, I could not hope to make myself heard half a mile off, amid the howling of the dying storm, and by people fast asleep. There was nothing for it, therefore, but to make myself as comfortable as possible, and remain where I was until morning. Fortunately,

I recollected having seen the ruins of a goat-shed not far distant, when I had landed on this spot with my gun two or three months before. With some difficulty, and some pain to my feet from thorns, I discovered this relic of a hovel. Part of the roof was yet entire, and sheltered me from the wind.

The door was lying inside, and this I made my bed. Then, having wrung out my shirt and flannel-waistcoat, and returned thanks to the Almighty for preserving a life not, perhaps, sufficiently prized by the owner, I lay down completely exhausted and fell asleep.

Awaking at daylight, I started off through the woods, stiff and hoarse with cold, but light of heart; and having reached the Canning, succeeded at last in making myself heard by the farmer opposite, who took me across in his boat, breakfasted me, and lent me his clothes, and finally conveyed me to Perth, where I found my friends preparing to go in search of my body.

CHAPTER XXIII.

THE DESERT OF AUSTRALIA.——CAUSE OF THE HOT WINDS.—— GEOLOGY.

I INTEND in this chapter* to give an explanation
of the cause of the hot-winds of Australia; to
throw out a suggestion on the most likely mode of
prosecuting discovery towards the interior; and to
conclude with a slight sketch of the geology of the
colony. Before doing this I shall give a brief
account of a journey made by myself and Mr.
Maxwell Lefroy in search of the inland sea so often
talked of, and which a native promised to show to
us; so large, he said, that when he stood on one
shore he could not see the other. Although this
sea turned out to be a pure fiction, the journey was
not entirely useless, nor altogether uninteresting.
As this sea was probably not more than 200 miles
distant from York, according to the reckoning of
the native, who said it was "ten sleeps off,"
I judged that one month's provision would be
sufficient.

Accordingly, Mr. Lefroy and myself started on
the expedition, on horseback, taking with us a

* This chapter I owe to Mr. Henry Landor.

native boy, and a pack-horse loaded with flour, tea, and sugar, and other necessaries. It will be sufficient to state that we pursued a south-east course, crossing the Hotham, the Williams, and the Arthur rivers, and traversing an indifferent country, but in many places fit for sheep-grazing, before we came to the lake, or sea, of which we were in search. When we arrived at it, we were disappointed to find it not more than six miles long, although the natives, with their usual amount of exaggeration, had increased it to an illimitable ocean. Before descending from the high land to the plain in which the lakes are situated, we caught a distant glimpse of what appeared to be a grand and broad river, pursuing a winding course through a magnificently wooded valley, with its clear bright waters dwindling in the distance to a silvery thread. A nearer examination, however, dispelled the illusion, and the beautiful river turned out to be nothing more than a chain of shallow lakes, situated in a woody valley; and only in very wet seasons flowing from one to another.

We determined to follow the chain of lakes eastward, so long as our provisions should last, or as long as our horses could find food for themselves. We proceeded east for six days, passing numberless lakes, and observing that the chain divided, one branch of lakes running north-east, and the other due east. We followed the latter until we came to a lake called Dambeling, by far the largest we had seen, being about fifteen miles long by seven or eight wide, with a good sheep country on its northern bank, and a river, which we called the Lefroy, falling into its eastern end. The river was about thirty yards wide, with a clayey bed, and large fresh-water pools, and flowed from the east, through the worst country we had seen, it being an apparently endless desert, and level to the horizon. We went one day's journey into this inhospitable country, but the want of food for our horses, and our own unprepared state, prevented us from penetrating farther. On our return, we went for two or three days north, on the outskirts of the desert, before we turned westward on our way back to York.

The only land we crossed in this expedition was situated at the head of the Hotham and Williams. The area of this country is undoubtedly very great, but its average character is below the York district, although it is well adapted for sheep-grazing.

But the most interesting feature is the barren and desolate country to the east of Lake Dambeling, doubtless a continuation of the same sterile country seen by Mr. Roe, the Surveyor-General, east of York many years previously; and probably

from Mr. Eyre's observation, extending quite down
to the southern coast.   We had no means of ascertaining the width of this dreary country, but we
did not think it could be impassably wide because
the river Lefroy appeared to come across it.   This
river, in a geographical point of view, may be important, as the character of its bed, without trees,
more water-worn than the other rivers of the
colony, its size, and the direction from which it
comes, render it exceedingly interesting to determine how it is supplied.   The sandy nature of the
country on its banks, and for many miles east, and
the flatness of the country, preclude the idea that it
receives its supply of water from the immediately surrounding district.   It must either be supplied by a
country of a far better character to the eastward, or
it is the outlet of another and larger lake far in the
interior.   From the natives we could learn nothing
but that there were no kangaroos, no opossums,
and no water to the east ; but as their knowledge
never extends 100 miles, and they would tell any
lie to avoid going where they had no inclination to
go, their opinions are worthless.   It might be
worth the while of the colony to send forth another
expedition to determine the boundaries of this desolate country, as it is not improbable that a practicable rout might be discovered to South Australia
by means of the river and lakes.

The outlet of the lakes is into the river Beaufort, and possibly also into the Gordon. There is no doubt that in exceedingly wet seasons the whole valley is one continuous stream, when all the lakes would be united and present a truly magnificent appearance; but as the area of evaporation is so large, and the banks of many of the lakes are high, the quantity of rain must be enormous before the valley becomes filled with a running river. Lake Barbering, where the valley divides, has a steep shore, with three distinct marks of former water-levels. All the lakes have two or more shores, showing either a decrease of rain or an elevation of the land itself, probably both. Between the present and ancient shores there is a belt of swamp-oaks and tea-trees, which show that some length of time has elapsed since the water left its old levels.

The water to fill these large reservoirs must come down the river Lefroy, as the neighbouring country is too sandy to supply it in sufficient quantities.

No question in geography has presented a wider field for conjecture than the much-debated one of the nature of the interior of Australia. Is it desert, or water, or pasture? inhabited, or destitute alike of animal and vegetable life? The explorations of Captain Sturt, and the journey of Mr.

Eyre, would incline us to believe that the country is one vast sterile waste; but the journey of the latter is worth nothing as an attempt to expose the nature of the interior, since he never left the coast. It certainly shows how much suffering the human frame can endure; and whilst, as illustrative of Australian geography, it is valueless, it is highly creditable to the energies of the traveller.

The expedition of Captain Sturt has shown that to the north of South Australia the country is chiefly desert, totally incapable of supporting animal life : while the geological specimens of that traveller prove that the rich mineral strata of South Australia extend far beyond the pastoral boundaries of the colony. A reference to the journey of Mr. Lefroy and myself, from York to the south-east, will show that there exists a low level country running far beyond our farthest eastern point, which may afford abundance of water and pasture for any future expedition proceeding in that direction.

An expedition starting from these lakes in the *beginning of winter,* so as to take advantage of the first supplies of water, might advance far enough into the interior to discover at least the possibility of proceeding before the succeeding summer would render it impossible to return; for the lakes alone would not be sufficient to ensure a supply of good

drinkable water during the summer, as they generally become quite salt long before summer is over.
It would be necessary to find a good deep water-
hole for the party to remain at during the dry
season, and from which they could push out small
lateral expeditions as a sort of foundation for the
next season's main advance.   Expeditions in Australia require great circumspection. It is not the
most rapid traveller who will get the farthest, but
the most prudent and cautious. I consider it
quite possible to get across the island, either to
South Australia or to Port Essington. Most probably it would be easier to get to the latter than
the former.

From observations made on the rains and winds
in Western Australia, and careful inquiries on the
same subjects when I was in South Australia, and
on a comparison of the two, I am inclined to believe
that the climates of the two colonies assimilate. A
wet winter in one is a wet winter in the other.
Both receive their rains when the wind blows from
the north-west to south-west.   Thus the rains from
South Australia pass from the Indian Ocean over
Western Australia, and the whole island, to South
Australia. The hot wind of Western Australia
blows from the north-east; and, in fact, the hot
wind of both colonies comes from the same portion
of the great island.   That which is the hot wind in

summer in Western Australia is the cold wind in winter; and the same in South Australia. The reason is obvious. It is evident, from the fact that South Australia receives its rain from the Indian Ocean, that there are no mountains in the interior of sufficient elevation to intercept the clouds; that there are no mountains in the interior, is shown also by the absence of rivers emptying themselves into the ocean. From the observation of Mr. Lefroy and myself, we were led to suppose that the interior consisted for the most part of immense clay plains; the lower portion of these plains being hollowed into the large shallow lakes we meet with in our journey. Where the country is a little more elevated the plains are sand instead of clay. In winter these plains are covered with water, as the drifted leaves on the bushes testify; and the marks of water on the surface are very evident. Now, when the winter winds pass over these immense masses of water, the great evaporation renders them intensely cold; and they arrive in the colony laden, (if I may so unphilosophically express it,) with cold, caused by rapid evaporation. In summer these very plains are equally the cause of the hot wind; for when the rains cease, and the sun acquires his summer power, the water is quickly evaporated, the clay becomes baked, and the heat is reflected from the hard heated surface quite sufficiently to raise a thermometer to 110° in the shade. The wind is now driven towards the colony laden with heat from the cracked, baked, clay-plains in the interior; and thus it is, that at different seasons the same country produces such opposite effects. But although the general state of the interior is barren and unproductive, as I imagine, I do not suppose that it is entirely so. I believe there are many cases of good pasture land in the midst of this sterile country; fertile spots, small when compared with the vast area of indifferent country around them, but large in themselves. And these pastoral oases are more cultivated than the worthless land amid which they are placed. In these patches of good land there are always water-holes to be found, and water-courses well marked, conducting the surplus waters to the lakes in the clay plains. That there are such fertile spots in the Australian deserts is certain, for I have seen many of them myself, and they are mentioned also by the South Australian travellers. The similarity in most respects of vegetation in Western Australia and in South Australia, and the identity of many plants, proves also a country of good quality lying between the two colonies; by which such plants were conveyed from one country to the other. Thus, the so called white-gum is the same tree in both colonies; the *mungat*, or raspberry-jam tree, is common to both; and also to the plains of New England, in New South Wales, where (I understand) it acquires a larger size than in Western Australia. The manch is another tree also common to the two colonies; so is the black-wattle. The grasses are many of them alike. But this similarity is not confined only to the vegetable kingdom. The birds and animals are many of them also alike. The white and the black cockatoo are common to the three colonies, as are many kinds of the smaller parrots, the kangaroo, and the kangaroo-rat, the numbat, the opossum, the native cat, and many others. And this is not only true of animals of great locomotion, or birds of long flight, as the pigeon or cockatoo, but equally so of the opossum, the quail, and the wild-turkey. The quail and the turkey are birds chiefly found in grassy lands, and neither fly to any great distance : at least the quail never does; the turkey will when much disturbed, but not otherwise. Also the water animals, as the tortoise, are to be found in both colonies; but not the platypus, which is confined to the country east of the great river Murrumbidgee and its tributary the Darling.

The natives are also alike in feature and habits, evidently the same race, with language similar in character, in both countries, with similar weapons and methods of procuring food; having also similar customs and laws.

Now, I infer from these facts, that the population, animal as well as vegetable, proceeded from one country to the other; and that many forms of vegetation in the two colonies possess no greater difference, than the difference of soil and latitude may account for; and that it may therefore be possible for men to find a route from one country to the other, by carefully noting and following the lay of the water-courses, the direction of the oases, and the nature of the geology of the country; for that no impenetrable desert exists between the countries, is evident from the passage of vegetables and animals from the one to the other. What will be the benefit, some one may ask, when such a route is discovered? Why, independent of the knowledge gained to geography, there will be the great practical good of opening the boundless pastures of Western Australia to the flocks of the already overstocked lands of the other colonies. To Western Australia the gain would be great; and to South Australia it would be equally advantageous, as it would maintain the value of stock there, which will rapidly fall when no more land can be found fit for occupation. Even with all the rapid increase of population which the great mineral abundance of that colony will continue to

create, sheep will multiply faster than the population, until they become of the same low value as in
New South Wales, where, if there be no run sold
with them, they are not worth more than the value
of the wool on their backs.

It is therefore most desirable that attempts should
be made to find a stock route from the western to
the eastern coasts.

Intra-tropical Australia is more abundantly supplied with rivers, and of a larger magnitude, than
any out of the tropics, the Murray alone excepted ;
and doubtless a journey across the island within the
tropic would present fewer difficulties than one
direct from Perth to Sydney, or Adelaide ; but,
excepting for the advancement of geographical
knowledge, there is no object to be gained by such
a journey. The best way is along the valley of the
lakes, guided as the party proceeds, by the nature
of the country.

I earnestly hope that an expedition will be sent
to make some effort to penetrate the great extent
of an unknown country, lying east of Western
Australia, as it is an object well worth the attention of the Government, or of the Geographical
Society.

The geology of Western Australia is not very
interesting, as the country is entirely of primary
formation to the east of the Darling range of hills :

the granite every where crowning the summit of the hills, and the immense plains consisting entirely of granitic sand, or of hard clay containing nodules of primary rocks. This formation, which does not in Western Australia consist of the stratified primary series, as in South Australia, cannot be expected to yield the abundant mineral riches that the strata of South Australia exhibit. Probably gold may be met with, and copper and lead may be found in the Koikunenup Range, which is not entirely a granitic range, but is, I believe, capped with clay slate. The level country lying between the Darling hills and the sea is of a much more recent formation; but has not been sufficiently examined to determine its age precisely, though I imagine it will be found to belong to the pliocene tertiary formations. Certainly it contains many shells of species now living in the neighbouring ocean; and the limestone ridge running parallel with and close to the coast, and which in the colony is falsely called magnesian limestone, contains a great proportion of modern shells. The country lying between the hills and the sea contains many beds of lignite; one of which, at Nornalup, on the south coast, is more than two feet thick, and shows itself on the face of the cliff on the north shore of the estuary. Following the line of coast in any part of Australia, the geologist cannot fail to be much struck

by the evident marks of a gradual elevation of the
land; he will every where see the marks of the sea
on the cliffs, at a considerable height above its present level. At Cape Chatham, on the south coast,
these sea-marks are visible 300 feet above the present level of the ocean; and can be seen on the
face of the rocks, in the hills at some distance from
the coast. On my journey to Nornalup, I discovered
a lake containing shells in abundance, which appeared to me, and were also considered by the late
Dr. Hinds (Surgeon, Royal Navy) a skilful concho-
logist, to be a littoral species, common to the shores
of various parts of the globe. These shells, of no
interest in themselves, become excessively interesting as evidence of a connexion once existing between
this lake and the ocean, from which it is now at
least forty miles distant. This lake is not more
than 100 feet above the present level of the ocean,
and entirely separated from any other lake or
river. How, therefore, could these marine shell-
fish be living in a salt lake, unless they had continued to exist there from the period when it was a
portion of the ocean itself? That many generations
of them had lived and died in this spot, was quite
certain, from the abundance of dead shells on the
shores of this very interesting lake. Nor is the
evidence of elevation confined to the coast; all the
lakes seen by Mr. Lefroy and myself have ancient

shores much higher than the present waters ever reach. The same evidence of elevation is to be seen in the harbour of Sydney, and in Spencer's Gulf, in South Australia. At the head of the latter the shingle and rolled-stones clearly show that the gulf has formerly run much farther inland: probably to Lake Torrens, the superfluous waters of which are now discharged into the head of the gulf. The whole plain of the Murrumbidgee has been, at not a very distant date, beneath the ocean; as the Madrepores, and other fossils in the limestone cliffs of the river testify. Earthquakes have been felt in South Australia since its settlement. A very intelligent gentleman there told me that he had noted eleven since his arrival; quite perceptible enough to leave no doubt as to their character. Probably the country was elevated at each shock, in a slight degree; and perhaps before the volcano of Mount Gambier became extinct the elevatory movements were more rapid. Be that as it may, I am quite convinced that they are going on at this moment; and it would be well to make marks on the cliffs in various parts of the coast, at the present sea-level, in order to determine, after the lapse of years, the rate of elevation.

CHAPTER XXIV.

COLONIAL GOVERNMENT.

WE have already observed that a vast deal of discontent prevails in colonies. With all the natural advantages of a fruitful soil and a heavenly climate, colonists are always dissatisfied with their position; because, in a pecuniary point of view, they are always poor. And why are they so? The answer is a startling one. The excess of their abundance is the first cause of their poverty; the instability of their government, the second. They possess more than they can dispose of, and are borne down by the weight of their possessions. Place the markets of England and the labour of Ireland within their reach, and they would become *millionnaires* were they to cease to be colonists; but so long as they continue to be colonists, governed by a Power altogether distinct from that which rules over Englishmen in their native land, they will continue to be helpless, oppressed, and poverty-stricken.

They alone, among British subjects, are living under an absolute Monarchy; the caprices of which render property insecure and of uncertain value; neutralizing industry, paralyzing enterprise, and crushing with fatal authority the energies and the spirits of the people.

In the absolute recklessness of colonial rule, no sooner does private enterprise raise its head, and throw out the first feelers on the way to wealth, than a watchful government steps forward, and careful only to secure gain to itself, crushes out (in the first feebleness of existence,) the germ of vitality.

In all new countries in which the sources of wealth are imperfectly developed, the expense of applying the means necessary to their development is so enormous, as to leave but small profit to the speculator. Labour is always dear in new countries, where there is so large an outlet afforded to the labourer to escape from the toils of servitude, and become himself an occupant or an owner of the soil. All that he gains by the exchange is an ideal independence; which is, unhappily, but too attractive to the uneasy spirit of modern improvement.

The prosperity of a colony is the aggregate of individual wealth. The prosperous advance of the colonist, is, therefore, the first duty of a superintending Government. But the first aim of that watchful guardian is ever to wring from the settler as much as may be extracted by pressure. The lowest demand for land, which would be dear at half-a-crown an acre, is eight times that amount. No sooner does the settler, by his science or industry, discover some lucrative opening, than government steps in with its restrictions, its taxes and duties, and at once cuts down the budding promise. If the design be to bring to light the mineral wealth of the country, royalties are immediately imposed; and no chance of profit is left to the speculator when the rents are raised according to the probabilities of success. It is the same with all other speculations; no one will embark, even in a timber-trade, when he knows that he is placing his capital at the mercy of a grasping and short-sighted Government.

How much more lucrative, and how much more statesman-like would it prove, were our rulers to display as much good policy as the peasants of Norfolk, who do not pluck their geese until they be well feathered! Colonists, like cabbages, should be allowed to acquire the necessary strength, and attain the proper dimensions, before they be seriously operated upon. You might then cut and nick them with reasonable hope of their sprouting forth anew.

But the worst evil of an absolute Government

arises from the destruction in the minds of the people of all faith and confidence in its truth and honour.

One Secretary of State countermands the edicts of his predecessor; and as the Executive Government of a colony is composed of the paid servants of the Crown, and is merely the machine of the Secretary for the time being, the ordinances which it promulgates are distinguished by only one uniform feature —the announcement of broken promises and betrayed faith.

The inhabitants of colonies, disappointed and deceived, have no trust in their rulers, and dare not invest their capital in enterprises which may be ruined in a moment by an arbitrary edict. At one period, for instance, they may have been induced, upon the faith of the Government, to purchase remission tickets, which entitle the owner to a certain quantity of land wherever he may choose to select it. A succeeding Government confines this right of selection within certain narrow limits; whilst another decides that the holder shall be allowed to purchase with these tickets only land that is entirely valueless. At one period men are encouraged to attempt the production of colonial spirits; but no sooner is a large amount of capital expended, than it is made illegal to distil. Some parties are permitted to purchase land at a distance

from the capital : and after years of toil and expense are deprived of all protection from the
Government, and allowed no compensation for its
withdrawal.

But it were vain to attempt to enumerate the acts
of broken faith on the part of an absolute Government, from whose decree there is no appeal, and
from whose oppression no redress. The moral evil
to colonies is crushing and fatal.

The best informed among English statesmen
know nothing of colonies : but their hardihood in
legislating for them is, unhappily, equal to their
ignorance. It was only last year (1846) that the
bill for the government of Western Australia was
(according to newspaper report) opposed in the
House of Lords by a noble duke, on the ground, as
his grace alleged in an animated and interesting
speech, of the wretchedly immoral state of the
colony, arising from the system of transportation,
which so deluged the country with convicts that it
was now a perfect hell upon earth ! A noble lord,
then *Under-secretary for the Colonies*, apologised,
with the best grace he could assume, for this
lamentable state of things, and assured the noble
duke that the Government was quite aware of the
evil, and was turning its attention to a remedy for
it. Had any one of the noble lords present known
anything at all about the subject of the debate, he

might in a few words have relieved the anxiety of the Government, by informing it that Western Australia is not, and never has been, a penal settlement—that convicts are not sent thither for punishment; that even a single bush-ranger has never been known within the territory; and that, in the words of an Adelaide journal, " it is as free from stain as any of the rural districts of England."

Another Australian colony (that of Port Phillip) calls for the attention of Government more imperatively, perhaps, than any other of these settlements. At present an appendage to Sydney, but situated at a most inconvenient distance from that capital, it is compelled to remit thither between fifty and one hundred thousand pounds annually for rates, taxes, and duties, not a tithe of which ever finds its way back again. It is deprived of roads, bridges, and all public works of importance, solely because it is friendless at home, voiceless and unrepresented. Might Englishmen be made to feel that interest in colonies which in general they are ever ready to accord to the unfortunate, they would glow with indignation at the wrongs, the injustice, and the oppression under which the inhabitants of distant settlements bend in silence. " If you don't keep your colonies in a state of dependence," are the memorable words of Lord Stanley, in May, 1846, " of what use are they ?" Such has ever been the

narrow-minded and unstatesman-like policy of the
British Government. And yet even the infant
colonies of the empire, though fettered, cramped,
and swathed like the young progeny of the Esquimaux, are useful still to the Mother Country. They
afford the best market for her produce; and when
freed from the pressure of their bonds, like
plants released from the torturing confinement of
their earthenware prison, and allowed to extend
their roots abroad in the free soil of Nature, they
will display new strength and viridity, and bring
forth fruit in increased abundance. Her Majesty's
present Secretary of State for the Colonies (Earl
Grey) entered upon his office with truly liberal and
right-minded views, which, we trust, will be carried
out into operation wherever found necessary and
practicable. "There can be no doubt," said his
Lordship in the House of Lords, shortly before
taking office, "that in our colonial empire we have
the advantage of possessing warm friends and allies
in all quarters of the world, who, commanding
great natural resources, are united in heart and soul
to defend our trade and our interests, and to take
part with us in all contests against our enemies.
We have garrisons of the cheapest kind in every
quarter of the universe. On the other hand, the
colonies have this inestimable advantage—they have
the glory and security to be derived from an in-

timate connexion with the greatest, the most civilized, and the most powerful nation on the face of the earth. They have the glory—and they feel it to be a glory—of calling themselves British subjects, and feeling that in defence of their interests and best rights, the power and might of this country are ready at any moment to be called forth and exercised in their behalf. This is a substantial advantage of the most important kind to the colonies; and they are fully sensible of it. And if with this we pursue a liberal policy, and extend to them the dearest privilege of Englishmen—*the privilege of self-government, and do not vexatiously intermeddle with their internal affairs;* in short, if we pursue a liberal policy towards them, both commercially and politically, we shall bind them to us with chains which no power on earth may break, and the connexion between the parent state and those great dependencies may continue until they far exceed us in population."

These are generous sentiments and profound truths, and they have shed the bright beams of Hope over that vast colonial empire to which they refer.

In legislating for colonies, let it not be forgotten that one of the chief drawbacks to their prosperity is the want of confidence in the stability and permanency of existing regulations. There can be no success, and there can be no safety, whilst those regulations and laws are liable to the influence of peculiar views or individual caprice. It is the people themselves, for whose government the laws are intended, who should be allowed to impose, to modify, or to expunge them.

The predominating evil in colonies is THE WANT OF CONFIDENCE AND FAITH IN THE GOVERNMENT.

CHAPTER XXV.

ONE OF THE ERRORS OF GOVERNMENT. — ADVENTURE OF THE
BRAMBLE.

It has ever been considered one of the first
principles of good government, that a frequent and
ready communication and intercourse should be
maintained between the ruling power and the possessions subject to its authority. The first act of
Roman sway was ever to lay down good lines of
road through the conquered country; and nothing
has tended so much to maintain the authority of the
United States over the Red Indians of America, as
the formation of roads through the wilderness.
The rulers of Great Britain entertain the opinion
that when they have once seized upon a distant
country, and thrown into it a handful of troops and a
few of their importunate friends, with the title of
government officers, they have done all that is required of them. They wait with resignation for
any account that may be brought of the progress of
the new colony, by some wandering merchant-
vessel. Despatches, frequently dated twelve months

previously, during which time they have been
making the tour of all the oceans at present known
upon the globe, are brought to Downing Street;
and are then thrown aside, or at least are never
attended to, probably because they are too old to
be deemed interesting.   No matter how pressing
and immediate the wants of the colony, chance
alone affords the opportunity of making their necessities known at home.   Letters and despatches
accumulate in the Post-office; no vessel arrives
bringing intelligence from England, or offering to
take away a mail: the Colonial Secretary, having
exhausted every official resource in the way of mental occupation, looks out at the window, and medi-
tates upon quail-shooting.   His Excellency the
Governor, questions the possibility of adding another despatch to the hundred and fifty already
composed in illustration of the art of making despatches, as Soyer makes soup, out of nothing ; and
oppressed by the subject, becomes dormant in his
chair of state ; the clerks in the neighbouring
offices no longer exhibit the uplifted countenance
which, as justly observed by Sallust, distinguishes
man from all other creatures ; nothing is to be seen
of them but masses of hair in wild profusion, and
right hands extended on the table, still mechanic-
ally grasping steel-pens, whilst every face lies flat-
tened upon a paper-case, and sleep and silence,

broken only by sighs and snores, reign throughout the building. Universal stagnation prevails among government people ; and merchants and store-keepers appear to be much in the same condition. The only person in office who is kept in a constant state of fever, is the unhappy Post-Master-General, who is hourly called upon to state when he is going to make up a mail for England. In vain he apologizes for the non-arrival of ships ; there is something radically wrong in his department, for which he is expected to answer ; and dark denunciations are muttered in his ear, until worn out with anxiety and nervousness, he loses his appetite, and gradually withers away, like grass in the oven.

And when at length a vessel arrives accidentally from Van Dieman's Land, or perhaps from America, the Master at first demurs about taking a mail, under the idea that it may convey letters giving information of the state of markets that he desires should be known only to himself and his employers ; but finally consents ; and then, having received the mail on board, carries it about with him from port to port, until, at the conclusion of a long voyage, having occasion to empty his vessel in order to smoke out the rats, he discovers the forgotten boxes, and conscientiously sends them ashore.

But if it be vexatious and inconvenient to have only this uncertain means of despatching our letters

to England, how much more annoying is it to have
no regular and stated time for receiving them from
home! What could be more painful than to have
to wait twelve months before you can receive an
answer to an inquiry; and what more destructive
to the interests of commerce? How many fluctua-
tions are there in the state of the markets during
those twelve months!

It is one of the greatest of evils to have no
regular post-office communication between the
Mother Country and her colonies, and the interests
of trade in both greatly suffer by it.

Much has been said lately of establishing steam
communication with Sydney. A committee of
Sydney merchants has been appointed in London
to consider the subject, and the restless and indefatigable Lieut. Waghorn has written a pamphlet
showing how it may be done, provided the Government will contribute £100,000 per annum towards
the project. He proposes that a branch line of
steamers shall be established, to proceed from Sincapore by the north of New Holland, touching at
Port Essington, and through Torres Straits to
Sydney, and probably on to Van Dieman's Land.
But why follow such a route as this, through the
most dangerous channel in the world, where even
steamers would have to lie-to at night (as the
Lieutenant admits), and where light-houses would

have to be erected and kept up at an extravagant cost? Why take such a route, which presents not a single place to call at, except Port Essington, a miserable spot, intended only as a kind of refuge for shipwrecked mariners, possessing no commercial or agricultural inhabitants, and only enjoying the advantages and the society of a Governor, a handful of soldiers, and three white women? Why insist upon expending so much public money, and encountering so many dangers, without conferring a single additional benefit upon the Australian colonies, when the route by the south of New Holland is so obvious, so practicable, and so superior? The projectors talk of making Port Essington a depôt for coal; but why not make this depôt in Western Australia? During the summer months, from 1st October to 1st April, the steamers might touch at Fremantle; and during the winter months, at Port Gladstone, fifteen miles to the southward, affording a sheltered harbour where ships may ride securely within one hundred yards of the shore. Coal mines will probably soon be at work in the colony, vast beds of that mineral having been discovered, thus offering every inducement to steam-vessels to touch here. Nor could anything be more advantageous, considering the great interests that England now has at stake in these seas, than to form a general depôt in this colony, where her

Majesty's steamers and ships-of-war might refit on occasion. As there is no other spot in all New Holland, Van Dieman's Land, or New Zealand, where first-rate ship-timber may be obtained, and where *iron, coal*, and *copper*, are also procurable in abundance, this colony offers advantages for the formation of a Government Dock-yard and depôt (at Port Gladstone), that must be acknowledged by every unprejudiced person.

Objections may be raised to doubling Cape Lewin during the winter season; but let the steamers stand well out to sea, and there would be no difficulty. The time lost would not exceed that spent in lying-to in Torres Straits during the night. Our colonial schooner, the 'Champion,' goes round Cape Lewin at all seasons.

We would propose that the mail steamers, instead of branching off from Sincapore, as proposed by Lieut. Waghorn, should depart from Point de Galle, Ceylon, make direct for Swan River, there take in coal, and pass on to Adelaide, South Australia, and thence to Van Dieman's Land, .where they might put the Melbourne and Sydney mails on board of the steamer already plying between Van Dieman's Land and those places. By this route the Sydney people would receive their letters quite as soon as though their interests alone had been consulted, according to the desire of the

disinterested committee before alluded to; whilst
Van Dieman's Land would gain a few days, and
South Australia and Western Australia would
be allowed to share· in the general advantage,
from which they would otherwise be entirely ex-
cluded.

But the Government and the public would also
be gainers by the route which we suggest. It
would be much cheaper to them, because it would
be much more profitable to the company that carried it out. The colony of South Australia is now
a populous country, and becomes more so every
year; but the Steam Company would carry no passengers and no goods for South Australia (perhaps
not even for Van Dieman's Land), if the route to
Sydney were to be by Port Essington and Torres
Straits. The two colonies of South and Western
Australia deriving no benefit from such a course,
could give no support to the company. Government hitherto has resisted the efforts of the Sydney
merchants, and refused to sanction the proposal of
Mr. Waghorn, but chiefly upon the ground of
expense. And there is no doubt that Ministers
would be guilty of a gross misdemeanour, were they
to consent to apply £100,000 per annum of the
public money in furtherance of a scheme designed
for the exclusive benefit of a single colony. It is
the duty of Government to see that any sum which

may be granted shall be so applied as to confer the most extensive benefit upon all the Australian colonies. That measures ought to be immediately taken to ensure a regular communication between the home country and every one of her colonies is a matter of no doubt to us. The want of this has long appeared to be one of the grand errors of colonial legislation. Let us hope that the day is not far distant when this crying evil shall be remedied. Now that steam navigation has come so generally into use, there is no valid reason why it should not be made the means of uniting together, as it were, the different outposts of the empire, drawing them more closely towards their parent country as to a common centre. It is full time that a greater appearance of sympathy were exhibited at home for those distant settlements which have now become the principal markets for British produce, and which, therefore, deserve something more at the hand of Government than what they have so long been accustomed to find— alternate periods of tyranny and neglect.

By far the greater portion of English merchant- ships are engaged in trading to the colonies; our manufactures there find their principal mart; our surplus population is there cheaply provided with maintenance and a home. These are the grounds on which the colonies lay claim to the fostering care of the Mother Country, and we trust the days are at hand that will see it afforded.

The first step must be to ensure a regular and frequent intercourse between the countries, without which there can be no real protection; without which there is no sufficient encouragement given to trade; and the parent state can therefore reap but little advantage, comparatively, from a colony whose powers are only imperfectly developed.

Since the above remarks were written, accounts have reached England of the arrival at Fremantle of her Majesty's surveying vessel ' Bramble,' Commander Lieutenant Yule, after passing some time in Torres Straits and on the coast of New Guinea.

Mr. Yule having kindly placed the notes of his voyage at the disposal of a friend in the colony, they were partially published in one of the local journals in the month of January last. The portion relating to Torres Straits is instructive. The ' Bramble' sailed from Port Jackson about the end of December 1845, in company with the ' Castlereagh' tender, Lieut. Aird, Commander. Touching at Moreton Bay, Mr. Yule visited his old acquaintance, Captain Wickham, R. N., late in command of H. M. S. ' Beagle,' and now a settler on the Brisbane. In the words of the journal referred to, " the ' Bramble' proceeded slowly to the northward, being much delayed by the bad

sailing of the tender." The voyage presents
nothing worthy of notice, until the arrival of the
ships in Torres Straits, when it is impossible to help
being struck with the commentary which Mr. Yule
unconsciously affords upon the *perfect safety* of
that passage, now so much vaunted by the advocates of the northern route. While the ' Bramble'
and ' Castlereagh' were lying off Sir Charles Hardy's
Islands, the latter being deficient in ballast, Mr.
Aird was despatched with the boats to look for
the *wreck* of the ' Maid of Athens' and the *wreck* of
the ' Martha Ridgway,' with the view of procuring
some; and having failed in discovering the former,
and therefore in procuring a sufficient supply, he
was again sent to the *wreck* of the ' Sir Archi-
bald Campbell' for the same purpose. So much
for Torres Straits!

Mr. Yule strongly recommends Cairncross Island
as the best station for obtaining wood and water
for vessels navigating the straits, there being abundance of both easily procurable, and even large
timber, if required. On this island they shot four
megapodii, and observed many of their nests, some
of which Mr. Yule describes as being twelve feet
high, and upwards of fifty feet in circumference.

On Friday, the 10th April, they made the coast
of New Guinea, which presented a low and thickly-
wooded coast-line, backed by mountains of mag-

nificent height and beauty; the country being apparently very rich, with many villages, embowered in cocoa-nut trees, scattered along the shore. While coasting along, in search of a convenient place to land, they encountered a native vessel of most extraordinary size and character, which we will allow Mr. Yule to describe in his own words :—

"At daybreak, as the sun was rising, I was very much struck with the grandeur of some very distant mountains in a south-eastern direction—one in particular, the outline of whose summit was only visible above the intervening clouds; immense ranges of mountains were also distinctly visible this side of it, extending in a N.W. and S.E. direction. It is seldom the rising sun has disclosed to my sight so splendid a view as then presented itself; but in a few minutes, when the sun's disk appeared, the beautiful scene vanished, leaving only inferior cloud-topped mountains visible, together with the rich and undulating foreground. We shortly afterwards saw the strange sail seen last night. Although she was much nearer, she proved more unaccountable than before. As there was not sufficient wind to enable us to weigh, I resolved to send Mr. Pollard in the second gig to take a nearer view of this extraordinary vessel. I watched the boat until Mr. Pollard must have gone nearly five miles from us, when the boat's sails appeared a mere speck when close to the wonderful stranger. On this officer's return, he informed me he had approached within bow-shot of the vessel, which proved to be a gigantic double canoe, which he conceives must have measured fifty or sixty feet long, kept apart and together by a platform from fifteen to twenty feet broad, which extended nearly the whole length of the canoes, the after-end being square with the sterns of the boats; six or eight feet of this was left clear for the three steersmen, who guided the vessel with three long paddles over the stern.   With the exception of this part of the platform, the whole was covered by a strong, well-built house, made of cane, the roof being flat, and about five or six feet above the platform.   This roof answered the purpose of an upper deck, affording the crew the means of conveniently walking on it.   This extraordinary craft was propelled by two large mat sails, each spread between two bamboo masts, the heels of which were fixed in the same step, the mastheads being spread (athwartships) from twenty to thirty feet asunder, the sail being triangular between these bamboo masts, which were supported by diagonal shores fore and aft on either side; besides these two large sails, the canoe had numerous smaller (square) ones suspended from the principal masts; there was also a small square sail forward.   The whole of the spars and rigging was ornamented with a sort of flags and streamers.   Mr. Pollard thinks that he saw about forty or fifty people on the roof, several of whom were in the act of stringing their bows; except this precaution on the part of the strangers, there was no demonstration of hostility. After taking a good view of this most extraordinary canoe, Mr. Pollard returned; and she ultimately was wafted out of sight.   Whence she came, or where bound, still remains to me a problem.

"At noon I obtained the latitude, which was 8° 3′ S.; longitude, by chronometer, 145° 28′ E.

"In the afternoon the 'Castlereagh' was visited by two small canoes, with eight men, who had come off from a village we discovered abreast of us.   The natives brought off a few cocoa-nuts and some bows and arrows, which they readily bartered for such trifles as were given in exchange."

The lofty mountain which so much excited Mr. Yule's admiration, was named by him Mount Victoria, and between it and the shore were several ranges of inferior altitude, which gave him "every reason to believe that the lower regions were well watered and fertile."

Having fixed upon a favourable spot for commencing his triangulation behind a promontory which served to conceal them from the view of a native village which they saw at no great distance, Mr. Yule went ashore in the first gig with five seamen and one marine, accompanied by Mr. Sweetman, in the second gig, with three seamen and two marines, all well armed, and proceeded to hoist the Union Jack and take possession of the place in the name of her Majesty Queen Victoria. Having successfully performed this duty, and obtained the observations he required, Mr. Yule thought it high time to return on board; but the surf had in the meantime increased so heavily, that in the attempt the second gig was swamped, and every thing in her, including the arms, lost, except the quintant and chronometer, the boat herself being with difficulty saved by being towed outside the surf by the other gig. The rest of the adventure we shall give in Mr. Yule's own words :—

"At this time I observed the 'Castlereagh' about two miles beyond Cape Possession, under sail ; I therefore made signs to Mr. Wright, in the first gig, to tow the second gig towards the 'Castlereagh,' which I concluded would attract Mr. Aird's attention. In this I was not mistaken, as the 'Castlereagh' was immediately anchored about a mile and a half off, and her boats sent to the relief of ours.   In the interim I determined that every thing which was washed on shore should be collected together, after which we all huddled close under a bush near the beech, whence we could see our boats and be hid from the view of the natives as much as possible.   The 'Castlereagh's' boats having at length closed with the 'Bramble's, the second gig was soon baled out, when all four boats pulled up abreast of us outside of the surf, which had continued to increase ; the 'Castlereagh' at the same time weighed, which I confess alarmed me much, as I knew very few persons could be left on board after she had dispatched two boats' crews ; I therefore concluded we were discovered by the natives beyond Cape Possession.   I was in a few moments confirmed in my fears by seeing Mr. Andrews prepare to push his boat through the surf.   I waved him back, when he energetically pointed towards Cape Possession.   I fully understood his signs (that natives were coming), but still waved him off, as I knew his gallant attempt to relieve us would fail, and that he and his boat's crew would be added to those already in distress on shore ; he, however, pushed through the surf, when, as I expected, this boat was upset, and all his arms, ammunition, &c. lost.   At the same moment we observed crowds of natives coming round the point of Cape Possession, armed with spears, clubs, and stone axes.   Our arms and ammunition had been all lost or destroyed ; our situation was therefore most defenceless, and, I may say, our retreat hopeless ; those boats at the back being unable to afford us the least relief.   I then thought it best to show no signs of fear or mistrust, but to make friends with the natives, and amuse them, until the next tide should enable a boat to back through the surf. In the interim, Mr. Andrews, with his four men, and assisted by some others, made three attempts to launch his boat, which failed, and she was ultimately dashed in pieces against the rocks.   I advanced alone with playful gestures, waving a branch of green leaves, in token of peace.   One man pointed a spear at me, but the others stared at me with more wonder depicted on their countenances than ferocity. I then offered them some bits of tobacco, which they would not approach near enough to take from my hands. This shyness, unfortunately, did not continue long; for when the main body came up, amounting to eighty or ninety men, armed, they became troublesome, and laid their hands on everything they could get hold of that was lying on the beach. To these robberies I attempted to put a stop, and made them some presents instead; but the savages must have known our helpless condition, and became every moment more daring and rapacious; and, to add to our tribulation, we observed two large canoes, each containing thirty or forty men, come round Possession Point, and heave to between the 'Castlereagh' and the boats, as if with the intention of cutting off the latter. The 'Castlereagh' could not unfortunately take advantage of her guns by firing grape or canister, as we were completely intermixed with the natives. At this critical stage of our anxiety, the second gig, at all hazards, was veered through the surf, and, to our great joy, four or five men were drawn off in safety. A second attempt was made, and succeeded. Then came the awful moment for us who waited for the last trip; for only a few moments before, I baulked a native when taking a deliberate aim at one of our last men who embarked. The natives now, seeing our numbers decrease, laid hands on us in the most violent manner. My quintant was first wrested from my coxswain, who in a tone of grief made known the circumstance. I immediately turned round and exclaimed 'Oh! don't part with that;' but it was too late; and when I endeavoured to recover it, I found a club wielded over my head. In making my escape from this wretch I was secured by four others, who first took the government micronometer, which was slung round my neck. I then endeavoured to struggle out of their clutches, and escape with the pocket chronometer and note-book, but these, as well *as every article of clothing I had about my body*, were stripped off; when the second gig was opportunely again backed in, and in this forlorn state Mr. Pollard, the two marines, and I, waded off, and were dragged into the boat. We then went on board the 'Castlereagh,' which was at anchor about a mile from the shore; the canoes slowly made off to the north-westward, after we had embarked. The boats having been hoisted up and secured, we got the anchor up and proceeded out to the 'Bramble,' and anchored close to her at 6h. 30m. p.m. I immediately afterwards returned to the 'Bramble,' truly thankful for our having escaped with our lives. The loss of instruments grieved me exceedingly, particularly as the nature of the coast rendered it next to impossible to effect a safe landing to attempt their recovery. From the account I heard of the ferocity of the natives where the 'Fly' had been surveying last year on this coast, I confess I fully expected death would be my fate in a few minutes, and thought of the similar position poor Captain Skying was in when murdered at Cape Roso. If we had been possessed of six or eight muskets and plenty of ammunition, I think the natives might easily have been checked, but being defenceless, my only hope was to dissemble my fears and amuse them, to give us time until we could effect our escape. These people varied in complexion from black to a light copper colour; they appeared well made and active; all of them were ornamented, but some much more so than others; their ear-rings were made of rings of tortoiseshell, a number of them being fastened together, and suspended to the lower parts of the ears, in which are holes stretched so large as to admit a man's thumb being passed through them; the cartilage dividing the nostrils is perforated in like manner."

This adventure of our old friends of the 'Bramble' appears to me sufficiently interesting to excuse my having wandered through Torres Straits in order to record it.

CHAPTER XXVI.

SCIENTIFIC DISCOVERIES.——KANGAROO HUNTING.——EMUS.——LOST
IN THE BUSH.

THERE can be no doubt as to the truth of the
axiom that "facts are stubborn things." Right or
wrong, they seem to persist in a resolution to
force conviction upon a man however reluctant he
may be.

Sturdy facts are never wanting in support of
erroneous views; and more false conclusions are
drawn from them than from the subtlest arguments
of the sophist.

When your theory is once confirmed by a fact,
the question is considered decided, and no further
argument is admissible. I had two theories not
long ago, the pursuit and investigation of which
gave me a good deal of pleasure; they were built
upon facts, and therefore they were indisputable.

My first theory was upon the amount of evaporation at Perth during the summer months.

The excessive dryness of the atmosphere proved
that the evaporation at the end of the rainy, or

winter season, must be very great indeed. My friend, Mr. H., had an hygrometer, which he kept in a small room adjoining that in which he usually sat; and this hygrometer afforded the ground-work for our theories. It proved most satisfactorily that the evaporation exceeded every thing of the kind known in any other part of the globe. It was clear that our atmosphere was drier than that of a brick-kiln when burning its best. But the great beauty and novelty of the theory was, that the evaporation was greater at night than in the day time.

This certainly puzzled us a good deal at first; but when once you are sure of your facts, it is astonishing how soon you come to mould your theory so as to make it perfectly agree with them, and manage to reconcile yourself to the most startling contradictions. After satisfying himself of the truth of the fact—that the evaporation was really greater by night than by day—Mr. H. proceeded to prove philosophically that nothing could be more reasonable than such a circumstance. From all that I could make out of his arguments, which were extremely logical and ingenious, it seemed clear that as every thing in this country is diametrically opposite to every thing in the old country, it was perfectly consistent with the regulations of nature in Australia, that evaporation should be greater at night than during the day-time. Moreover, he placed great reliance upon the attraction of the moon.

For my part, seeing that facts were on his side, I embraced his views with ardour; and went about as an apostle, proclaiming the new tidings far and wide. It was one of those astonishing truths in science that come suddenly and un-expectedly upon mankind—like those connected with electricity—that take the reason captive, and are beyond the reach of human investigation. Men usually appeared incredulous when the theory was first broached to them; but when convinced of the fact, as proved indisputably by the hygro-meter, they were compelled to acknowledge the truth, and forthwith looked upon it as a matter of course.

As the weather grew warmer—when the ther-mometer stood daily at about 86° in a cool room—the nocturnal evaporation increased. At length it grew to such a pitch, that the tube of the hy-grometer containing the water was exhausted in a couple of nights. Notwithstanding the astonish-ment of Mr. H., he was enraptured at the trium-phant confirmation of his theory. He devoted every moment he could spare from public duties, to the compilation of a learned and voluminous treatise upon the subject. He looked upon him-

self as destined to be considered one of the
master-philosophers of the age, the promulgator
of a new and wondrous theory, based not only
upon sound argument, but upon long observation
and indisputable facts. When any one ventured
to raise a doubt, he would smile with that ineffable
sweetness which distinguishes a man conscious of
his superior knowledge and sources of information.
I, his enthusiastic adherent, picked up the crumbs
of instruction that fell from his table; and dealt
forth mysterious hints of the scientific errors about
to be corrected by the observations and treatises
of Mr. H., who was now generally known to have
forwarded an account of his discoveries to some of
the learned Societies of London; and the English
papers were perused with avidity, in the hope of
finding that due honour had been paid to his
merits.

As he walked along the streets he was looked
upon with additional reverence. He had raised
the renown of Western Australia, and was now
considered to be at once its *decus et tutamen*. The
idlers who congregated in small knots about lun-
cheon-time at the corners of the streets, began to
talk of a statue in the market-place.

Suddenly, however, the philosopher secluded
himself from the vulgar gaze. The public wondered, and then became alarmed. The philosopher

had taken to his bed. After some days I was admitted to his presence, and found him greatly enfeebled for want of rest. It was evident there was something that weighed upon his mind. After many ineffectual efforts, many sighs and some blushes, he faltered forth a confession that he feared our theory, (he seemed now, for the first time, kindly solicitous to share the merit of the discovery,) of evaporation being greater at night than in the day-time, was not well founded. An electric shock, shivering the funny-bones of both elbows, could not have startled me more. What did he mean? He continued, that one night whilst engaged upon a new hygrometrical treatise, he had sat up till a very late hour; the door of the room which contained the instrument was open, and the light from his lamp fell directly upon it. Absorbed in profound speculations, his eye occasionally rested upon the little instrument which stood upon a table. There it was—the pillar of his fame. It seemed to dilate in dimensions until it rivalled the column in the Place Vendôme, and on the top of it was a figure, less sturdy than that of Napoleon. Suddenly his vision was broken, and his thoughts were recalled from the future to the present, by seeing a living object move along the table, and quietly approach the foot of his column. Appalled and paralyzed, he sat immovable whilst he beheld an actual mouse, unrestrained by any scientific considerations, place its profane snout in the bowl of the hygrometer, and drink deliberately until its thirst was satisfied. It then retired, and other mice soon came trotting along the table and did the same.

Mr. H. is a man of great self-control. He did not tear his remaining locks, or commit any other rash act, but with all the calmness of despair he set fire to the unfinished treatise, and saw it consumed; then he retired to bed, a desolate individual, and rose not again for several days.

My next theory was entirely my own. I claimed all the merit of it, and felt the utmost pangs of jealousy when any one ventured to assert that *he* had long ago suspected it. Built upon a solid foundation of facts, I maintained an opinion entirely at variance with that of Professor Owen and certain Parisian professors, and satisfied myself, at least, that the young of the kangaroo, and of other marsupial animals, is produced, not in the usual way, but from the teat of the dam. And although this theory is, and must be erroneous, I can even yet scarcely bring myself to believe it so—with such fidelity do we cling to error. There are many men in the colony who have been for years in the constant, almost daily, habit of killing kangaroos, and they have consequently had opportunities of

observing the young ones in every stage of de-
velopement.　Females have been killed with young
ones hanging to the nipple, about half an inch
long—the form not fully developed, a mere fœtus,
presenting no appearance of active vitality.　The
nipple to which it is attached is not merely placed
in the mouth of the fœtus, but extends into its
stomach, where it serves the purposes of the um-
bilical cord in other animals, whilst the lips grow
round it, so that it cannot be removed without
rupturing the skin.　A little older, and it becomes
evidently possessed of vitality—a quickened fœtus.
The pouch of the doe is closed up until the birth
of the young one; and gradually enlarges to accom-
modate the inhabitant.

There are other marsupial animals, of the size of
rabbits, that are found with eight or ten young
ones, or rather small fœtuses, similarly attached to
the nipples of the parent.

Now I could not conceive how creatures with
long sharp claws, though provided with flexible
wrists or joints, should be able to take up the newly
produced little lump of inanimate flesh, and thrust
a long, soft, yielding nipple down into the depths
of the stomach.　I collected a number of *facts* to
prove the contrary—but the question is now considered to be set at rest by the observations of
French naturalists, and therefore I have quietly

strangled my theory, but am still occasionally haunted by its ghost.

I may mention here that male kangaroos are sometimes found provided with pouches; but these, I conceive, are *lusus Naturæ*.

This allusion to kangaroos (being good for nothing else) may serve as an introduction to a hunting excursion. A party of us started from Perth, equipped in the manner already described in the chapter upon Wild Cattle.

We rode to the Canning to breakfast, at the house of the ———s, where we found the table ready spread with coffee, grilled fowls, eggs, ham, &c. The room was a good one, having French windows, looking out upon park-like scenery, among which the Canning River pursued its lazy course. There was also a piano belonging to the sister of our hosts, then absent on a visit. One of her brothers informed us that he had availed himself of her absence to abstract sundry of the wires from the piano in order to make bell-wires, which he thought was turning the piano to good account.

After breakfast we loaded our bullock-cart with our goods, and left it in charge of a servant whom we appointed to meet us at a certain spot where we were to bivouac for the night. The only disagreeable part of travelling in Australia is the scarcity of water, except at the end of winter, when all the gullies are filled. Unless, therefore, the ground be well known, it is always advisable to take a native, who can inform you where the pools or springs are situated. Four of us set out, well mounted, and attended by a native on foot, and five kangaroo dogs. These dogs are descended from a cross between a bloodhound and a greyhound, and combine strength, fleetness, scent, and sight. As it was the middle of winter (late in June) the air was cool and pleasant, and the sun bright and joyous, as he always is here. We were all in high spirits, anticipating excellent sport, as the country to which we were going abounds with game of great variety—kangaroos, emus, quail, and turkeys, or bustards. A rough coarse scrub, interspersed with small quantities of grass, overspread the sandy soil. The only animal we saw for some time was an opossum, which the native discovered in a tree and climbed up for. I examined its pouch, but there was no young one within it. At length we caught a glimpse of a kangaroo hopping along at a distance, and we galloped off in full chase, but he was too far ahead for the dogs to make anything of it; so we lost him. Disconcerted and vexed we drew together again after a short run, but had scarcely done so before we emerged upon an open prairie, where on our right we beheld three kangaroos hopping away

at a gentle pace. The kangaroo uses only his
hind legs in running. The leg presses the ground
from the hock to the toes, and its strong sinews
enable the animal to bound forward with immense
leaps; the heavy tail vibrating behind keeps him
steady. Four of the dogs rushed after the game,
followed by all the horsemen, at full gallop,
hallooing and shouting vociferously. A more
animated sight could scarcely be conceived; three
graceful kangaroos bounding away in a line, with
four large greyhounds laying well after them, and
the hunters chiveying along, and dashing through
brushwood and thickets like whirlwinds. The
kangaroos, however, fairly beat us; they gained a
thick wood, dashed through it and into a swamp
beyond, and there we lost sight of them. We all
returned to the side of the wood, and waited for
the dogs, who came back with hanging heads and
drooping tail, completely blown. All returned but
one—the oldest and most sagacious of them. He
had not gone with the four which followed the
heels of the kangaroos, but had made a short cut
to the left, so that he was in the wood almost as
soon as the kangaroos, whilst the other dogs were
still a long way behind. We waited patiently for
old Tip (of whom honourable mention has been
made before); his master, Tom H., asserting confidently that he had killed. At length, as we were

standing talking together, we suddenly perceived
Tip among us. His master examined his mouth,
and declared he had killed; then saying, "Show,
Tip, show!" the dog turned round, and trotted off
before us; and going into the swamp took us to
the spot where the kangaroo lay dead.

It is not all kangaroo dogs that can be taught to
show game, and those that do so are therefore
highly prized. It is a very pleasing sight to
observe how proud a dog is of this accomplishment.
He will come quietly back to his master, and
oftentimes lay himself down as if he were afraid
the other dogs should suspect he had got something to tell, and would run off in search of it.
And when his master gives the signal, he deliberately proceeds to lead the way, snarling at the
other dogs whenever they run before him, and seem
likely to arrive first at the spot. Sometimes he
tries to deceive them by going in a wrong direction,
and when the others have started off, full of eagerness, as if they themselves (the senseless fools!)
were inviting people to follow, and were anxious to
show them the game, the old dog will rapidly turn
aside, evidently laughing in his sleeve, and dash
forward to the spot where he left the carcase.
There you will find him standing over it; and as
you ride up he will give a faint wag of his tail, as
though he were glad that you are pleased with

him, and yet he cannot help feeling that he is not properly rewarded. His gaunt ribs and melancholy eye speak of his hungry stomach; he seems to remember that he receives from his rough master more kicks than caresses, but still he does his duty, and will do so to the last; and denies himself even a mouthful of the prey, which, but for him, would lie undiscovered in the thicket. I used to know an old show-dog who displayed so much thought and sagacity, that I never was in his company without feeling for him a certain degree of respect. Whenever struck by brutes of lower order than himself, he did not howl or display his· teeth, but slunk aside with a look of deep sorrow and reproach.

In the evening we bivouacked near a small pool of water, where the cart joined us, according to previous arrangement. The horses were tethered out and fed; a good fire was kindled, and with kangaroo steaks, cold fowls and ham, and brandy and water, we managed to make a tolerable supper. A fence against the wind was constructed of upright sticks, and leaves of the black-boy (Xanthorea, or grass-tree) resembling rushes, only brittle; and with a good fire at our feet we were exceedingly warm and comfortable. The wild dogs uttered their doleful, wailing cries around our camp during the night, and caused our own frequently to sally forth and give them chase.

We had kangaroo curry for breakfast next morning; and having fed our horses, and sounded to saddle, set out again in pursuit of game.

Proceeding across some plains, interspersed with swamps and thickets, we soon perceived a herd of about a dozen kangaroos feeding and hopping about. Keeping a covert in line before us, we tried to get near them, but they soon made off, bounding away like a herd of deer, which they much resemble at a distance. The dogs started after them at full speed; and with loud halloos and bounding hearts the horsemen spurred their steeds, and scoured along the plain. There are, unfortunately, no fences in this country, but there are a thousand worse obstructions—fallen trees, thick clumps of black-boys extending right across the plain, and therefore not to be avoided; woods through which the game dashes at speed, and where you must follow at the risk of striking head or limbs against the trunks or branches of trees, or else you will be thrown out. Then of course you don't like to be last, and you don't like to allow the gallant captain, who is spurring at your side, the opportunity of bragging at mess that he alone kept near the dogs, which you know he would be delighted to do. So, determined to ride against the captain at any rate, you keep your horse and yourself well together, and flinch at nothing;

dashing through thickets, tearing over rough
ground, steering between trees, ducking your head
under boughs, and twitching up first one leg and
then the other to save them from being smashed
against black-boys or banksias.   You clear the
wood, and emerge again upon a plain; the kangaroos are bounding along, some three hundred yards
in advance, the dogs lying well up to them; and
now the latter have fixed upon one of the herd,
whom they pursue with resolute fierceness.   The
others escape into friendly thickets, but the doomed
one, an old buck, some six feet in height when
resting on his haunches, still holds out, though his
enemies are fast gaining upon him.

At length, finding escape impossible, he makes
for a broad mahogany tree, where he suddenly
comes to bay.   The dogs hesitate to rush in upon
him, his eye gleams with such deadly ferocity,
whilst he sits erect upon his haunches, ready to
dart the long claw of his hind leg into the first
assailant who comes within reach.

A kangaroo in this position is no despicable
enemy.   He has great power in his limbs; and if
he happens to strike a dog with his claw, he
inflicts a grievous wound, and sometimes tears out
his entrails, and kills him on the spot.   He rushes
at men with the same fury, and tries to clasp them
with his fore-paws whilst he strikes at them with

Isaac A.Hirty St. Ivanʸ 1st 1841.

E.Radclyffe sc

DEATH OF THE KANGAROO.

his hind-legs. I rode up to the animal in question, dismounted, and struck him a rap on the head with a broken bough, as he rushed towards me with a fierce hissing noise. As he staggered at the blow, the dogs darted upon him and quickly despatched him.

We had several other good runs before luncheon, and then baited our horses, and allowed them to rest for two or three hours. Whilst riding towards our bivouac in the afternoon, a native who was walking at my side, and who had accompanied us all day, stopped suddenly, and, pointing with his finger, said, "Emu!" About a mile distant across the prairie were two of those large birds quietly feeding. The dogs were immediately called together, fresh vigour seemed to animate the whole party, and we proceeded to give chase in high spirits. Emus are sometimes shot with the rifle, but the usual mode of obtaining them is by hunting them with kangaroo dogs. If you happen to come near enough to them without raising alarm, they may frequently be detained, and even attracted almost up to your stirrup, by *whistling*. I have known this to be repeatedly tried with success. When you begin to whistle, the emu lifts up its head and listens with attention; soon, delighted with the sound, he walks leisurely in the direction from which it comes; then, perceiving a human

being, he pauses, seems irresolute, and finally walks
round and round you in circles gradually lessening,
until he approaches within a few yards. If his
confidence be not repaid with a bullet, he will, after
gratifying his curiosity by a good stare, quietly
walk away through his native woods. Emus are
frequently speared by the natives, who, by taking

care to stand stock-still the moment the creature
lifts up its head, manage to approach within a few
yards of them while feeding. Though the savage
may have his hand raised in the act of throwing
the spear, he remains fixed in that attitude whilst
the emu takes a survey of him. Perceiving only
an object without motion, the bird takes him for a

tree, and continues to graze, falling a victim, like other innocent things, to a misplaced confidence in its own security.

The emus ran fast, and gave us a long chase; but at length the headmost dog caught hold of the extended flapper of one of the birds, and arrested its progress; the others, coming up, soon pulled him to the ground, and by the time we reached the spot he was dead. The feathers from the tail were distributed among the party, and placed in our caps; and the legs being cut off, the rest of the bird was abandoned. The legs alone afford any meat, which is by no means a delicacy, and resembles coarse beef. Whilst the process of cutting up was going on, my attention was attracted to the movements of old Tip, who had stolen away from the party, and was now, *ventre à terre*, scouring along the edge of a belt of trees about a quarter of a mile from us. His master in vain tried to recall him, and I set off to see what he was about. Following him through the wood, I perceived him at the other side in hot pursuit of half-a-dozen kangaroos, that were bounding away some hundred yards ahead of him. It was in vain to attempt to recall him, so I foolishly followed the chase, though it was leading far away from the direction I wanted to take. Old Tip held on unflaggingly, as though this were his first run that day; and for nearly two miles we dashed along through woods and across prairies, until I began to wish myself back with my friends.   At length we lost the game in a vast swamp, covered with thick underwood, in which my horse floundered for some time in a fearful manner. Thinking it worse to return than to push through, we struggled on, in momentary danger of sinking for ever, and after great exertions got upon solid ground again.   When dismounted, to rest the horse, who panted and trembled with the efforts he had made, I called for Tip till the woods rang again, but all in vain.   At last I saw a single kangaroo, a fresh one of immense size, break cover, with Tip about forty yards in his rear.   In the ardour of the chase, all prudential considerations were given to the winds; and cheering on the gallant hound, I followed the game more determinedly than ever.   And what a race that villain kangaroo led us !—through thickets where my hunting-shirt was torn into strips, my arms and legs covered with bruises, and my face lacerated with boughs that were not to be avoided.   The villain doubled like a hare, and led us in such various directions, that I fancied we must have turned upon our steps and gone past the spot where I had parted from my friends.   Unless a man be very well accustomed to the bush, he is certain to lose himself in a few minutes.   One clump of trees is so like another—the thick swamps, the open plains, all bear such a general resemblance to one another, that you feel quite confounded whilst trying to recollect whether you have really seen them before, and can form some tolerable guess as to your position. The kangaroo was now approaching the foot of the long, even, uninteresting range of the Darling Hills; his pace was slow, he made his leaps with difficulty, and would soon have been caught, had not poor Tip been equally dead beat.

It was evident the old dog could scarcely drag himself along, but still he refused to give in. My horse, exhausted with floundering in the swamp, was completely knocked up; and for some time I had only been able to push him along at a jogtrot. Still I was no more willing to give up the chase than old Tip. It seemed to have become a point of honour that I should not desert the hound; and, moreover, feeling myself completely lost, I did not like to part from my companion; and, above all, it would never do to let the kangaroo escape after all the trouble he had given us. So we all three continued to work along as best we could.

At last my poor horse happened to set his foot in an empty water-hole, and too weak to recover himself, came down on his shoulder and side with great

violence. I threw myself off as he fell, but could not
save my foot from being crushed beneath the saddle,
and so both horse and man lay extended on the
ground. I could just see the hound and kangaroo
still struggling onward, and almost close together.
The horse made no attempt to rise, and I tried in
vain to extricate my foot; at length I managed to
flog him up, and then raised myself with difficulty.
I had not suffered much damage, though bruised,
and in some pain, but my poor horse had sprained
his shoulder, and was completely *hors de combat.*
On looking about for the chase, I fancied I could
perceive the dog lying on a little rising ground, a
few hundred yards distant; and leaving the horse, I
hopped after the game. On arriving at the spot, I
found the kangaroo and the dog lying side by side,
both alive, but completely exhausted; the one
unable to do any injury, and the other to get away.
Securing the dog with my handkerchief, I sat down,
waiting till he should be able to walk. In a few
minutes the kangaroo lifted up his head, and looked
about him; the dog sat up, panting as though his
heart would burst, and took no notice of the other.
The kangaroo, scrambling to its feet, hopped away
a few yards, and then stood still again. " Go along,
old fellow ! " said I, " you have done us abundance
of mischief, but it would be criminal to kill you
when I cannot carry home even your tail—so fare-

well!" Off he jumped, and was soon lost to view, leaving us alone—three miserable cripples, far from any shelter, and (so far as I was concerned) not knowing at all how to rejoin our friends. Tip being now able to limp on three legs, and myself upon one, we returned to the unhappy steed, who remained where I had left him, hanging down his head, and looking the image of woe.

In vain I tried to determine the direction I ought to take; trees and swamps were on all sides of me, and I could not decide whether my friends were now on my right-hand or my left. I remembered that our place of rendezvous appeared to be nearly opposite an opening in the hills, some six or eight miles distant; but there were openings in the hills on each side of me, and which was the one to be sought I could not determine. I therefore resolved to retrace the foot-marks of my horse, if possible; and set out leading the animal, having Tip limping at my side, and every now and then looking up as though he felt for the ill plight in which we all appeared. It soon became evident that the horse must be left behind; and therefore removing his saddle and bridle, I placed them at the foot of a tree, and gave him his liberty.*

* Six months afterwards he was caught among the horses of a settler on the Serpentine, perfectly sound and in excellent condition.

After going some distance, I came within view of an extensive swamp, which I fancied formed part of that I had had so much difficulty in crossing. Turning to the right, I followed its course for some time, hoping to get round it, but it seemed to extend towards the hills, cutting off all farther progress. The sun was now about to set, and getting desperate, I plunged into the thicket, and tried to push through the swamp. There was no water, but the immense quantities of bind-weed, and other thickly-growing plants, quite defied every attempt, and I was obliged to turn back again. Tip and myself had now to retrace our steps. It was getting dusk, and the state of affairs looked uncomfortable. Again we tried in vain to cross the swamp, which soon afterwards receded farther from the hills, and left a broad plain before us, which we traversed in the course of half an hour.

My foot seemed to get better with exercise, but night had now set in, and it was useless to attempt making farther progress, when we could not distinguish an object thirty feet in advance. I now found myself stumbling up a rising ground covered with trees; and here I lay down, with Tip at my side, to wait as patiently as possible for morning. The dog, I imagine, had found some water in the swamp, as he did not now seem to be suffering from thirst as I was myself. He was soon asleep, and I

envied him, for hours elapsed before I could find
repose. The land-wind, sweeping down from the
hill-side, moaned through the trees; the rising moon
shed her sickly and distorting light upon the bushes
around; and bruised and stiff, hungry, thirsty, and
uncomfortable, I felt by no means delighted with
my quarters. A fire would have been agreeable, but
there were no means of procuring one. Sleep at
last befriended me, and I did not wake until the
sun began to shed his first rays upon the tops of
the trees.

On rising I found myself exceedingly stiff, and
by no means in good condition for walking, but
there was no choice; and when Tip had got upon
his legs, and given himself a good stretch and yawn,
and licked my hand, as much as to say he had no
intention of leaving me in the lurch, we started on
our doubtful journey. In vain I tried to encourage
the dog to lead the way; he would not stir from my
side. Only once he darted after a kangaroo-rat,
and caught it before it had gone twenty yards.
This afforded a breakfast which I envied him.
I now pushed on towards the coast, but was continually intercepted by thick swamps impossible to
penetrate, and turned from the right direction.
I looked about for water, and found some at length
in a muddy hole. It was most refreshing, and revived my spirits, which had begun to flag considerably.

Mid-day was long past, and I was still rambling over plains of coarse grass, penetrating into woods, and struggling through swamps; worn almost to death with fatigue and hunger, and the pain of my ankle, now greatly swollen, I sat down at last at the foot of a mahogany-tree, in order to gain a little rest.

I knew that the hills were behind me, and the sea must be somewhere before me, but as to my precise locality, and the distance of the nearest settler's house, I was quite at a loss. In vain I tried to satisfy myself as to whether I was much to the south of the bivouac. I was growing dizzy with hunger and weariness, and no longer felt any wonder at the confusion of mind which seizes upon those who are lost in the wilderness. During the day, I had repeatedly "cooeyed" as loudly as I could, in the faint hope of attracting the attention of my friends; but no voice responded.

It was now nearly five o'clock in the evening, and I had the prospect before me of spending another night in solitude, and felt some misgivings as to whether it would not be the last of my existence.

I tried to struggle on a little farther, as it was possible that I might be close to some farm on the Serpentine; but it was difficult to move along. Tip seemed to be getting tired of this slow progress; he grew fidgety, and I fancied he had formed the base resolution of leaving me to myself. Suddenly he started off upon our traces, and I was alone without a friend.

In a few minutes I heard behind me a distant shout, and immediately afterwards a loud " cooey " met my ear. Oh how thankfully I heard it, and answered it as loudly as I could ! And then, having returned grateful acknowledgments to the Almighty for this seasonable relief, I began to walk towards the sounds, which were repeated from minute to minute. Not long afterwards I perceived a party of natives, followed by men on horseback, emerging from the trees. The latter galloped towards me, waving their hats, and shouting with friendly joy. It is due to Tip to state that he reached me first, and gave his congratulations with warm sincerity.

My friends had started at day-break with the natives, who had tracked my footsteps without once losing the trail. They had found the horse grazing near the place where I had left him, but he was too lame to be removed ; the natives had fully accounted for every trace ; they perceived that the dog and kangaroo had lain side by side, and that the latter had recovered first, and got away. They found and brought with them the saddle and bridle, and followed my steps to the swamp, through which they saw I had not been able to penetrate. And so they tracked me during the whole of the day, whilst I

was only going farther and farther from my friends.
I had wandered much more to the south than I
expected; and now, mounting a horse, we all rode
to a house on the Serpentine, where we were hospitably entertained, and where I continued until
able to return to Perth.

CHAPTER XXVII.

THE COMET.——VITAL STATISTICS.——METEOROLOGY.

ONE evening in March, 1844, whilst standing at my gate enjoying the pleasant balmy air and the conversation of a friend, our attention was attracted to a luminous appearance in the sky immediately above the horizon. We fancied that a large ship must be on fire not a great distance from the coast.

The next evening, happening to leave the house at an early hour, my eye was immediately caught by a grand novelty in the heavens. A magnificent comet extended itself over an entire fifth of the firmament. Its tail reached to the belt of Orion, whilst its nucleus, a ball of fire resembling a star of the fourth magnitude, was scarcely a degree above the horizon. It looked like a fiery messenger rushing headlong down from the very presence of GOD, bound with dread tidings for some distant world. Beautiful, yet terrible messenger, it seemed to leave its long, fiery trace behind it in its passage through the heavens. The soul of the spectator was filled with the sense of its beauty, whilst admiration was sublimed into awe. Speaking to us strange and wonderful things of the hidden Holy of Holies which it seemed to have left, it passed on its headlong journey of billions and trillions of miles with the glad speed of a love-inspired emanation from the Most High. It left us to wonder at its transient visit, and to wish in vain for its return.*

Whether it had or not any effect upon the season, I cannot say, but the ensuing six months were the most unhealthy period ever known in the colony. The natives, who were greatly alarmed by the sudden appearance of the comet, declared that it would cause many people to be *mendik* and die—so universal is the belief in the portentous and malign influence of these phenomena.

In general, as I have before observed, the climate is most salubrious. " The Comparative Statement of Deaths to the Population" proves the vast superiority of Western Australia in this respect, not only over Great Britain, but over neighbouring colonies. I refer to the able, interesting, and carefully-prepared Reports of G. F. Stone, Esq. the Colonial Regis-trar - General of Births, Marriages, and Deaths.

---

* This comet, having exactly the appearance I have de-scribed, was visible nearly a week, gradually disappearing in the northern heavens.

Taking his data from the Parliamentary Reports of 1836, he deduces the following

Comparative Statement of Deaths to the Population.

Western Australia	1 death in	94$\frac{24}{41}$
Van Diemen's Land	1 „	65$\frac{121}{130}$
Cape of Good Hope	1 „	60$\frac{1}{4}$
England	1 „	46$\frac{3}{4}$
Mauritius	1 „	44$\frac{3}{5}$

The opinions of medical men, published in different reports, a few of which happen now to lie before me, may prove interesting to some readers, and I therefore extract them briefly :—

J. M. JOHNSON, Esq. M.D. Surgeon of H. M. S. 'Sulphur :'—

" During the three years that H. M. S. 'Sulphur' was employed on that station (Western Australia) not a single death, and very few important cases of disease occurred, notwithstanding the very great exposure of her men. When exploring the country for several days, and sometimes weeks, they have been exposed to the sun; fatigued in the evening after a day's excursion, slept in the open air, (and that repeatedly in wet weather,) and suffered no inconvenience. I have no hesitation in stating that such a life in any other climate would have been productive of the most serious sickness."

WILLIAM MILLIGEN, Esq. M.D. Surgeon 6th Dragoons :—

"I have met with several individuals here, who, on leaving England, were great sufferers from dyspepsia, and diseases of the digestive organs, who have recovered their health in a wonderful degree since their arrival. Children thrive remarkably well; and I may add that every description of live stock, although collected from different countries—England, India, America, Africa, &c.—find here a congenial temperature."

JOSEPH HARRIS, Esq. Acting Government Surgeon :—

"Nothing can be more delightful than the climate generally; and its invigorating influences on the human constitution, especially those of Europeans, render it more fit for invalids than any other in the world. Several persons arrived in the colony suffering from pulmonary and bronchial affections, asthma, phthisis, hæmoptysis, or spitting of blood, hopeless of recovery in England, are now perfectly restored, or living in comparative health—measles and small-pox are unknown."

W. H. SHOLL, Esq. Government Surgeon, *pro tempore* :—

"From pulmonary complaints we are happily free; and even when these have gone to some length in other countries, removal to this climate has been of the highest possible benefit. Children are exempt from the diseases common to them in England;—small-pox, measles, scarlet-fever, and hooping-cough, are unknown here."

W. P. DINELEY, Esq. Surgeon of Fremantle Gaol:—

"We have almost a cloudless sky, a clear dry atmosphere, and a climate unsurpassed by any in the world."

Dr. FERGUSON, of Australind:—

"We have no fevers or epidemics here."

By the Registrar-General's Report for 1843, it appears that the *births* in Western Australia are about 1 to $24\frac{83}{158}$, which is a very high rate. Those readers who are fond of statistics will be pleased to learn the following rather curious fact:—In the year 1836, males were in respect to females, as about five to three, but during the following seven years, females increased 21 *per cent.* more than males; and the continued preponderance of female births promises speedily to adjust the balance of the sexes.

The Registrar-General, in his Report for 1844, makes the following interesting observations:—

"Supposing the whole population of the colony

were now grown up and unmarried, out of every 100 males, as many as 67 could find wives.

" Supposing the total population *under twelve* were now of age, and wished to marry; out of every 100 males 97 could find wives.

" Supposing the total population *of Perth* were now grown up, and unmarried, 87 out of every 100 males could find wives.

" But supposing the population *of Perth under twelve* were grown up, and wished to marry, out of 100 *females*, only 85 could find husbands."

The temperature of the atmosphere is exceedingly dry, and therefore the heat is not oppressive, though the thermometer may stand at a high degree.

A rainy day in February or March is an extremely rare occurrence at Perth, though not unusual at Australind, a hundred miles southward.

In the hottest weather, farm-labourers work all day in the open air, and feel no more inconvenience than reapers do in England. This is owing to the dryness and elasticity of the atmosphere.

I have no recorded observations of a late date, but the following table is extracted from the journal of an obliging friend, Robert Dale, Esq., who, when a Lieutenant in the 63d regiment, was stationed some years in the colony.

The thermometer was kept in a cool house at Perth, from March, 1830 to June 1831.

MONTHS.	No. of Fine Days.	No. of Rainy Days.	No. of Showers.	Maximum Height of Thermometer.	Medium Height of Thermometer.	Minimum Height of Thermometer.	REMARKS.
1830.							
March . . .	28	2	1	88	71	58	
April . . .	23	0	7	87	70½	54	
May	17	6	8	84	64½	45	Fine weather at commencement of the month.
June	18	5	2	76	56	40	Five days not accounted for.
July	14	9	8	65	49½	30	
August . .	9	8	7	76	57	38	Seven days not accounted for.
September .	17	2	4	80	62	44	Ditto ditto.
October . .	19	5	6	78	62	46	One day not accounted for.
November .	23	3	4	93	73½	54	
December .	26	—	5	103	82½	62	The thermometer was lower than what is marked in the minimum column.
1831.							
January . .	28	—	3	106	87	68	
February. .	26	1	1	102	82	62	
March . . .	30	—	1	96	78	60	
April. . . .	28	—	2	98	73	48	
May	21	2	8	78	61	44	At this season frequently a heavy dew during the night.
June	14	9	7	70	52	38	

CHAPTER XXVIII.

THE BOTANY OF THE COLONY.

BARON HUGEL, Dr. Lindley, and Sir William Hooker, have published lists of Western Australian shrubs and plants, but the most complete and elaborate work on the botany of Western Australia is the series of nineteen letters published in the " Inquirer," by Mr. Drummond, of Hawthornden, in the colony, and from them we shall compile the present chapter; but, interesting as they are in their fullest and most minute details to botanists, it is possible that they may be *too* descriptive and extend too much into detail for general readers, and we shall therefore abstain from giving a catalogue of the various indigenous plants, and confine our remarks to the more useful ones.* The first to which Mr. Drummond alludes is the blackboy, of which there are several varieties. The glaucus-leaved York blackboy is, however, the most impor-

* This brief compilation is the work of Alexander Andrews, Esq.

tant, and grows thirty feet in height without a branch. It is considered by the settlers the best material for thatch, and the young and tender leaves are found to be an agreeable vegetable, and also fodder for horses, goats, sheep, and cattle. The natives are particularly fond of the blackboy, whilst its sound old flower-stalks furnish them with the means of obtaining a light by friction. The native yam, of the class *Diœceæ*, is stated by Mr. Drummond to be the finest esculent vegetable the colony produces. The *fungi*, or mushrooms, are also palatable to the Aborigines; one species belonging to this order, and named the *Boletus*, is remarkable for possessing the properties of German tinder, when well dried, and for emitting a radiant light in its natural state.

There are seventy species of grasses. The genus *stripa* has several varieties, of which the seeds are injurious to sheep, penetrating into the wool, and sometimes into the carcase and causing death. By adopting the precaution of shearing before the seeds are ripe, this mischief is however obviated. Another description is distinguished as *elegantissima*, from its beautiful appearance, and is used as a decoration, and for ornamenting rooms.

The bulrush of Scripture is found here, and is used by coopers to stanch their work. A large jointed rush has also been found of great service, and introduced in the walls of houses to advantage, and some varieties of the *Restiaceæ* are useful in thatch work ; and in his sixth letter, Mr. Drummond mentions the buttack as very useful in tyings. A climbing species of the *Thysanotus*, near the Moore river, is much used by the natives as food. The Madge and the Guardine are roots from which the natives extract nutritious food ; the pigs are also fond of them, and besides these there are other white roots used as food by the natives.

The oak-leaved *Chenopodium* is supposed to contain essential oil ; it was formerly used by the settlers as a vegetable, and is proved to contain carbonate of soda, so that, as Mr. Drummond suggests, " it would be worth inquiry at what price we could afford barilla as an export." The *Erythræa Australis* is, we are informed, a good substitute, and is used as such, for hops ; and one species of tobacco is indigenous to the colony. The sowthistle of Swan River was, in the early days of the settlement, used as a vegetable, but is now eaten only by the domestic animals, by whom it is much relished. As a salad, it is said to be scarcely inferior to endive. The *Helicrysum*, a biennial of the Vasse district, is a grateful fodder for horses, and the *Morna nitida* for goats, sheep, and cattle, as are also several species of *Picris* and other shrubs. There is also a native celery, which forms a poor substitute for that of Europe; two varieties of this species are mentioned—the *Conna*, of which the roots are eaten by the natives after being peeled, and the *Kukire*, the root of which resembles the carrot in appearance, with the smell and colour of the parsnip. The wild carrot is also an excellent vegetable, and from its root rich wine has been extracted. The order *Eryngo* has a species of which the roots when candied have great restorative powers. Of the *Hederoma latifolia*, Dr. Lindley remarks, that its half-ripe fruits, if sent to Europe, would give several original and valuable scents to the perfumer.

Of the sea-weeds, one particular species, supposed to be the *Fucus amylæceus*, thrown in great quantities upon the coast, is mentioned as forming when boiled, sweetened, and spiced, a nutritious and beautiful jelly of a fine rose colour; and as it appears that it may be dried without injury and preserved for years, it would be of value as an export.

The catalogue of indigenous fruits is not very extensive, but one species, belonging to the order *Epacrideæ*, is reported to bear very palatable berries. The Vasse apple, of the size of a peach, is stated when boiled with sugar to be an agreeable sweetmeat.

Another fruit, of the species *Mesembryanthe-*

mum, is of a less pleasing flavour; but one of the same species, resembling the English gooseberry, is said to be delicious. Mr. Drummond also records the discovery, southward of the Vasse, of a non-descript shrub of about five feet in height, and bearing fruit as large as a middle-sized plum, of a fine purple colour, covered with a rich bloom, and having a stone similar to the plum. It is reported to have a pleasing taste. This completes the list of fruits, which Mr. Drummond acknowledges to be imperfect, as the cultivation of the vine, olive, currant, and other imported fruits has withdrawn the attention of the settlers from the native productions; and we shall now pass to the smaller classes of the *Eucalyptus* tribe. *The Doatta* is a species of this class, and the bark of its root is much relished by the natives, having a sweet and pleasing taste, as is also the trunk of the red-gum; and its leaves, washed in water, form an agreeable beverage. They also collect a description of manna from the leaves of the York gum, which yields a considerable quantity of saccharine matter. The common green wattle of the genus of *Acacia* is found plentifully on the alluvial flats of the Swan, and the bark is much used for tanning; and the gum-wattle of the same order produces so great a quantity of gum as to demand the attention of exporters. Another shrub of this order is found in the Vasse district, and produces galls similar to those of the oak, which might also be collected for exportation. The gum of some of these species is used by the natives as food, and the seeds, when ground, give them a tolerable substitute for flour.

Instead of entering more at large into dry botanical details, I will transfer to these pages a letter from my respected friend, Mr. James Drummond, the botanist already alluded to, which perhaps will prove more acceptable to the general reader.

This letter was published at the time in the local journals.

"DEAR SIR,—I send you a few extracts from a journal of observations which I made in a journey to the north, in company with Mr. Gilbert, the ornithologist.* My sons had heard from the natives that a considerable river and lakes of fresh water were to be found about two days' journey to the north of their station on the Moore River; and in company with Captain Scully, the Government Resident of this district, they determined to explore the country in that direction. Mr. Phillips and some other gentlemen who were to be of the

---

* Mr. Gilbert, an enthusiastic naturalist, and an amiable and highly respectable man, was treacherously murdered by natives to the North-East of New Holland, whilst engaged upon a scientific expedition.

party, as well as Mr. Gilbert and myself, arrived at
the station too late; I shall therefore principally
confine my observations to Mr. Gilbert's transac-
tions and my own.

" We left Hawthornden on the 22d August, and
slept at the residence of Captain Scully, who had
set out some days before to join the exploring
party. On the 23d we proceeded on our journey
to the north, and in about five or six miles we
examined some remarkable masses of granite rocks
a little to the right of the road which is formed by
our carts and horses passing to and from the Moore
River. Mr. Gilbert found a small but curious
fresh-water shell in some pools of rain-water on the
rocks, and I found two plants which I had not
seen before. In about eleven or twelve miles from
Captain Scully's we reached a permanent spring
called Yoolgan, where there is excellent grass, and
where we stopped to dine and feed our horses.
Soon after leaving Yoolgan, we met with Mr. Phillips and Mr. John Mackie returning; they had
arrived at our station a day too late for the party;
we therefore knew that our hurrying on to join
them was useless. In ten or twelve miles from
Yoolgan we reached Yeinart, a tea-tree swamp,
where there is grass and water to be had throughout the year. The night threatened to rain, but
we arrived too late to do much in the house-making

way; fortunately, the rain kept off until daylight, when we soon covered our house with tea-tree bark, and determined to stop for the day, which I consider the best way, as no collections can be made when it is raining, and provisions and everything get spoiled. It cleared up about ten o'clock, and we went to visit a brushwood swamp, where my son Johnston had shot several specimens of a beautiful species of kangaroo with a dark-coloured fur, overtopped with silvery hairs, called *Marnine* by the natives : we saw plenty of tracks of the animals, but could not see a single specimen. On the top of a hill to the north of the swamp I succeeded in finding two very distinct species of *Dryandra*, new to me. I also found a fine species of *Eucalyptus* in flower, which is distinguished from the *Matilgarring* of the natives, the *Eucalyptus macrocarpus* of Sir W. T. Hooker, by having lengthened recurved flower-stalks; the flowers are rose-coloured.

" On the 25th we proceeded on our journey. I observed two new species of acacia near Yeinart. We mistook our road, and made our old station at Badgee-badgee, where we stopped to dine and feed our horses. I also found some curious aquatic plants in the pools of water among the rocks at Badgee-badgee. After dinner we succeeded with difficulty in tracing our road to our present station on the Mouran pool, the cart tracks being nearly obliterated by the trampling of the sheep. On arriving, we found that the exploring party had returned, and that Captain Scully and my son James had left, on their return, about half an hour before our arrival. The mutilated specimens of plants brought home by the party, and the accounts of some which were left behind, determined me to visit the new river myself, after botanizing a day in the vicinity of the station, where I found a fine glaucus-leaved *Anadenia*, and Mr. Gilbert got specimens of the blue kangaroo, and several small new quadrupeds—one of them apparently a true rat, almost as large and mischievous as the Norway rat. Having got two natives, one of whom (Cabbinger) had been with the party to the north, we started on the 27th, and slept at a spring called Boorbarna. On the way I found a species of the common poison which I had not seen before, and a beautiful *Conospermum*, with pannicles of blue flowers varying to white. I was informed, by my son Johnston, that a plant like horehound, but with scarlet flowers, in tubes about an inch long, grew on the top of a stony hill to the north of the spring; I went and found the plant, which belongs to *Scrophularinæ;* I also found a *Manglesia*, allied to *Tridentifera*, but having the leaves more divided; I also found a beautiful blue climbing plant, a species of *Pronaya*, on the top of the same hill.

On the 28th, soon after setting out on our journey, I found two splendid species of everlasting flower, of which my son Johnston had been the original discoverer; one, with golden-yellow flowers varying to white, has the flowers in heads different from anything of the sort I have seen before, and will, I think, form a new genus of *Compositæ ;* and the other, with pink flowers, growing two feet high, something like *Lawrencella rosea,* or *Rhodanthe Manglesii,* but if possible finer than either. In nine or ten miles to the north of Boorbarna, we crossed a curious tract of country, covered with what I considered a variety of quartz, which breaks with a conchoidal fracture, but it has very much the appearance of flint; in many places the pieces were large, with sharp angles; my sons complained that it injured their horses' feet, but by alighting, and leading our horses over the worse parts, I did not perceive any bad effects from it. This tract of country produces some interesting plants; a splendid *Calathamnus,* with leaves nine inches long, and showy scarlet flowers, was found by my youngest son, and I got plenty of specimens.

" With regard to a new *Banksia,* allied to *Aquifolia,* which he found here, I was not so fortunate, and he brought home no specimens. After crossing several miles of this quartz formation, we came upon an extensive flat of strong clay, covered with *Euca-*

lyptus, and some curious species of acacia; we crossed a considerable river, or brook, running strong to the west, and about two miles, after crossing this brook, we made the river we were in quest of at a place called Murarino by the natives. Near the river I found a splendid plant, which had been first observed by my son Johnston; he took it for a *Lasiopetalum,* but I expect it will prove to be a species of *Solanum;* it grows two or three feet high, with large purple flowers, with calyxes like brown velvet; the leaves are irregularly shaped, acuminate, about two inches long, and an inch and a half wide at their broadest parts; the stems are prickly, and all the leaves covered with a down, as in *Lasiopetalum.* I am uncertain about the genus, not having seen the seed-vessels, but whatever that may be, it is of our finest Australian plants.

" We stopped to dine on the river, and in about four miles farther to the north, we reached two fresh-water lakes called Dalarn and Maradine. Ducks of various sorts were here in thousands, and the water-hens, or gallinules, which visited the settlements on the Swan some years ago, were plentiful. Mr. Gilbert shot three or four at a shot. I found a fine *Bæchia,* which had been first found by my son James, and a curious new plant belonging to *Compositæ,* but not yet in flower. The appearance of the country about these lakes, of which there are several besides

those I have named, and the plants which grow
about them, which are generally met with at no
great distance from the sea, seem to prove that the
lakes are at no great distance from it, and that the
Darling Range does not extend so far to the north.
No hills of any description appeared to the west;
from the top of a hill to the east, two remarkable
hills appeared, apparently about thirty miles to the
north; one of them was observed by my son to
have a remarkable peaked top, and they supposed
they might be Mount Heathcote and Wizard Peak.
We saw, as we came along, a high hill, which the
natives called Wangan Catta; they said it was three
days' walk to it; it lay due east of our course.

" On the 29th, we returned on our track for about
seven miles, until we reached the first running
river we met on our journey to the north. Our
guides agreed to take us back by a different route,
and to take us to a hill where a curious species of
kangaroo called ' Damar ' by them, would be met
with. My son Johnston has shot several of these
animals about a day's walk to the east of our
station on the Moore River. We therefore ascended
this river in a course S.E. by E., and soon after we
were upon its banks, we came upon a grassy country; three or four miles up we stopped to dine
and feed the horses, at a place called Nugadrine;
several pairs of beautiful falcons, the *Falco Nypo-*
lencus of Gould, were flying over us, and Mr. Gilbert

succeeded in shooting one of them. After dinner, we proceeded in the same direction for nine or ten miles ; we soon crossed the tracks of Captain Scully and my sons on their return ; they had gone up the main or northern branch of the river, and had found but little grass while they followed its banks ; but they had passed over a great deal of grassy land in crossing the country from it to the Moore River.

" We travelled for ten or eleven miles through a splendid grassy country, and met with a large tribe of natives, several of whom had never seen white men before ; they were very friendly, and offered us some of their favourite root, the wyrang, which grows abundantly among these grassy hills. They made so much noise, that we wished to get some distance from them to sleep, but they all followed us and encamped near, many of the single men sleeping by our fire. In the morning of the 30th I went to the top of a hill, near our bivouac, while Mr. Gilbert was superintending the preparations for breakfast, and clipping the beards of some of our new friends. After breakfast, we started direct for our station on the Moore River; the natives who were with us as guides considering our stock of flour insufficient to proceed any farther in the direction of the hill where they expected to find the Damars. For almost the whole of this day we travelled over the most splendid grassy country I have ever seen in Australia; the hill-sides, as far as we could see in every direction, were covered with beautiful grass, and of a golden colour, from the flowers of the beautiful yellow everlasting flower which I have described in a former part of this letter, which is only to be found in the richest soil. After reaching our station, I was a day or two employed in drying my specimens of plants. My son Johnston pointed out a most beautiful new *Dryandra*, which he had discovered on the top of a hill near the Mouran-pool; I have named the species *Dryandra floribunda*, from its numerous blossoms, which almost hide the leaves; it grows twelve or fifteen feet high, and in such abundance, that the side of the hill on which it grows actually appears of a golden colour for several miles. I consider it the most beautiful species of the genus yet known for cultivation.

" I am, Sir,

" Your obedient servant,

" JAMES DRUMMOND.

" P.S.—Our course generally by compass from Hawthornden to these lakes has been several points to the west of north. The natives informed us, when at the lakes, that they could reach the sea-coast long before sunset.

" *Hawthornden Farm, Toodyay Valley.*"

CHAPTER XXIX.

MISFORTUNES OF THE COLONY.

MANY causes have unhappily united to keep
Western Australia from rising into notice and
importance with that rapidity which has marked
the career of the other Australian colonies. The misfortunes of the first settlers, attributable in a great
measure to flagrant mismanagement, deterred intending emigrants from tempting the like fate.
The man who had the largest grant of land in the
colony allotted to him—a monster grant of 250,000
acres—made so ill an use of the means at his command, that nothing but misery and misfortune has
ever attended his steps. The funds with which he
was intrusted might have been applied with the
happiest effect, both for the advancement of the
colony and of his own personal fortunes. The
people whom he brought out, chiefly mechanics and
labourers, to the number of four hundred or
upwards, were sufficient to have formed a settlement of their own. By an unhappy fatality, the
early settlers were landed on a part of the coast

the most unfavourable in the world for their purposes. The whole country around them was a mere limestone rock. Here, however, the town-site of Clarence was fixed upon, but scarcely a yard of land was to be found that afforded space for a garden. No attempt was made to sow grain, or plant potatoes, to provide for the wants of the following year.

The people lived upon the provisions they had brought out with them. The four hundred workmen being left by their principal without direction or employment, soon consumed in riotous living the abundant stores left at their disposal, and too soon found that destitution is the inevitable consequence of idleness and folly. Many perished miserably of want and sickness, and many others effected their escape to Van Dieman's Land, where they gave a melancholy account of the wretchedness of those who were unable to flee from the scene of their errors.

The active intelligence, and unremitting exertions of the Governor, Sir James Stirling, at length ameliorated the condition of the unfortunate settlers. He removed the seat of Government to Perth, and explored the neighbouring country in every direction in the hope of finding tracts of land sufficient for the support of the people under his charge. The flats of the Swan River afforded all the facilities he required; but the settlers were greatly intimidated by the treacherous attacks of the natives, and were very reluctant to separate from the main body. In consequence of these fears, many consumed their capital in their present support, instead of applying it in the formation of farms, and laying the ground-work of future prosperity. Provisions being all imported, were sold at high rates, and the hesitating colonists became unavoidably subservient to the cupidity of the traders.

In addition to these misfortunes, no man liked to lay out his money in building a house upon land which might not eventually be allotted to him. He lived therefore, with his wife, children, and servants, miserably under a tent, until the surveyor-general should be able to point out to him the land which had fallen to his share, in the general lottery of the Government. In many cases this was not done for one or two years after the formation of the colony, in consequence of the lamentably inefficient force placed at the disposal of the able and indefatigable surveyor-general; and even then, the boundaries of the different allotments were not permanently defined. This state of incertitude had the most fatal effect, not only upon the fortunes, but upon the moral condition of the settlers. Those who had come out resolutely bent upon cultivating their own land, and supporting themselves and families by their manual labour, refused to make the necessary exertions upon property which might eventually belong to others for whom they had no desire to toil. Waiting, therefore, in their tents on the shore, until the Government should determine their respective locations, they passed the time in idleness, or in drinking and riotous living; and when at length they obtained their Letters of Allocation, they found themselves without money or any means of subsistence, except by hiring out their manual labour to others more prudent, or more fortunate.

Other accidental circumstances have combined to retard the progress of the colony. From ignorance of the seasons, many lost their crops, and were obliged consequently to expend the last remains of their capital in procuring necessary supplies. From the same cause, vessels which brought emigrants to the colony were not secured during the winter season in the safest anchorages, and being exposed to the fury of the north-west gales, were, in too many instances, driven ashore and completely wrecked.

Again, too, there has always existed a strong desire on the part of Western Australia to connect herself with India, conscious that there are great facilities of communication between the countries, from favourable trade-winds, and that her own climate is perhaps better suited to invalids than even that of the Cape. This desire has been met by several influential gentleman of Calcutta, and on two occasions, vessels were freighted and despatched from that city to the colony, in the hope of establishing a mutually advantageous connexion, and on both occasions the vessels were lost on the voyage. At length a small establishment was effected near Australind, by the agents of Mr. W. H. Prinsep, for the purpose of breeding horses for the Indian market; and we most sincerely hope success will ultimately attend the enterprising effort. Indian officers have occasionally visited the colony; but they have naturally received unfavourable impressions, from being unable to find those accommodations and luxuries to which they had been accustomed.

The settlers will not build houses and lay out their money on the mere speculation of gaining advantage by the visits of Indian officers, but if once there appeared a reasonable prospect of early remuneration, every convenience would be provided, and every comfort ensured to visitors. Living is now extremely cheap, and there is a profusion of vegetables and fruits of every kind. There are plenty of good horses and pleasure-boats, and there are the amusements of fishing, and hunting the Kangaroo and Emu.

The misconduct of some, and the misfortunes of

others of the early settlers, tended to bring about
calamities which were echoed throughout Great
Britain, and for many years had the effect of turning the stream of emigration away from these shores.
Other causes have also contributed to this end. The
Government plan of giving grants of land to emigrants, proportioned to the capital which they
introduced into the colony, was good to a certain
extent, but the object was perverted, and the boon
abused. In almost all instances, men received a
much greater quantity of land than they were justly
entitled to. Every article of provisions, furniture,
and household effects, and even wearing apparel,
were taken into account. The valuations were
made by friends and neighbours, who accommo-
dated one another, and rated the property of the
applicant at a most astounding price. The consequence has been, that large grants of land have
fallen into the hands of those who have never lived
upon them, or spent anything upon their improvement, beyond a fictitious amount which they were
required to specify to the Government before they
could obtain possession of their deeds of grant.
These original grantees have clung to their lands
with desperate tenacity, in the hope that some day
their value will be more than nominal. The idea
that all the best portions of the colony are in the
hands of a few great unimproving proprietors, has

been one reason why emigrants have turned away from it.

But this provision, which has so long been an evil to the colony, may now be looked upon, thanks to the narrow-minded policy of the Home Government, as an advantage. These original grants, which have proved so little beneficial to the owner, and so highly detrimental to the community, are now far more easily obtainable by the emigrant than the surrounding crown-lands. The policy of the Government has entirely changed with regard to the disposal of waste.lands in the Australian colonies; instead of giving them away with a lavish hand, it has for some years been the practice to throw every obstacle in the way of intending purchasers.

They are now valued at one pound per acre, though it is well known, even at the colonial office, that five acres of Australian land are requisite to maintain a single sheep; and as the average value of sheep in all these colonies is six or seven shillings, it scarcely requires the head of a Secretary of State to calculate that every one who buys land for the purpose of feeding his flocks upon it, must be content to purchases it at an irreparable loss of capital. In consequence of this wise regulation, no purchase of crown-lands are now made in any of the Australian colonies, except of town allotments, which have a factitious value, altogether irrespective of the qualities of the soil. It is now that the holders of large grants find purchasers, as they are extremely willing to sell at a much lower rate than the crown. In Western Australia alone, however, are these grants to be found; and here excellent land may be purchased at three shillings an acre. Thus the careless profusion of one government, and the false policy and unhappy cupidity of another, have proved the means of placing this colony in a better position in some respects than any other.

Western Australia has been unfortunate also in having had no powerful company to support her cause in England. The neighbouring colony of South Australia, with a much less extensive territory, and without any natural superiority in the quality of the soil, was immediately puffed into notice by the exertions of her friends at home.

But whilst the settlers at Adelaide and their patrons in London, proclaimed to the world the advantages of the new colony, they scrupled not to draw comparisons between it and the Western settlement, that were neither flattering nor just to the latter. Not content with elevating their own idol with pæans and thanksgiving, before the gaze of a bedinned public, they persisted in shouting out their scorn and contempt at the pretensions of their unhappy neighbour. The public, with its usual discernment, gave implicit credence to both fables. Western Australia had met its contumelious detractors with silence; and the false statements were therefore looked upon as admitted and undeniable. But notwithstanding the injurious misrepresentations of enemies, and her own injurious silence, this colony has been quietly and steadily progressing, until she has laid for herself a foundation that no envious calumny can shake. The last blow she has received was from the failure of the settlement at Australind; a subject that I intend to treat of in a separate chapter.

So many misfortunes and untoward accidents have combined to prejudice the emigrating portion of the British public against Western Australia, that no voice is ever raised in her behalf, and scarcely any literary journal condescends to acknowledge her existence. And yet, notwithstanding the veil of darkness that conceals her from Northern eyes, there is perhaps no spot in the world that contains so eminently within itself the elements of prosperity and happiness. A climate more genial, more divine than that of Italy, robs poverty of its bleakness and its bitterness. Absolute want is never felt, and those who possess but little, find how little is sufficient in a climate so productive and so beneficent.

The purity and elasticity of the atmosphere induce a continual flow of good spirits.

To all the fruits of Italy in most abundant profusion, are added the productions of the East.

The regularity of the seasons is so certain, that the husbandman always reckons with confidence upon his crops. No droughts interfere, *as in the other colonies*, to ruin his hopes. The vintages, annually increasing and improving, are equally free from disappointment.

It must not, however, be denied that there are many natural disadvantages which can never be overcome without a much larger population.

In the first place, the only good harbour on the Western coast has only just been discovered—June 1846—and is at least thirty-five miles distant from Perth, the capital. Then, secondly, all the superior land of the colony is situated about sixty miles back from the capital, and the farmers therefore have a considerable distance to convey their produce to the port; and part of that distance the roads are extremely bad.

There is another objection to the colony in the opinion of intending emigrants, which arises from a small plant, or shrub, of the order *leguminosæ*, a deadly poison to sheep and cattle. This plant grows over the colony in patches, but is now so well known, that accidents very seldom occur from it, shepherds being careful not to allow their flocks to feed in its vicinity. It is however to be observed, that neither sheep nor cattle will feed upon this plant unless they be very hungry, and other food be wanting. It is very seldom indeed that cattle, which are sometimes left to roam at large over the country, are found to have perished from pasturing upon it. This plant has no injurious effect upon horses; but these animals have in several instances been poisoned by eating the leaves of a small plant described as resembling the *ranunculus*, which grows in small quantities in the Southern portion of the colony. A gentleman once informed me that he was riding up from Australind on a favourite and very fine horse, which he allowed to feed, during several hours of rest, on a spot where this plant unfortunately grew. On mounting to resume his journey, the horse seemed full of spirit; but he had not proceeded a mile before it stumbled, and was with difficulty kept from falling. A little farther on, after proceeding with evident difficulty, it fell, to rise no more, and died in a few hours of violent inflammation of the kidneys.

However alarming these drawbacks may seem to people at a distance, they are only lightly considered in the colony. Fatalities are very rare among the flocks and herds, and many diseases which prevail in New South Wales are entirely unknown among us.

CHAPTER XXX.

THE RESOURCES OF THE COLONY :——HORSES FOR INDIA——WINE——
DRIED FRUITS——COTTON——COAL——WOOL——CORN——WHALE-OIL
——A WHALE-HUNT.——CURED FISH——SHIP TIMBER.

THE geographical position of Western Australia
makes it one of the most desirable colonies of the
British empire. The French would be delighted to
possess so advantageous a station in that part of
the world, whence they could sally forth and
grievously annoy our shipping-trade. Vessels
bound for China and the Eastern Islands pass
within a few days' sail of the colony. For my
part, I confess I should feel by no means sorry
were we to fall into the hands of the French for a
few years, as they would not hesitate to make such
lasting improvements as would materially add to
the importance of the settlement. It requires that
Government should be made to feel the value of
this colony as a naval station before it will rise into
anything like consequence. The anchorage of
Cockburn Sound, lying between Garden Island and
the main land, presents a splendid harbour, where
hundreds of ships of war might lie throughout all

weathers in perfect safety. Enemy's cruisers passing along the coast cannot come within Garden Island from the south, and they would scarcely venture without a pilot from the north, except with a great deal of deliberation and caution, so that small vessels might readily slip away and avoid the danger; and numbers of ships might lie so close under Garden Island, that they never would be perceived by men-of-war reconnoitring the coast.

There is no other colony in Australia so admirably situated with respect to other countries. The Cape of Good Hope is four or five weeks sail distant; Ceylon about twenty days; Calcutta, Sincapore, and Batavia are all within easy reach. In exporting live-stock, this is of vast importance; and in time of war a central position like this would afford an admirable place for vessels to repair to in order to refit. With the finest timber in the world for naval purposes in unlimited profusion; with a soil teeming with various metals; with harbours and dock-yards almost ready made by the hand of Nature, all things requisite for the wants of shipping may be obtained whenever a Government shall see fit to resort to them.

It must doubtless surprise many that more has not be done in a colony possessing such natural advantages. The reason is, that the prejudices which have so long prevailed against this settlement have retarded the progress of immigration, and the small number of inabitants has ever precluded the possibility of any great effort being made by the colony itself.

Public opinion in England must turn in its favour before it can rise from obscurity into importance; but public opinion is never in favour of the poor and deserted. Time, however, will eventually develope those resources, which at present lie dormant for want of capital and opportunity.

The proximity of this colony to India peculiarly marks it as the most advantageous spot for the breeding of horses for that market. From Van Dieman's Land or New South Wales, ships are generally about eight weeks in reaching an Indian port, and must proceed either by the north of New Holland, through the dangerous navigation of Torres Straits, or by the south and west, round Cape Lewin. Either route presents a long and rough passage, highly detrimental to stock, and of course increasing the cost of the horses exported. The voyage from Fremantle may be performed in half the time, and the animals will therefore arrive at their destination in much finer order, and with much less loss.

It is well known that none of these colonies afford better or more extensive pasture-ground for

horses and cattle than ours. Nothing is wanted
but capital and population to produce a thriving
traffic in horse-flesh between this settlement and
India.

There is every reason to believe that Western
Australia will one day become a great wine
country. Its vineyards are becoming more numerous and extensive every year, and the wine produced in them is of a quality to lead us to believe
that when the art of preparing it is better understood, it will be found of very superior quality. It
will, however, be a new kind of wine; and therefore, before it will be prized in Europe, prejudices
in favour of older wines have to be overcome.
Soil and climate combined, give to different wines
their peculiar flavour. The vines which in Madeira
produce the wine of that name, when brought to
another country, even in a corresponding latitude,
and planted in soil that chemically approaches as
closely as possible to that which they have left,
will produce a wine materially different from that
called Madeira. So with the vines of Xeres and
Oporto; of Teneriffe or Constantia. Different
countries produce wines peculiar to themselves;
and the wine of Western Australia will be found to
be entirely *sui generis*. All that I have tasted,
though made from the poorest of grapes, the
common sweet-water, have one peculiarity; a good

draught, instead of affecting the head or flushing the
face, causes a most delightful glow to pervade the
stomach; and it is of so comforting a nature, that
the labourers in harvest prefer the home-made
colonial wine to any other beverage. Every farm-
settler is now adding a vineyard to his estate. The
olive is also being extensively cultivated. In a
few years' time, dried fruits will be exported in
large quantities; but we almost fear that the
colonists are giving too much of their attention to
the cultivation of grapes and other fruits. In
addition to exports, on a large scale, of wool, horses,
timber, and metals, these articles of commerce are
not undeserving of attention, but they should not
be brought so prominently forward as to form the
principal feature in the trade of the colony. Wine
and fruit countries are always poor countries; let
us think of substantials first, and of wine and fruit
only by way of dessert.

Cotton is a plant that grows extremely well in
this colony, and might be cultivated on a large
scale, and doubtless with great success. Mr. Hutt,
the late governor, whose constant anxiety to
promote the interests of the settlers in every way
must long endear him to their memories, always
appeared extremely sanguine as to the practica-
bility of making this a great cotton country.

But Western Australia contains, perhaps, greater

internal wealth than that which appears on the surface.
She abounds in iron, which must some day come
into the Indian market; and as the metal lies close
to the surface, it may be obtained without much
expenditure of capital.   There is no doubt, also,
that she is equally rich in copper and platina, but
capital is wanting at present to enable the settlers
to work the mines.   Soon, however, companies
will be formed, and operations will be carried on
rivalling those of South Australia.

Extensive fields of excellent *coal* have lately been
discovered, and will prove the source of vast wealth
to the colony.   Steam-vessels in the Indian ocean
will be supplied with coal from Western Australia;
and the depôts at Sincapore, Point-de-Galle, and
perhaps at Aden, will afford a constant market for
this valuable commodity.

The staple export of the colony is, of course, at
present wool.   Our flocks, unfortunately, increase in
a much greater ratio than the inhabitants, and thus
the scarcity of labour becomes severely felt.   A
large flock becomes an evil, and men are burdened
and impoverished by the very sources of wealth.
The expense of maintaining becomes greater
than the returns.   The emigrants who are most
sure of improving their condition in a colony, are
those men who begin as shepherds, and, having
established a good character for themselves, under-

take the care of a flock upon shares; that is, they receive a certain proportion—a third, and sometimes even a half—of the annual increase and wool, delivering the remainder to the owner at the seaport, ready packed for shipping. These men, of course, soon acquire a flock of their own, and then abandon their original employer to his old embarrassment, leaving him, (a resident probably in the capital, and already a prey to multitudinous distractions,) to find out a new shepherd on still more exorbitant terms. As large grants of land may be obtained by tenants for merely nominal rents, or in consideration of their erecting stock-yards or farm-buildings in the course of a term of years, there is every inducement to men of this class to become settlers.

The houses in some districts are built of clay, or prepared earth, rammed down between boards, and thus forming solid walls of twelve or eighteen inches in thickness, that harden in a short time almost to the consistency of stone. The windows and doorways are cut out of the walls. These edifices are built at a very cheap rate; and when laths or battens are fixed inside of them, may be covered with plaister, and either whitewashed or painted.

Besides the extensive sheep-runs of the colony, there is an unlimited extent of excellent corn-land. The crops in the Northam, Toodyay, and York

districts—though inferior to those of the midland
counties of England, for want of manure, and a
more careful system of husbandry—are extremely
fine; and there is land enough, if cultivated, to
supply the whole of the southern hemisphere with
grain.

The sea on the western coast of New Holland
still abounds with whales, although the Americans
for many years made it one of their principal
stations, and have consequently driven many of the
animals away. The whale is a very suspicious and
timid creature, and when it has been once chased it
seldom returns to the same locality. The Americans tell us that Geographe Bay, about twenty
years ago, abounded with whales at certain seasons.
Many of them came there apparently to die, and
the shore was covered with their carcases and
bones. About the month of June, the whales
proceed along the coast, going northward; and
then visit the various bays and inlets as they pass,
in pursuit of the shoals of small fish that precede
them in their migration. They generally return
towards the south about six weeks afterwards, and
at these times the whale-fishery is eagerly pursued
both by the Americans and the colonists. Bay-
whaling is followed with various success at Fremantle, Bunbury, the Vasse, Augusta, and King
George's Sound.

At these times swarms of sharks of enormous dimensions infest the coast. At the Vasse, they were so numerous in 1845, that the men in the boats became quite cowed by their audacity. Were a whale killed in the evening, two-thirds of it would be eaten before morning by the sharks. The monsters (sometimes thirty feet in length) would follow the whale-boats, and strike against them with their snouts and fins; until the men were so intimidated that they even refused to go in pursuit of a whale which otherwise they might easily have captured. Mr. Robert Viveash, one of the principals at this station, told me, among other anecdotes, that one day, standing on the deck of a small schooner, watching the evolutions of an enormous shark, he saw it seize the rudder with its teeth in a kind of frenzy, or else in mere sport, and shake it so violently that the tiller, striking against some heavy object on deck, was actually broken in two pieces. It is a well-authenticated fact, that some years ago a shark, playing round a whaling vessel of upwards of 300 tons, whilst lying at anchor during a calm, got entangled in the buoy-rope of the anchor, and in its efforts to free itself actually tripped the anchor. The people on board, perceiving something extraordinary had happened, hove up the anchor, and brought the struggling shark to the surface. Having

thrown a rope over its head and secured it by a
running bowline knot under the pectoral fins,
the fish was boused up to the fore-yard; and its
length was so great, that when its nose touched
the yard, its tail was still lashing the water.

There is something highly exciting in the chase
of the whale. I have watched the proceedings for
hours from Arthur's Head, the high rock between
Fremantle and the sea. A man stationed here
on the look out, perceives a whale spouting about
six miles off, between the main-land and the opposite islands. He immediately hoists a flag, and
makes signals indicating the direction.

The crews of six whale-boats, which have been
lying ready on the beach, with their lines carefully
coiled in a tub, and harpoon and lances all at hand,
assemble like magic. The boats are launched, and
pulling rapidly out of the bay, each with its own
particular flag flying at the bows; the steersman
leans forward, and gives additional force to the
stroke-oar by the assistance of his weight and
strength; the men pull strongly and well-together;
the boats dance over the flashing waves, and silence
and determination reign among the crews. The
object is to meet the whale, and come down upon
him in front; none but a lubber or a knave would
cross his wake; for his eyes are so placed that
he can see laterally and behind better than straight

before him, and the moment he detects a boat in pursuit he begins to run. The lubber crosses his wake, because he has not steered so as to be able to avoid doing so; the knave, because either out of spite to his employer, or because he is bribed by an adverse company, is desirous that the fish should be lost. If the boats are a long distance astern when the whale begins to run, pursuit is useless, and the men return, hoping for better luck another time.

The boats come round Arthur's Head almost together. The men, knowing that many hours of severe toil are probably before them, pull steadily, but not so as to exhaust themselves at the outset. At length one boat creeps out from the rest; the others gradually drop into line, and the distance between each widens perceptibly. The last boat, a heavy sailer, is half-a-mile astern of the first. From the boats, your eye wanders to the spot where the whale was last seen to blow. For some time you can discern nothing, and fancy he must be gone off to sea again. At last a thin white column of vapour is perceptible; the animal is carelessly sporting about, unconscious of danger. The first boat draws rapidly down upon him; it approaches nearer and nearer. The fish has disappeared, but his enemies seem to know the direction in which he is going, and are ready awaiting him when he returns to the surface. You now perceive him

blowing close to the first boat, the steersman of
which draws in the steer-oar and runs forward,
whilst the men have all peaked their oars, and
remain quiet in their seats. The steersman has
seized the harpoon to which the long line of coiled
rope is attached; in a moment he has plunged it
into the animal's side. Starting at the stroke,
away it darts; the line flies out of the tub over
the bow of the boat; the men begin to pull, in
order to ease the shock when the line is all run out;
and now away they go, the whale drawing the
boat after him at such speed that the water flies off
from the bows in broad flakes.

After running upwards of a mile, the fish dives
down to the bottom; there he remains some
minutes, until compelled to return to the surface
for breath. His reappearance is heralded by a
column of water spouted from his nostrils.

Two of the boats are able to approach near
enough to allow lances to be thrown at him, which,
penetrating through the blubber, pierce his vitals,
and cause him to run again as swiftly as before.
Again he sinks, and again appears on the surface;
the column which he now spouts forth is tinged
with red. The boats again approach, and more
lances are driven into his sides, but he is not yet
subdued; he breaks away from the assassins, and
tries once more to escape; but, alas! his strength

and his life-blood are fast ebbing away; his breath begins to fail, and he cannot remain long beneath the surface.

He comes up suddenly in the very midst of the boats, and, as he rolls from side to side, he strikes one of them with his fin, staving it in and making it a wreck upon the water. The drowning men are picked up by their companions, and the whale is again pursued. He is now in the death-flurry, spinning round and round, and lashing the sea into foam with his broad tail. He is still; and now the boats venture to come close up to the carcase, and fixing grapnels in it, with tow-lines attached, they form in a line, and commence towing their conquest to the shore, singing as they row, their measured pæans of victory.

When the blubber is cut off and tryed out, it produces from three to ten tons of oil.

Besides whales, there are immense quantities of fish upon this coast. The best kind are called tailors, and have a good deal of the mackerel flavour; and snappers, which somewhat resemble cod-fish. The mullets and whitings are better than those on the English coast, but every other fish is much inferior in flavour to those known in England. We have nothing to equal salmon, turbot, soles, cod, or mackerel; nevertheless, a snapper of twenty pounds weight is a very eatable fish.

They are caught in great quantities, salted and exported to the Mauritius, where they are acknowledged to be superior to the fish imported from the Cape of Good Hope. Snapper-fishing is not bad sport, as they bite freely. They go in immense shoals, and it is not an uncommon thing to catch twenty-hundred weight at a single haul. When H. M. S. 'Challenger,' was lying in Cockburn Sound, some of the men with a very large seine-net, caught two thousand fish at a single haul—averaging five pounds a-piece. This is almost incredible, but it is related on good authority.

The fresh-water rivers have no fish but a small craw-fish, that buries itself in the ground when the bed of the stream is dry; and a flat-headed, tapering fish called a " cobbler." This is about twelve inches long, and has a sharp, serrated bone an inch in length on each side of its head, that lies flat and perfectly concealed until an enemy approaches. This bone is hollow, like an adder's tooth, and contains a virulent poison, which is injected into the wound, and causes intense pain for several hours. Men are frequently stung by these wretches, whilst wading through the water.

There are several valuable kinds of wood in this colony, which do not exist in South Australia or New South Wales. We may mention the sandal-wood, which now finds a market in Ceylon, where it fetches about £22 per ton; but if it were sent direct to China, (its ultimate destination,) it would obtain probably £35 per ton. Sandal-wood is burnt in large quantities in China, as a kind of incense. There is another highly-fragrant wood peculiar to this colony, called by the settlers "raspberry jam," from its resembling that sweet-meat in its scent. A small quantity sent to Tonbridge-Wells, was worked up into boxes, and highly approved of by the cabinet-makers, who gave it the name of "violet wood."

One of the most beautiful trees in the colony is called the peppermint-tree; its leaves, which are very abundant, resemble those of the willow, and, on being rubbed, smell strongly of pepper-mint. It bears a small yellow flower. There is much reason to believe that this is of the same species as the tree which yields the valuable Caje-put oil, and it is highly desirable that an endeavour should be made to distil this oil from the leaves.

Many of the vegetable productions of Western Australia appear to correspond with those of Java and others of the Eastern Islands, modified by the difference of climate.

The timber adapted to ship-building purposes, extends in vast quantities down the line of coast, and is of three kinds, all varieties of the eucalyptus. The *tooart* in the districts of Bunbury and the

Vasse, and the *blue-gum* which abounds at Augusta and Nornalup, are woods of large size, and remarkably hard and close-grained in texture. It is well adapted for keel-pieces, stern-posts, capstan-heads, and heavy beams: and its fibres are so closely matted and interwoven together, that it is scarcely possible to split it. It grows in lengths of from 30 to 60 feet, and measures from 15 to 30 inches in diameter.

But the wood most highly prized and most easily attainable, is the *Jarra,* which grows upon the entire range of the Darling Hills, distant from sixteen to twenty miles from the coast, and extends over a country averaging at least twenty miles in breadth. It was for a long time erroneously called mahogany by the settlers, as it takes an excellent polish, and is extremely useful for cabinet purposes. A small quantity recently sent to England for the purpose of being worked up with furniture, has been thus reported upon :—

"We have just inspected about two tons of wood brought to this town (Leeds) under the name of Swan River Mahogany. Some of the wood is firm and close in texture, with a very great abundance of cross mottle ;—in fact, it is quite crowded with figure. The colour is something like old Jamaica mahogany, and it bears a strong resemblance in some of its figures to the wood so cele-

brated by Messrs. Collard, as 'Ocean Wood.' We
are quite firm in our opinion, that it is NOT
mahogany, and do not know why it should be
nicknamed. Why not call it by its proper name?
—for it has sufficiently strong claims to maintain
its own independence.

" J. KENDELL AND Co.

" Cabinet Manufacturers, Leeds."

Mr. Bond, of the firm of Gillows and Co.,
cabinet manufacturers, 176 and 177 Oxford-street,
London, to whom a small quantity was submitted,
has also made an equally favourable report.
Messrs. Chaloner and Fleming, of Liverpool,
whose firm is one of the most extensive importers
of timber in the empire, have reported that they
" consider the specimens submitted to them to be
of rich figure, and very fine quality, although the
colour is rather dark. It is quite as fine in texture
as the best Spanish mahogany, and takes the polish
remarkably well."

It is not, however, as cabinet wood that
the Jarra is so highly valuable. It has been
found to be some of the best ship-timber in the
world. It is so extremely durable, that when it
is cut in a healthy state, it is never found to rot,
even though it be buried in the ground for years.
For seventeen years it has been constantly used in
the colony for a variety of purposes. As it resists

the white-ant, an insect that destroys oak and
every other kind of wood, and is never subject
to the dry-rot, it is invaluable for building purposes. Boats constructed of it, which have been
in the water during the whole of this period, and
entirely unprotected by paint, are still as sound as
they were when first launched.

It resists the sea-worm ; and our colonial vessels,
when hove down for repairs or survey at Sincapore,
Launceston, or other ports, have always excited the
admiration of the surveyors, and have been pronounced not to require to be coppered. This wood
is long in the grain, but very close and tough, and
not only makes very good planking, but excellent
beams, keel-pieces, and many other portions of a
ship. Growing without a branch to the height
of from fifty to one hundred feet, and from eighteen
inches to three feet and upwards in diameter, it
excites the admiration of all practical men ; and as
its properties have been so long tested, and are so
generally admitted in the southern hemisphere,
it is matter of no less surprise than regret that it
should be still unknown in the English markets.
Strong prejudice, and the interest of parties connected with the timber-trade in other countries,
have served to keep the inexhaustible forests of
Western Australia in the obscurity which has
hung over them from primeval times. Besides

this, although the Jarra wood exists not in other parts of Australia, and is confined to the Western coast alone, timber has been imported to England from New South Wales, and is very little prized there. Timber-merchants, therefore, who confound all the Australian colonies together, as most other people in England do, are willing to believe that the Jarra of Western Australia is the same as the Stringy-bark of New South Wales, and therefore worth little or nothing for ship-building purposes. The experience of seventeen years has proved the contrary. Not only have the valuable qualities of the Jarra been tested in vessels built in the colony, and employed in trading to the neighbouring ports; but men-of-war and merchant ships have been frequently repaired with it, and the wood so employed has always been highly esteemed when subsequently inspected abroad.

In the autumn of 1845, the " Halifax Packet," a barque of 400 tons, having parted from her anchor in a gale, and drifted ashore, underwent repairs at Fremantle, to the extent of about eleven hundred pounds. On being surveyed at the Port of London on her return home, the new timber, which had never been previously recognized at Lloyd's, though many efforts have been made to obtain that sanction, was allowed to remain in the ship as being perfectly serviceable. The following memorandum was addressed by the Surveyor of Lloyd's to A. Andrews, Esq., a gentleman interested in the welfare of the colony :

" The wood used in the repairs of the ' Halifax Packet' at Swan River, appears to answer the purpose very well. It is not found necessary to remove any part thereof.

" From the samples which I have seen of Swan River timber, I am of opinion that it will form a very desirable and serviceable wood in shipbuilding ; but this must be regarded as my private opinion, the Society of Lloyd's Register, to which I belong, not having as yet assigned any character to it in their rules.

(Signed) " P. COURTNEY, Lloyd's Surveyor.
" *Lloyd's, 24th February*, 1846."

This extraordinary timber grows to a size that would appear incredible to readers in England. It is perhaps only manageable and remunerative from 40 to 60 feet ; but in the southern districts of the colony—especially to the back of Nornalup and Wilson's Inlet—it is found growing to 120 and 150 feet in height, before the first branch appears. My brother and his servant, when exploring in that district, took refuge once from a storm in the hollow of an old Jarra tree, which not only sheltered themselves but their horses ; and the interior actually measured in diameter three times the length of the largest horse, an animal sixteen hands high and very long backed. This may appear an astounding assertion, but the following is not less so. The same parties found a Jarra tree which had fallen completely across a broad and deep river (called the Deep River) running between high precipitous banks, thus forming a natural bridge, along which a bullock cart might have passed !

Timber of such large dimensions is perfectly useless ; but there are, of course, trees of every size, growing in boundless profusion.

As Indian teak and African oak are now scarcely obtainable, we look upon our colony as a storehouse for the British navy ; and though we have hitherto vainly battled against prejudice and private interest to make this timber known to our rulers, the day will arrive when the wants of the naval service will compel men in authority to acknowledge the value of wood, which is most highly prized 'by all who have had the opportunity of testing its qualities.

It is due to the Lords Commissioners of the Admiralty to state, that on two occasions they have promised to receive a quantity of this timber, provided it were delivered at one of the royal dockyards, and to allow a fair price for it. But unfor-

tunately, there is so great a scarcity of labour and
of capital in the colony, that the settlers have
shrunk from the outlay necessary to perform what
would be, after all, only an experiment.

It cannot be supposed, that timber which has
been tested in every way for seventeen years, and
is known throughout Australia to be indisputably
first-rate for ship-building purposes, should be
condemned at home as unserviceable. But the
colonists know how many prejudices and interested
feelings environ the Admiralty; and in general
shrink from the experiment.

CHAPTER XXXI.

RISE AND FALL OF A SETTLEMENT. — THE SEQUEL TO CAPTAIN
GREY'S DISCOVERIES.——A WORD AT PARTING.

His Excellency the Governor having kindly invited me to be his companion on a journey which he proposed to make to the new settlement of Australind, about a hundred miles south of Perth, I set about making the necessary preparations. I borrowed a pair of saddle-bags, and having stuffed my traps into one side of them, loaded the other with a cold roast fowl, a boiled tongue, a pound of sausages, a loaf of bread, a flask of brandy, and sundry small packages of tea, sugar, cigars, &c.

When I looked at the result of my labours, the swollen sides of the leathern receptacle, I enjoyed a noble feeling of independence; as though I were now prepared to ramble through the world, and stood in no need of friendly welcome, or the doubtful hospitality of an inn.

Having breakfasted at five o'clock on a December morning (the middle of summer), and equipped

myself in a broad-brimmed straw-hat, and light
shooting-jacket, I mounted my steed, and sallied
forth from my gate, followed by the sympathizing
grins of Hannibal.

His Excellency, true to the hour, was mounting
his horse at the door of Government House—and
as the appearance of the whole turn-out was rather
unlike anything usually seen in Hyde Park, or even
connected with the morning drives of his Excellency
the Viceroy of Ireland, I may as well describe it.

The representative of our gracious Sovereign was
habited in his bush costume—a white hat, bare of
beaver, having a green veil twisted round it, a light
shooting coat and plaid trousers, shoes, and jean
gaiters. His illustrious person was seated on a
pair of broad saddle-bags, which went flap, flap
against the sides of his charger, as he jogged steadily
along at the usual travelling pace. On the pummel
of his saddle was strapped a roll of blankets for the
night bivouac, and to one of the straps was attached a tin-pannikin, which bumped incessantly
against his horse's mane. Round the animal's
neck was coiled a long tether-rope, which every
now and then kept coming undone, and the cara-
van had to halt whilst it was being readjusted.

Behind us rode his Excellency's man, no longer
the smug gentleman in a black suit, with a visage
as prim as his neck-cloth, but blazing in a red

woollen shirt, and grinning incessantly with amazement at his own metamorphosis. Strapped to his
waist by a broad belt of leather, was a large tin-
kettle, for the purpose of making his Excellency's
tea in the evening. Huge saddle-bags contained
provisions, knives and forks, plates, and everything
necessary for travelling in the Bush in a style of
princely magnificence. No scheik or emir among the
Arabs wanders about the desert half so sumptuously
provided. I could not help laughing (in my sleeve,
of course,) at the figure produced by the *tout ensem-
ble* of John mounted on his ewe-necked and pot-
bellied steed.

In excellent spirits we jogged along to the Canning, and then eleven miles farther, to a muddy
pool called Boregarup, where we baited the horses,
and lunched on one of his Excellency's cold meat-
pies. The water in the pool was not very tempting,
but we ladled a little out in our pannikins, and
mixing it with brandy, managed to drink it. The
want of water makes travelling in the bush during
summer a serious business. Frequently you find
a well, on which your thoughts and hopes have
been fixed for the last twenty miles, completely
dried up; and you have to endure thirst as well
as you can for some hours longer. Sometimes by
scraping the bottom of the well, and digging
down with your pannikin, you come to a little

moisture, and after waiting an hour, succeed in obtaining about half-a-pint of yellow fluid, compounded of mud and water. This you strain through as many pocket-handkerchiefs as you can command, and are at last enabled to moisten your baked lips.

On these occasions the traveller cares less about himself than his horse, and often have we served the latter out of our pannikin from holes into which he could not get his nose, whilst denying ourselves more than a little sip.

After lying an hour on our blankets in the hot shade, smoking a cigar, and waging incessant war with myriads of mosquitoes and sand-flies, we decided that it was impossible to continue any longer so unequal a conflict; and saddling our horses in haste, we beat a quick retreat, and felt much cooler and more comfortable whilst in motion. In the course of the afternoon we passed through a vast dry swamp many miles long. The reeds on each side of the track frequently reached to our heads, and prevented our seeing any thing else on either side of us; and when we did get a glimpse over the rushes level with our eyes, we could behold nothing but an immense plain of waving green, like a huge field of unripe wheat, edged in the distance by the stern outline of the ever-sombre forest of eucalyptus trees. This swamp is a terrible place to pass through in winter. It is nevertheless one of the royal post-roads of the colony; and the bearer of her Majesty's mail from Pinjarra to Perth, is frequently obliged to swim for his life, with the letter-bag towing astern, like a jolly-boat behind a Newcastle collier.

After emerging from the swamp, we passed through an extensive plain, covered with coarse scrub and thinly-scattered grass, and lined with forest trees and clumps of black-boys. When about half-way down it, we came upon a herd of wild cattle grazing at some two hundred yards' distance from the path. They seemed very much astonished at the appearance of three such picturesque individuals; and after gazing for a few moments, lost in wonder, they tossed up their heads, and trotted along-side of us, keeping their original distance. Having kept us company for about half-a-mile, they relieved us of their society, (which was not very agreeable, as we had no fire-arms,) by coming to a halt, and allowing us to proceed in peace, whilst they contented themselves with brandishing their horns and tails, and butting against one another in play.

That night we slept at the Dandalup, hospitably entertained by F. Corbet Singleton, Esq., M. C., the owner of a fine estate of twelve thousand acres, a good deal of it alluvial soil. Were the population such as it ought to be in this fine country; and the markets proportioned to the capabilities of the soil, nothing would be more agreeable than to live on a beautiful property like this, cultivating your corn lands and multiplying your flocks and herds. But as it is, unfortunately, a man is soon overdone with his own wealth. He has more corn than he can find a market for; more cattle than he can sell; and he is obliged to allow his land to run waste, and his herds to run wild, rather than be at the expense of farming on a great scale without adequate remuneration.

Let me advise emigrants to these colonies to turn their attention chiefly to the breeding of sheep and horses, which are saleable things in foreign markets. The growers of wool, and the breeders of horses for India will make their estates profitable; but large herds of cattle will produce nothing to the owner in a thinly-populated country.

The next day, after inspecting the farm, we proceeded with our host to Mandurah, crossing an estuary a quarter of a mile broad, but so shallow that the water did not reach above our saddle-flaps. And now (having parted from Singleton) we had to swim our horses across the mouth of the Murray River. After a little delay, a boat was found; with a couple of men to row it across, and removing the saddles and other things from

the horses' backs, we prepared for the passage.
His Excellency's Arab mare was destined to make
the experimental trip, and the Governor, with
many injunctions and misgivings, committed the
end of the tether-rope to the hand of his servant,
who belayed it to the stern of the boat, where he
seated himself, to act as occasion should require.
The boatman rowed till the tether-rope was out
at full stretch; his Excellency coaxed and entreated
the mare to enter the water, and " shoo-ed!" and
" shaa-ed!" and called her a stupid creature, whilst
I cracked my whip and jumped about, and rattled
my hat, and made as much noise as people usually
do on such occasions. The mare, on her part,
reared up, and flung herself back, and plunged
about, and showed so strong a determination not
to go down the broken bank, that we feared we
should never get her into the river. At last, however, we managed to back her into the water,
when she was dragged instantly out of her depth
and obliged to swim. The men pulled so fast
that she could not keep up with them, and giving
up the attempt, floated quietly on her side, to the
great horror of her master, who thought he never
should bestride her again, until he was relieved
by seeing her start to her feet in shallow water,
and scramble up the bank, dripping like a veritable
hippopotamus.

The other horses behaved better; and when we had ourselves crossed and remounted, we rode by the side of the river, or rather estuary, a distance of ten miles, till we came to a picturesque little spot called Mocha weir—a high bank, a clump of trees, a brawling brook, (unusual sight in this country,) and a patch of excellent grass.

Here we resolved to halt for the night. Each rider attended to his own horse, which, however, did not get much grooming, and then we prepared for the great business of life, and kindled a fire, filled the kettle with limpid water, drew out our various stocks of provisions, and arranged the dinner-table on the grass, and made every thing look exceedingly comfortable and inviting. Then we made tea, and invited each other to eat, and did eat without invitation; and joked and laughed, and felt considerably more happy and sociable than if vice-royalty had been real-royalty, and the green canopy of the trees were the banqueting-hall at Windsor Castle. The man munched his victuals at a small private bivouac of his own, within easy call, as he had to jump up every now and then, and bring the kettle, or wash the plates for the second and third courses. When the things were removed, we lighted cigars, and pleasantly discoursed, recumbent before the fire. Our beds were already made of black-boy tops, and, therefore we had nothing to do but await the hour of rest. The sun had disappeared, and darkness, closing around us, drew nigher and more nigh every moment, swallowing up object after object in its stealthy advance, and seeming about to overwhelm us in its mysterious obscurity. But John heaped logs of dry wood upon the fire, and nobly we resisted all the powers of Darkness. In the midst of that black solitude, our little circle of light maintained its independence, nor yielded to the invasion which had swallowed up all around it. Here was our Camp of Refuge, and here we felt snug, and secure, and at home; whilst all without our magic circle was comfortless and desolate.

Sometimes the active-minded John would dive, without apparent dismay, into the black and hostile-looking regions of Night, which seemed to close upon him as though for ever; and when we had resignedly given him up, a prey to the evil spirits that prowled around, he would reappear with startling suddenness, issuing forth into the light like some red demon of the woods, and bearing a huge log upon his shoulder—the spoils of his "foray-sack"—which he would fling down upon the fire, making it blaze up with sudden fierceness, and extending the circle of light for a few moments to a greater distance around, so as to give us a transient glimpse of things which were soon swallowed up again in darkness—like glimpses of the dead in dreams.

I must hurry on to Australind, merely mentioning that we passed two lakes not far from each other, one of which was fresh, and the other salt—salt as the Dead Sea. It is usual in this perverse country (though not so in this instance) to find a salt lake surrounded with good, and a fresh-water lake with bad land. Here it was bad altogether. The country, however, improved greatly as we drew towards Australind; and about ten miles from that place, we came upon a fine flock of sheep that seemed to be doing extremely well.

We now passed along the banks of the Leschenault estuary, on which Australind is situated; and soon we discovered three figures approaching on horseback. These proved to be M. Waller Clifton, Esq., the Chief Commissioner of the Western Australian Company, to whom the whole district belongs, attended by a brace of his surveyors as aides-de-camp—one mounted on a very tall horse, and the other on a very small pony. The Chief Commissioner himself bestrode a meek-looking cart-horse, which, on perceiving us in the distance, he urged into an exhilarating trot. His Excellency, seeing these demonstrations of an imposing reception, hastily drew forth his black silk neck-cloth from his pocket, and re-enveloped his throat therewith, which, during the heat of the day, he had allowed to be carelessly exposed. Gathering himself up in his saddle, and assuming the gravity proper to the representative of his sovereign, he awaited with as much dignity as his state of perspiration would allow, the approach of the Chief of Australind. As for myself, I plucked up my shirt-collar, and tried to look as spicy as possible.

The first greetings over, the two chieftains rode into the town side by side, as amicably as Napoleon and Alexander of Russia; whilst I fell to the share of the aides, and related the most recent news of Perth, and the last *bon mots* of Richard Nash, for their entertainment; receiving in return an account of the arrival of 400 male and female emigrants at the settlement the day before.

We were entertained, as every guest invariably is, right hospitably by Mr. Clifton and his amiable family.

Australind was then (December 1842) a promising new town. It was alive with well-dressed young men and women, who were promenading under the large forest trees which still occupied the intended squares and most of the streets. They had only landed from the vessel which had brought them some twenty-four hours before, and they were evidently variously affected by all they saw. Some appeared to be struck with the strange circumstance

of trees growing in the streets ; some looked aghast
at the wooden houses and canvass tents ; one
thought everything looked exceedingly green ; another fancied that a town built upon sand could not
possibly endure long. And he was right : for the
town has long since been deserted, except by half
a dozen families ; and the newly arrived settlers are
dispersed over the colony. This has not been the
fault of the Chief Commissioner, nor is it owing to
any inferiority in the soil, but to causes which I
intend briefly to explain, as there are many people
in England who are, or were, interested in the fortunes of this promising young settlement.

The Western Australian Company's grant of
land at Australind comprises 100,000 acres, among
which there is a large quantity of excellent pasture
and arable land. It is well watered, and generally
well adapted for the site of a new settlement. The
flats of the Brunswick and Collic rivers would
supply the whole colony, if thoroughly peopled, with
grain ; and there is abundance of feed for sheep and
cattle, even to the summits of the hills.

A great portion of this grant has been purchased
by the Company from Colonel Lautour, who, however, could not furnish a good title to it. Having
never performed the necessary improvements which
would entitle him to a deed of grant in fee-simple from
the crown, his right of possession became forfeit ;

and in April, 1840, Governor Hutt, though much interested in the success of the Company, of which his brother, the member for Gateshead, was chairman, thought himself obliged, in the conscientious discharge of his duty, to resume the estate for the crown.

This proved to be a most fatal proceeding. The Company's title to Colonel Lautour's grant had been confirmed by the Home-government, in November 1839, but, owing to the non-existence of regular post-office communication (that grand and inexcusable error, which allows the British Empire to be composed of a mass of unconnected settlements, dependent upon chance for intelligence and aid from the mother country), the news did not reach the colony until May or June following.

Accounts of the resumption of the grant by the Governor reached England, and not only perplexed the Company, but greatly disquieted the minds of the numerous individuals to whom they had sold land, to the value of nearly 60,000l. At this very time, too, unhappily, arrived Captain Grey in England, on his return from the expedition to the north-western side of New Holland, of which he has since published a clever and popular narrative. Captain Grey took an early opportunity of giving a somewhat lamentable account of the Company's land at Leschenault, or Australind, and a very glowing description of a district, many miles to the

north of Perth, between Gantheaume Bay and the
Arrowsmith River, which he had passed through on
his disastrous return.   He also expatiated, in most
precise terms, upon a splendid harbour which he
called Port Grey, and of which he made an elaborate sketch ; and on the 26th of October, 1840, addressed to Lord John Russell " a detailed description of that portion of the western coast of Australia which lies between Gantheaume Bay and the
River Arrowsmith, as it would be found useful in
enabling persons, intending to occupy that tract of
country, to arrive at correct conclusions regarding
its capabilities."   In the map of his route, published by Arrowsmith, Port Grey is laid down as a
spacious, well-sheltered harbour, with a convenient
point of land extending a couple of miles out to sea
from its northern extremity, and having a useful
reef of rocks projecting, most happily, to the same
distance, affording altogether a secure shelter for
shipping in seven fathoms' water.

The Directors of the Western Australian Company, alarmed at the account related of Australind,
perplexed by the proceedings of the local Government, and captivated by the description of Port
Grey, with its splendid districts of " rich flats," and
" fertile downs," determined to change the site of
their settlement.

Captain Grey describes two " flat-topped ranges,"

in the neighbourhood of this port, lying about twenty miles apart ; and in his diary of "Sunday, April 7, 1839," he says : " The country between these two ranges was an open grassy valley thinly wooded ; and *it appeared to be one of the most extensively fertile* portions of country which I had yet seen in Australia. After travelling for another mile over the sandy downs, we reached another romantic glen-like valley, bounded to the north and south by steep limestone cliffs ; we descended these cliffs, and at their base found, as in the last valley we had crossed, *extensive flats*, through which wound a water-course. All the hills I could see in the vicinity consisted of limestone, and for the whole distance I could see to the eastward (about seven or eight miles) the country appeared to be of the *most fertile* and picturesque character ; the hills were slightly wooded with large timber, and the valleys were nearly bare of trees and *covered with grass.* On ascending the limestone hills to the south of the valley, we found ourselves once more in open sandy downs ; after travelling three miles across these in a S. by E. direction, we again came to a valley of the same character as the one above described ; it ran from the same direction ; to the eastward we saw a fertile valley. * * * We halted for some time immediately at the foot of Mount Fairfax.

" We continued our route in the evening over

the sandy downs, which, at the distance of half a mile from the sea, terminated in cliffs. * * * After travelling three miles, we halted for the night.

" *Monday 8th.* The first three miles of our route lay over sandy downs, when we found ourselves in grassy, wooded plains, lying between the flat-topped range, and some dunes which bordered a bay," &c.

It is well known that people in the latter stages of starvation have constantly visions before their eyes of sumptuous entertainments, rich meats, and delicious wines. Captain Grey, who was then walking for his life, at a Barclay pace, with a very empty stomach, was probably labouring under a similar hallucination with respect to the country over which he passed; beholding flowery meads and fertile vales in districts which we fear would prove little attractive to a settler. He beheld fine flowing rivers and sheltered bays, which have since altogether disappeared, like the scenes beheld on misty mornings by Sicilian mariners.

His account of the country determined the Western Australian Company to change the site of their intended settlement. Calling together the purchasers of land at Australind, the Directors offered to return them the amount of their respective purchases, or allow them to take up new allotments in the very superior district of Port Grey. Almost all chose to reclaim their cash, and declined further speculation.

The Company now, towards the close of 1840, sent out Mr. Clifton, their " Chief Commissioner," with directions to remove the whole of their establishment then settled at Australind, to the new settlement of Port Grey. On arriving at Australind, Mr. Clifton was agreeably surprised to find the country much superior to what he had expected, after hearing Captain Grey's account of it. So differently do the same objects appear to different eyes! And perhaps Captain Grey had only viewed the sandy banks of the inlet, without having passed into the interior, and seen the flats of the Brunswick, &c. There is a very great deal more of worthless than of good land at Australind, which is the case throughout the whole of New Holland, in the very best districts. The general character throughout all the settled parts of the island, or continent, is bad, with scattered patches of good.

The Chief Commissioner, however, prepared to carry out his instructions, though with much regret, as he doubted greatly whether the proposed alteration would prove for the better. These preparations were put a stop to by a communication from his Excellency the Governor, informing him that the Government schooner had recently returned from a survey of the coast and district of the so-called Port Grey, and that no sufficient harbour could be discovered along the coast; whilst the country in every direction appeared barren and incapable of cultivation. Mr. Clifton therefore remained at Australind with his party, and used every effort and exerted every energy to found a flourishing colony. But unfortunately, the change of site to Port Grey, and then the return to Australind, and the various conflicting accounts promulgated by the Company themselves, now lauding and now condemning the two places in turn, operated so unfavourably upon the public mind that no more sales of land could be effected. It became, therefore, inexpedient to maintain the expensive establishment of Commissioners, Secretaries, and Surveyors at Australind, who were accordingly *congé'd* without much ceremony; and the Western Australian Company, like an "unsubstantial pageant," or Port Grey itself, "melted into air, thin air," leaving "not a rack behind." Yet not exactly so, for it has left behind, like some stranded wreck by the receding tide, a most worthy and high-minded family who deserved a brighter fate.

Such has been the lamentable result of Captain Grey's discoveries in Western Australia; for whether there be or not a good tract of land in the neighbourhood of Champion Bay, Captain Grey's denunciation of Australind, and his strongly-urged advice to the Company to change the site of their settlement, have undoubtedly been the chief causes of their failure.

Three expeditions have been sent to the scene of this Australian "Fata Morgana," in the hope of beholding it again, but like the door of the fairy palace in the rock, it is visible only to Prince Ahmed; and unless the Governor of New Zealand will himself found a colony there, it is most likely ever to remain desert and valueless. The first expedition was that in the Government schooner, in 1840, already alluded to; the second was made in 1841, by H.M.S. 'Beagle,' Captain Stokes, accompanied by the Chief Commissioner, Mr. Clifton. A careful survey was made of the coast as far north as the spot were Captain Grey was wrecked, and began his march southward, but nothing was discovered at all resembling the description given of Port Grey. The only bay in which a ship could lie, and that with very doubtful security, was Champion Bay; but unfortunately the country in every direction from this spot is most barren and miserable. Captain Grey travelled close along the coast-line, according to his journal, but those who have gone in search of his "fertile valleys" have penetrated some distance into the interior, without discovering anything but scrub and desert.

Captain Stokes, in his published " Letter to the Surveyor General of Western Australia," detailing his proceedings, mentions having " now seen and examined an extent of country little short of forty miles, nearly the whole of which deserved the character of sterility." In another place, he relates the discovery of "the only piece of grass of a useful nature seen in this route; it was, however, quite parched, and occupied a space of three or four acres."

Not being able to find any tolerable shelter along the coast besides Champion Bay, he concludes that it must be the spot designated as Port Grey; and after exploring the country behind it, with the effect just stated, he sailed away one morning towards the north-west, and meeting with a "favourable westerly wind," by afternoon was carried "past the bight south of Point Moore, sufficiently near to see that its shores were fronted with many sunken rocks." This also led to the conclusion that " Champion Bay is the port Captain Grey speaks of in his journal, placed in Arrowsmith's chart twelve miles south of its true position."

Since the date of Captain Stokes's survey, Captain Grey has himself virtually admitted

Champion Bay to be the locality visited by him. In a letter to that officer dated, "Government House, Adelaide, January 28, 1842," and published in the South Australian journals, Captain Grey observes, "I have attentively read your letter to the Hon. the Surveyor-General of Western Australia; and have also considered the observations made by you to me, relative to the error you suppose I have fallen into in mistaking the Wizard Peak of Captain King for the hill named by him Mount Fairfax, and I find I have certainly fallen into this error—a by no means unlikely one, considering the very similar character of the singular group of hills called Moresby's Flat-topped Range, and the circumstances under which I was journeying."

The hill, therefore, at whose foot Captain Grey halted on the afternoon of April 7, 1839, was not Mount Fairfax, but the Wizard Peak, or some other hill "to the north of Mount Fairfax." From thence the "sandy downs," (mentioned in the extract from his Journal that I have given above) over which he passed in the evening continued to within "half a mile of the sea," where "they terminated in cliffs." To have seen all this he must have been walking at no very great distance from the shore during that day's march. His object was to reach Perth as quickly as possible; and he steered in the most direct course—"south by east." We know, therefore, exactly the line of country traversed by Captain Grey—the "singular group called Moresby's Flat-topped Range" being unmistakeable.

In December, 1844, H. M. colonial schooner, 'Champion,' under the command of Lieutenant Helpman, R.N., accompanied by Mr. J. Harrison, Civil Engineer, &c., was again despatched by Governor Hutt to make further observations in the neighbourhood of Gantheaume Bay. Lieutenant Helpman says in his report, "I coasted close in from Champion Bay, collecting angles and soundings until in latitude 28° 10′ 30″, S. the low ridges of sand along the shore induced me to land, being then (as I concluded from the latitude given by Captain Grey) in the immediate vicinity of the estuary." This estuary is described by Captain Grey in his diary of the *fifth* April, who states that "for one mile we continued along *the rich flats* which bordered the estuary" . . . "we ascended the limestone range, and got a view of the country to the eastward, and found it *still grassy*, and exactly the same character as far as we could see. For the next five miles we continued along the top of the limestone range, the estuary still occupying the valley which lay to the west of us." . . . "At the end of a mile in a south by east direction, we found ourselves on the banks of a river, the Hutt, from forty to fifty yards wide, which was running strong, and was brackish at its mouth," &c. Such was the appearance of the estuary and of the Hutt River in the eyes of Captain Grey.

Lieutenant Helpman continues his report as follows :—

" On reaching the summit of the highest coast hill I found myself abreast of the centre of the inlet, which was void of water, but presented the appearance of a continuous sheet of salt as far as the eye could reach. Passing over the coast ridges, I came down, in about half a mile, to the edge of the estuary, and followed it in a southerly direction for about two miles, when I ascended another hill, from which I could clearly see the south end of it, which was covered with the same description of incrustation of salt.

"A gorge at the south-east corner of the estuary is probably where the Hutt River discharges itself during the rainy season, but there was no appearance of water in any part of the flat, which was about two miles wide between the hills and the south-east shore of the inlet.

" Observing that the north extremity of the estuary, as seen from the hill just referred to, presented some slight appearance of water, I was induced to examine it, and found the sand ridges

on the coast extremely low, nearly destitute of
herbage, but giving the idea of having had water
passing over them. This I judged to be the case,
from a few blades of very coarse grass which were
laid flat on the ground, as if from the effects of
running water.

" From the highest point of these ridges, notwithstanding the smoke from the numerous native fires,
the whole north end of the inlet was plainly seen
to be covered with salty incrustations, similar to
those previously referred to.

" I conceive the point of land near which these
latter observations were made, and where I landed
the second time, to be ' Shoal Point ' of the chart ;
but, except that it is very low, I see no cause for
its name, as the water was deep close to it, and
having only a few rocks close off its extreme west
point, within a quarter of a mile of the shore.

" Following close in from Shoal Point, the coast
is perfectly clear of dangers ; but I observed no
opening in the hills indicative of a river, nor could
I discover any bay or place of shelter for shipping
to resort to.

" Red Point, which is the western entrance of
Gantheaume Bay, is a very bold headland of considerable elevation, it is circular, and about four
miles in extent. I landed at the east end of the
red sand cliffs, taking a specimen of the rock.

"The land to the northward from this promontory is of a white sandy appearance, having ridges of sand hills along the coast of moderate altitude.

" The low state of the barometer, and the strong northerly winds, induced me to keep the vessel at a considerable offing. During the day the breezes were very fresh, and had it not been for the whale-boat with which I was furnished, I should not have been able to have effected a landing on any part of the coast which came under my observation. Under these circumstances, I was compelled most reluctantly to abandon the idea of spending much time in examining the interior.

" The *very dry state of the Hutt at this season* seems to indicate that but little water flows into it at any time; and I am disposed to fancy, that the lagoon, or estuary, owes its formation to the break-ing in of the sea over the low sand hills during the tempestuous gales of the winter months, more especially towards the north end of the inlet, where the sand ridges are lower than in any other part of the coast in that vicinity."

Thus the luxuriant country of Captain Grey, like the water-pools seen in the *mirage* of the desert, when approached, vanishes from the view of the traveller.

It is to be observed, that Captain Stokes and Lieutenant Helpman surveyed these districts in the

early part of the summer season—November and
December—when they were more likely to appear
fertile than on the 5th and 7th April, quite at the
end of that season, and just before the commencement of the winter rains.

Since the above passages were written, I have
read an account in the Perth journals of January,
1847, of the discovery of coal by the Messrs.
Gregory, about forty miles east of Champion Bay.
These gentlemen relate, that in journeying towards
the coast, they passed through a tract of country
capable of being settled. This may possibly be
Captain Grey's luxuriant district; and yet the district which he describes was close upon the coast.
It is also stated, that there is now ascertained to be a
corner of Champion Bay in which small vessels may
find a safe anchorage; and this is conjectured to be
that Port Grey whose existence has been so long
denied. But, although a few miles of country may
be found in this neighbourhood capable of supporting a limited number of flocks and herds, it is
certain that there is no such district here as would
suffice for the purposes of a colony of the magnitude contemplated by the Western Australian Company. The advice, therefore, given them to change
the site of their operations from Australind, or
Leschenault, to Champion Bay, or Port Grey, was
the most pernicious that could have been bestowed.

But it may certainly be doubted whether the principles on which the settlement of Australind was founded were in themselves of a sound and permanent nature. They were those propounded originally by Mr. Edward Gibbon Wakefield, and applied with extraordinary success to the formation and to the circumstances of the colony of South Australia. The most prominent features which they present are,—the concentration of population, and the high price of land.

The land in the immediate neighbourhood of Adelaide is very fine, and capable of supporting a dense population ; it was therefore perhaps, good policy to divide it into eighty-acre sections, valued at one pound per acre, which supported a body of agriculturalists, who found a ready and near market for their productions in the rapidly rising town. But there are few theories that will bear universal application ; and the mistake made in the case of Australind was, in expecting to obtain the same result from principles which were to be applied under very different circumstances.

The land adjoining the town-site of Australind is generally very indifferent, though the flats of the Brunswick and Collie Rivers afford perhaps some thousand acres of excellent land, but still not sufficient to maintain a large and dense population. The Company's property was divided into farms of

100 acres, and these were valued at 100*l.* each to the emigrants, who drew lots for the choice of site.

When the settlers arrived and took possession of their respective grants, they soon discovered that if they all produced wheat, there would certainly be plenty of food in the settlement, but very little sale for it; whereas, if they intended to become sheep-farmers, and produce wool for the English market, one hundred acres of land would not suffice in that country for the keep of fifty sheep. The sections of one hundred acres were, therefore, far too small for the wants of the settler, who found that, although he might probably be able to supply his table with vegetables, he had but small prospect of ever applying his capers to boiled mutton, or initiating his family into the mysteries of beef *à la mode*. Disgusted with the narrowness of his prospects, and recoiling from the idea of a vegetable diet, the sturdy settler quickly abandoned the limited sections of Australind, and wandered away in search of a grant of some three or four thousand acres, on which he might reasonably hope to pasture a flock of sheep that would return him good interest for the capital invested.

The Western Australian Company gave far too much for their land in the first instance, and were therefore compelled to set a much higher value upon it than it would bear. The ministers of the

Crown, who have adopted the principles of Mr.
Gibbon Wakefield, require one pound per acre
for waste lands; and the Company, though they
purchased their property from private individuals at
a somewhat lower rate, expected to sell it again at
the same price. There is very little land (in proportion to the vast extent of poor and of entirely
worthless land) throughout the length and breadth
of all New Holland, that is worth twenty shillings
an acre. In the more densely populated parts,
arable land is worth that sum, and often much
more; but in the pastoral districts, three shillings
an acre is in truth a high price.

It has long been acknowledged in New South
Wales, as well as in other parts of Australia,
that it takes from three to five acres to support
a single sheep throughout the year. An ewe-
sheep is worth about nine shillings; and if
you have to buy three and a half acres of land,
at three shillings, to keep her upon, the amount of
capital you invest will be nineteen shillings and
sixpence. The profits on the wool of this sheep,
after paying all expenses of keep, shearing, freight,
commission, &c., will be barely two-pence, or about
one per cent upon the capital invested. But then
you have her lamb? True, but you must buy an
additional quantity of land to keep it upon. Still
there is a gain upon the increase; and in process

of time the annual profits amount up to ten and even twenty per cent. But suppose the three and a half acres of land, instead of 10s. 6d. had cost 3l. 10s. 6d., it would then be perfectly absurd to think of investing money in sheep.

The course pursued by the home Government, in fixing the uniform extravagant price of twenty shillings an acre upon the pastoral lands of Australia, is probably more the result of ignorance of their real value than of a desire to check or prevent emigration to that country. It is an ignorance, however, that refuses to be enlightened, and has therefore all the guilt of deliberate injury.

The monstrous demand of twenty shillings an acre for crown-lands, has not only had the effect of deterring capitalists from embarking in so hopeless a speculation, but has grievously wronged the existing land-owners, by raising the price of labour. When land was sold at five shillings an acre, a fund was accumulated in the hand of the local Government that served to pay for the introduction of labouring emigrants. That fund has ceased to exist in New South Wales and in Western Australia. The value of labour has therefore risen, whilst the value of agricultural produce, by the increase of the supply beyond the demand, has grievously diminished. The advocates of the Wakefield system triumphantly inform us that

there never can be a labour-fund in any colony in
which private individuals are able to sell land at
a cheaper rate than the Government.

They point to South Australia, and bid us note
how different is the state of things there, where
land universally is worth a pound an acre or more.
But to us it appears, that as the character of the
soil is much the same throughout these countries—
if anything, being superior in Western Australia,
where there are no droughts, and where the wool
produced, though the worst got up, from the want
of labour, is stated by the London brokers to
be pre-eminent in quality—that colony would most
naturally be sought by the emigrant in which the
price of land is the most reasonable. It is not
the high price of land that has caused the prosperity of South Australia. Every one who is well
informed on the subject, is perfectly aware, that
in 1841 and 1842, before the discovery of copper-
mines, South Australia was universally in a state
of bankruptcy. Never was a country so thoroughly
smitten with ruin. Almost all the original settlers
sank in the general prostration of the settlement,
and never again held up their heads. The inhabitants slunk away from the colony in numbers ;
and property even in Adelaide was almost worthless. The holders of the eighty-acre sections produced far more of the necessaries of life than

the non-producing population required; and the neighbouring colonies were deluged with the farm-produce of the bankrupt agriculturalists of South Australia. This model colony afforded itself the most signal refutation of the truth of the Wakefield theories; and the whole world would have been compelled to acknowledge the falsehood, but for the opportune discovery of the mineral wealth of the colony. It is to its mines that South Australia owes its good fortune, its population, and its riches, and not to any secret of political economy bestowed upon it by adventurous theorists. According to the opinion of these philosophers, New South Wales and Western Australia can never again by any possibility possess a labour-fund, because the private owners of large grants of land, which they obtained for nominal sums, can always afford to undersell the Crown. So long as the Crown refuses to sell for less than a pound an acre, this will certainly be the case; but the day will doubtless come when our rulers will condescend to enquire into the necessities of those over whose fortunes they preside; and will adopt a policy suited to the actual circumstances of the case, and not vainly endeavour to apply, universally, abstract opinions which have long been proved to be, in almost all parts of Australia, totally useless and inapplicable. *The only way to raise a labour-fund in these colonies is, by offering crown-lands to the emigrant at the lowest market price.* The Crown could always afford to undersell the private land-speculator, and might establish a permanent fund for the introduction of labour, by selling land at a low rate, AND RESERVING A RENT-CHARGE, IN THE SHAPE OF A LAND-TAX——OF ONE HALF-PENNY PER ACRE. Thus, every grant of five thousand acres would pay an annual tax to Government of 10*l.* 8*s.* 4*d.*; and would, therefore, in a very few years, accumulate a fund sufficient to supply itself with a labouring population. When it is remembered how very small was the original cost to the owners of most of the lands in Western Australia, there will not appear much hardship in imposing this tax upon all the private property of the colony, as well as upon lands to be hereafter sold by the Crown. This course of legislation would infuse new vitality into the colony; and at the end of the short period of five years, the tax might be suspended as regards all lands purchased by individuals *prior to the passing of the Act,* but continued for ever upon lands purchased under the Act, and in contemplation of having to bear such a rent-charge.

This is the only way by which emigration can be insured to the colonies of New South Wales and Western Australia; and the time will sooner or later arrive when this suggestion will be adopted, though it may not be acknowledged.

Her Majesty's present Secretary of State for the Colonies is the first really liberal minister we have had; and to him the distant and struggling settlements of Australia look with reviving hope. THE OBJECTS MOST EAGERLY SOUGHT BY THOSE COLONIES ARE—A NEW SYSTEM OF GOVERNMENT, WITH LESS OF COLONIAL-OFFICE INTERFERENCE; A REGULAR POST-OFFICE COMMUNICATION WITH ENGLAND; AND A TOTAL REFORM IN THE EXISTING REGULATIONS FOR THE SALE OF CROWN-LANDS, WITHOUT WHICH, IN COUNTRIES PURELY PASTORAL AND AGRICULTURAL, THERE CAN NEVER AGAIN BE FORMED A FUND FOR THE INTRODUCTION OF LABOUR.

In the hope of making colonial subjects more familiar to the general reader, and more popular than they are at present, I have perhaps given to this little work a character so trifling as to make it appear unworthy of the attention of political philosophers; and yet, inasmuch as it points out some of the wants of a large body of British subjects, whose fortunes lie entirely at the mercy of distant rulers, who have but little sympathy with a condition of which they possess but a most imperfect knowledge —it is a work (inadequate though it be) not altogether undeserving of the consideration even of Statesmen.

NOTE TO CHAPTER XXX.

————

I AM happy that this work will become the medinm of informing the Colonists of Western Australia of one of the most promising events that has ever happened to that country.

The ship-timber of the Colony, a trial cargo of which arrived in England this month, (October, 1847,) has just been admitted into the Royal Navy. A highly favourable report has been made upon it by the Government surveyors, and it is pronounced admirably adapted for kelsons, stern-posts, great beams for steam-frigates, and other heavy work. If a company be formed, on good principles, and under proper management, a timber trade for the supply of the Navy will be found most lucrative.

The principal portion of the labour should be performed by Chinamen, to be obtained from Sincapore.

For this great boon, the Colonists are indebted to LORD AUCKLAND, the First Lord of the Admiralty, for his ready acquiescence in agreeing to receive the timber, by way of experiment; to Mr. G. H. WARD, the Secretary, for the kind attention he has paid to

G G

every request made to him on the subject, notwithstanding that he has been sufficiently pestered to have wearied the patience of the most amiable of mankind; and, above all, to our late Governor, Mr. HUTT, and his brother, the Honourable Member for Gateshead, who have been indefatigable in their exertions to promote the weal of the Colony.

THE END.